Electrical principles for installation and craft students

Consulting Editor

M. R. Ward

Vice-Principal, South East London Technical College

Electrical principles for installation and craft students

G. Birchall
Garretts Green Technical College

G. S. Stott
Garretts Green Technical College

McGRAW-HILL Book Company (UK) Limited

London · New York · St Louis · San Francisco · Auckland
Bogotá · Düsseldorf · Johannesburg · Madrid · Mexico · Montreal
New Delhi · Panama · Paris · São Paulo · Singapore · Sydney
Tokyo · Toronto

Published by McGRAW-HILL Book Company (UK) Limited

MAIDENHEAD · BERKSHIRE · ENGLAND

07 094269 2

34567WC 79876

PRINTED AND BOUND IN GREAT BRITAIN

Contents

Preface

The book is intended primarily for second- and third-year Electrical Craft Students. It covers fully the Electrical Principles and Associated studies syllabus of the Electrical and Electronic Craft Studies Course Part II, and the Electrical Installation Work Course B. To assist the students in maintaining continuity, much of the relevant Electrical Principles of the first-year syllabus is also covered.

The book is written completely in SI units and follows the recommendations of the Council of Technical Examining Bodies recommendations on SI Symbols, Abbreviations, and Conventions. Wherever possible the questions and worked examples are based on the new metric standards for electrical equipment.

There are over 150 worked examples and over 320 problems for the student to solve, many of which have been based on past examination papers.

We are grateful to the City and Guilds of London Institute, the Union of Lancashire and Cheshire Institutes, and the Union of Educational Institutions for permission to publish questions based on past examination papers. The answers and worked solutions for these questions are those of the authors and are in no way the responsibility of the examining bodies.

In the majority of worked examples the numerical values and constants have been tabulated at the commencement of the solution. The conversions and incidental calculations have also been included at this stage. Experience has shown that this method tends to reduce the possible sources of student errors.

G. Birchall
G. S. Stott

1. Drawing

A drawing is a means of communicating information to other people. To enable engineering drawings to be easily understood by other engineers it is essential that they conform to agreed standards, as detailed in the British Standard No. 308, Engineering Drawing Practice.

All engineering components are three-dimensional, that is they have length, breadth, and height, but when producing sketches or drawings of these components they have to be drawn on paper, which has only two dimensions.

1.1 Types of drawings

Simple components can be drawn to appear three-dimensional by using either pictorial, oblique, or isometric representation.

Pictorial drawings are drawn in perspective and can be viewed from any angle. They are difficult to draw, since parallel lines must converge to a common point, and are not often used for engineering drawings, Fig. 1.1(a).

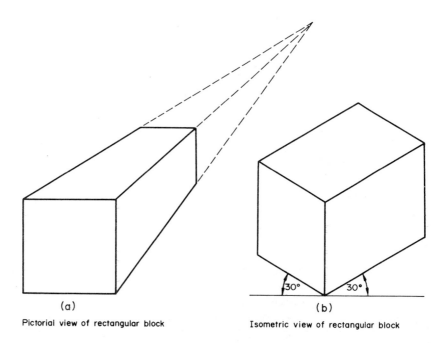

(a)

Pictorial view of rectangular block

(b)

Isometric view of rectangular block

Fig. 1.1. Pictorial and isometric projection

1

Isometric drawings are constructed using a T-square and set square, as are most engineering drawings. This method is easier than pictorial since all parallel lines are drawn parallel to each other, which often gives the impression that the top rear portion of the component is oversize. The component is tilted at 30° to the base and viewed from one edge, as shown in Fig. 1.1(b). Drawing of circles on the sides of a component drawn in isometric projection requires some construction work since they will not appear as true circles. One of the simpler construction methods is shown in Fig. 1.2.

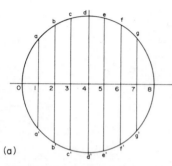

(a)

Draw a circle, using compasses, to the size required. Divide the horizontal axis into a number of equal-spaced parts 1,2,3,4, etc. Draw vertical lines through points 1,2,3,4, etc.

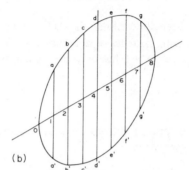

(b)

Draw vertical axis and axis at 30° to the horizontal. Mark spaces 1,2,3,4, etc. equal to the spaces on figure (a) as shown. Draw a vertical line through each point. Using compasses or ruler mark points a a', b b', etc. so that 1a, 1a' 2a, 2a' are the same length as on figure (a). Join points a,b,c,d, etc.

Fig. 1.2. Construction of isometric circle

Oblique drawings are an alternative to isometric, and are particularly useful where the component can be positioned so that any circles appear in the front face of the component. The circles will then appear as true circles and can be drawn with compasses, as shown in Fig. 1.3.

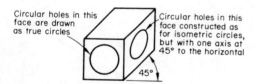

Circular holes in this face are drawn as true circles

Circular holes in this face constructed as for isometric circles, but with one axis at 45° to the horizontal

45°

Fig. 1.3. Oblique view of rectangular block

Orthographic drawings are used when components possess too much intricate detail to be shown clearly by any of the previous methods. Drawings for most engineering components are usually drawn using orthographic projection.

An orthographic drawing does not appear to have any depth. Separate views are drawn looking at each face of the component. Most components can be drawn by showing only three views:

2

(a) a front view—called the front elevation,

(b) a view on one side—called the side elevation, and

(c) a view looking down on the component—called the plan.

There are two systems of projection in use:

First angle projection where each view shows what would be seen by looking at the far side of an adjacent view.

Third angle projection where each view shows what would be seen by looking at the near side of an adjacent view. Figure 1.4(b) shows the third-angle orthographic projection of the component shown in Fig. 1.4(a). Note carefully the positions of the three views. Third-angle projection is to be preferred since the side elevation is placed adjacent to the side of the front elevation that it represents.

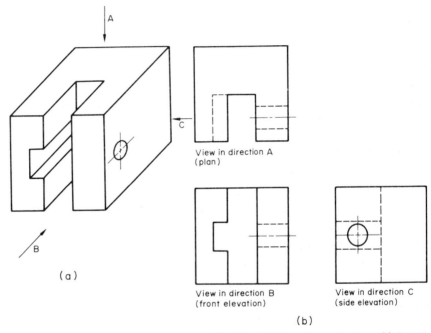

View in direction A
(plan)

View in direction B
(front elevation)

View in direction C
(side elevation)

(a)

(b)

Fig. 1.4. Orthographic projection — third angle

1.2 Drawing techniques

Equipment. The essential equipment required to produce an engineering drawing is a rule, 60° and 45° set squares, T-square, drawing board, compasses, and pencils. For use on normal types of paper H or 2H pencils are suitable, and these must be kept sharp to produce a clear line on the drawing.

Types of lines. The types of lines used for the various parts of the drawing are given in Fig. 1.5.

3

Type	Example	Application
Continuous — thick	————————	Visible outlines
Continuous — thin	————————	Dimension or projection lines
Short dashes — thin	– – – – – – – –	Hidden details
Chain — thin	—·—·—·—	Centre lines
Wavy — thick	∿∿∿	Break lines

Fig. 1.5. Types of lines used on engineering drawings

Dimensioning. Each necessary dimension required to enable the component to be manufactured should be given on the drawing and should appear only once. Recommended methods of dimensioning are given in Fig. 1.6.

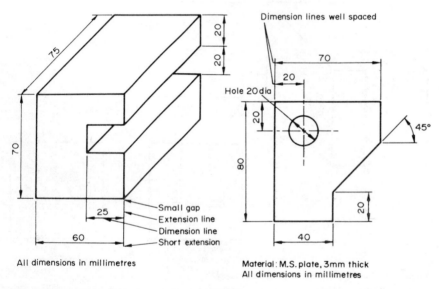

All dimensions in millimetres

Material: M.S. plate, 3mm thick
All dimensions in millimetres

Fig. 1.6. Method of dimensioning engineering drawings

1.3 Circuit diagrams

When drawing electrical circuit diagrams the symbols used to represent the various components should be in accordance with British Standard No.3939. A selection of the more common symbols likely to be encountered by installation engineers is given in Fig. 1.7.

Figure 1.8. shows a typical circuit diagram following the recommendations of B.S.3939. Further examples will be found in the electrical chapters of this book.

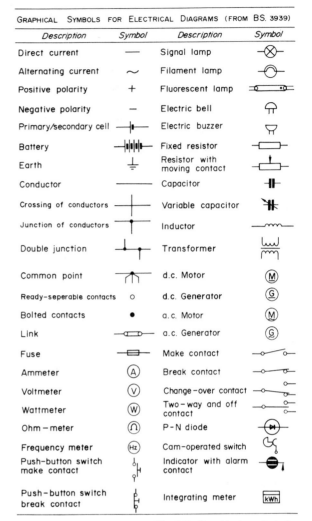

Description	Symbol	Description	Symbol
Direct current	—	Signal lamp	
Alternating current	∼	Filament lamp	
Positive polarity	+	Fluorescent lamp	
Negative polarity	—	Electric bell	
Primary/secondary cell		Electric buzzer	
Battery		Fixed resistor	
Earth		Resistor with moving contact	
Conductor		Capacitor	
Crossing of conductors		Variable capacitor	
Junction of conductors		Inductor	
Double junction		Transformer	
Common point		d.c. Motor	
Ready-seperable contacts	o	d.c. Generator	
Bolted contacts	●	a.c. Motor	
Link		a.c. Generator	
Fuse		Make contact	
Ammeter		Break contact	
Voltmeter		Change-over contact	
Wattmeter		Two-way and off contact	
Ohm-meter		P-N diode	
Frequency meter		Cam-operated switch	
Push-button switch make contact		Indicator with alarm contact	
Push-button switch break contact		Integrating meter	

Fig. 1.7. Graphical symbols for electrical diagrams

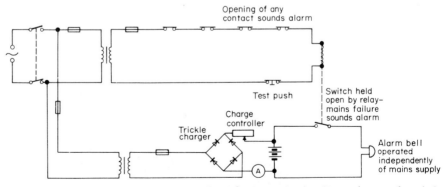

Fig. 1.8. Alarm circuit — illustrating use of symbols

5

2. Calculations

2.1 Transposition and evaluation of formulae

Transposition. The general rule for transposing formulae given in the form of equations is that any mathematical operation applied to one side of the equation must be applied to the other side of the equation. This can, for the work covered in this book, be generalized in the following operations:

(a) Any term or group of terms added or subtracted from other terms can be transposed to the other side of an equation, by writing it on the other side of the equation with a reversed sign, i.e., + to −, etc.

Example 2.1. $\quad E = V + iR \quad$ transposing iR gives,

$$E - iR = V$$

Example 2.2. $\quad R_0 = R_1 + \dfrac{R_2(R_1 + R_0)}{R_0 + R_1 + R_2} \quad$ transposing $\dfrac{R_2(R_1 + R_0)}{R_0 + R_1 + R_2}$ gives

$$R_0 - \frac{R_2(R_1 + R_0)}{R_0 + R_1 + R_2} = R_1$$

(b) Any term or group of terms multiplied or divided by each other (but not part of terms which are added or subtracted) can be transposed to the other side of an equation by cross-multiplication.

Example 2.3. $\quad f^2 = \dfrac{1}{4\pi^2 LC} \quad$ transposing f^2 and LC gives

$$LC = \frac{1}{4\pi^2 f^2}$$

Example 2.4. $\quad R = \dfrac{R_1 R_2}{R_1 + R_2} \quad$ transposing $R_1 + R_2$ and R gives

$$R_1 + R_2 = \frac{R_1 R_2}{R}$$

Note: Neither R_1 or R_2 in the denominator can be cross-multiplied on their own.

(c) The same power or root can be applied to both sides of the equation.

Example 2.5. $I^2 R = P$ transposing R gives

$$I^2 = \frac{P}{R} \quad \text{taking the square root of both sides gives}$$

$$I = \sqrt{\frac{P}{R}}$$

Note: The negative root can usually be ignored.

Example 2.6. $Z = \sqrt{R^2 + X_L^2}$ squaring both sides gives

$$Z^2 = R^2 + X_L^2$$

Example 2.7. $PV^n = C$ transposing P gives

$$V^n = \frac{C}{P} \quad \text{taking the } n\text{th root of both sides gives}$$

$$V = \left(\frac{C}{P}\right)^{1/n} \quad \text{or} \quad \sqrt[n]{\frac{C}{P}}$$

(d) Any term contained in more than one term can be taken out as a common factor.

Example 2.8. $V = IR + Ir$ taking out I as a common factor gives
$$V = I(R + r)$$

Evaluation. When it is required to find the value of a quantity contained in a formula the following stages should normally be carried out:

(a) Write down the formula.

(b) Insert the given values.

(c) Evaluate any parts which can easily be simplified.

(d) Transpose so that the quantity being evaluated is on the left-hand side of the equation and complete the evaluation.

Example 2.9. Evaluate the resistance R_2 from the formula

$$\frac{1}{R} = \frac{1}{R_1} + \frac{1}{R_2}$$

when $R = 3 \cdot 5 \ \Omega$ and $R_1 = 4 \cdot 6 \ \Omega$:

$$\frac{1}{R} = \frac{1}{R_1} + \frac{1}{R_2}$$

$$\frac{1}{3 \cdot 5} = \frac{1}{4 \cdot 6} + \frac{1}{R_2}$$

7

Using reciprocal tables, $0.2857 = 0.2174 + \dfrac{1}{R_2}$:

$$0.2857 - 0.2174 = \dfrac{1}{R_2}$$

$$0.0683 = \dfrac{1}{R_2}$$

$$R_2 = \dfrac{1}{0.0683} \; \Omega = \underline{14.64 \; \Omega}$$

Example 2.10. Evaluate the temperature t_1, from the formula

$$\dfrac{R_1}{R_2} = \dfrac{1 + \alpha t_1}{1 + \alpha t_2}$$

when $\quad R_1 = 60, R_2 = 50, \alpha = 0.004$ and $t_2 = 20°C$

$$\dfrac{R_1}{R_2} = \dfrac{1 + \alpha t_1}{1 + \alpha t_2}$$

$$\dfrac{60}{50} = \dfrac{1 + 0.004 \, t_1}{1 + 0.004 \times 20}$$

$$1.2 = \dfrac{1 + 0.004 \, t_1}{1.08}$$

$$1.2 \times 1.08 = 1 + 0.004 \, t_1$$

$$1.296 = 1 + 0.004 \, t_1$$

$$0.296 = 0.004 \, t_1$$

$$t_1 = \dfrac{0.296}{0.004} \; °C = \underline{74°C}$$

Example 2.11. Evaluate the voltage drop V_R across a resistor in an a.c. series circuit from the formula $V_R = \sqrt{V^2 - V_X^2}$ when $V = 240$ V and $V_X = 140$ V:

$$V_R = \sqrt{V^2 - V_X^2} \qquad \textit{Note:} \text{ this could be worked through using } (V^2 - V_X^2)^{1/2}$$
$$\text{refer to example 2·7}$$

$$= \sqrt{240^2 - 140^2} = \sqrt{57\,600 - 19\,600} = \sqrt{38\,000}$$

$$= \underline{194.94 \; V}$$

2.2 Graph plotting

A graph gives a visual indication of the variations between two related quantities. The variation in one of the quantities will depend on how the other quantity varies, and they are therefore called the dependent and independent variables respectively, Fig. 2.1(a).

The relationship between the two quantities should be tabulated.

x				$\cdots$
y				$\cdots$

These quantities should then be plotted on the graph axes using small dots for each point.

The scales should be chosen so that the graph is as large as possible on the graph sheet and so that the values are easy to plot, i.e., let 10 mm = 10, 20, or 50 units, etc.

Graphs can be divided into two groups:
(a) those which possess no regularity and do not follow a definite law,
(b) those with straight lines or curves where one set of values is a function of the other set.

Most experimental results follow certain laws and the graphs are usually either smooth curves or straight lines.

In these graphs a smooth curve or straight line is drawn through the mean of the points. This method enables any small errors in instrument readings to be averaged out.

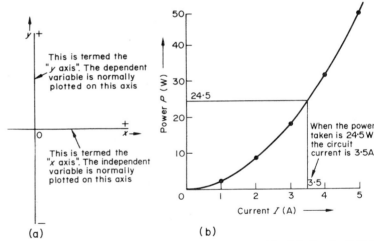

Fig. 2.1. Graph plotting

Example 2.12. The power P (W) taken by a certain electrical circuit for various values of circuit current I(A) are given in the following table. Construct a graph of P against I. Estimate from the graph the value of the circuit current when the power taken is 3·5 W, Fig. 2.1(b):

I (A)	0	1	2	3	4	5
P (W)	0	2	8	18	32	50

9

2.3 Linear graphs

These are straight line graphs which follow the general law $y = mx + c$.
y and x are variables; m and c are constants which represent the slope of the graph and the value of y when $x = 0$ respectively, Fig. 2.2.

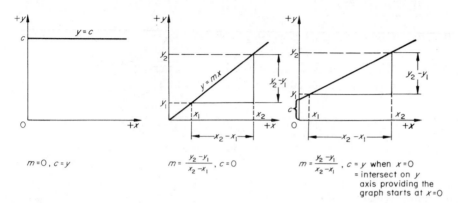

Fig. 2.2. Linear graphs

Example 2.13. An experiment carried out on a wheel and axle lifting machine gave the following results:

Load (N)	40	60	80	100
Effort (N)	10	13	16	19

Construct an effort-load graph and determine the approximate law relating these quantities, Fig. 2.3.

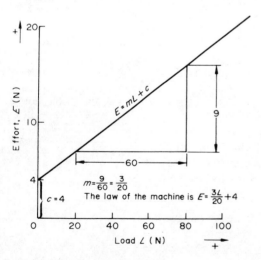

Fig. 2.3. Solution to example 2.13.

2.4 Basic trigonometrical ratios and graphs

The basic trigonometrical ratios are the sine, cosine, and tangent. These are given in terms of the ratios of two of the sides of a right-angled triangle, Fig. 2.4(a).

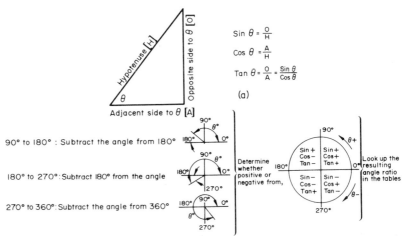

$$\text{Sin } \theta = \frac{O}{H}$$

$$\text{Cos } \theta = \frac{A}{H}$$

$$\text{Tan } \theta = \frac{O}{A} = \frac{\text{Sin } \theta}{\text{Cos } \theta}$$

(a)

90° to 180° : Subtract the angle from 180°

180° to 270°: Subtract 180° from the angle

270° to 360°: Subtract the angle from 360°

Determine whether positive or negative from,

Look up the resulting angle ratio in the tables

Angular measure can also be expressed in radians where 2π rad = 360°. In order to evaluate trigonometrical ratios of angles given in radians the angle must first be converted to degrees from values given in tables or by using the relationship 1 rad = 57°18′.

(b)

Fig. 2.4. Trigonometrical ratios

The numerical values of these ratios for angles between $0°$ and $90°$ can be obtained from trigonometrical tables.

Examples 2.14.
(a) $\sin 60° = 0.866$, (b) $\cos 45° = 0.7071$, (c) $\tan 80° = 5.671$.
Values of ratios for angles greater than $90°$ can be found by applying the rules shown in Fig. 2.4(b).

(d) $\sin 210° = -\sin(210° - 180°) = -\sin 30° = -0.5$.
(e) $\cos 300° = \cos(360° - 300°) = \cos 60° = 0.5$.
(f) $\tan 135° = -\tan(180° - 135°) = -\tan 45° = -1$.

Trigonometrical ratio graphs are curves of the ratios plotted against the angle, Fig. 2.5.

Amplitude, frequency, and phase. A multiple A of the ratio is called the amplitude, a multiple n of the angle is called the frequency and an angle ϕ added to the angle, results in a horizontal phase displacement of the waveform from the basic wave. These effects can be represented graphically as shown in Fig. 2.6.

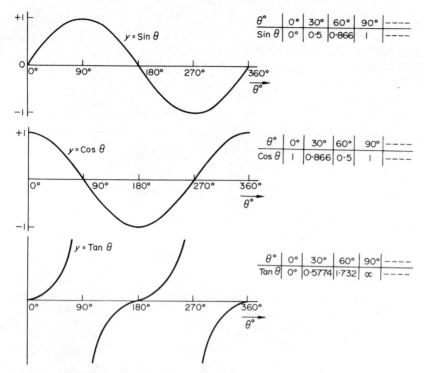

$\theta°$	0°	30°	60°	90°	----
Sin θ	0°	0·5	0·866	1	----

$\theta°$	0°	30°	60°	90°	----
Cos θ	1	0·866	0·5	1	----

$\theta°$	0°	30°	60°	90°	----
Tan θ	0°	0·5774	1·732	∞	----

Fig. 2.5. Trigonometrical graphs

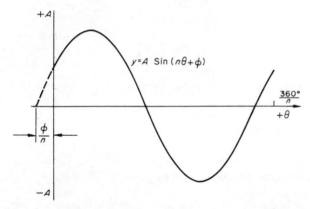

Fig. 2.6. Amplitude, frequency, and phase

2.5 Addition and subtraction of graphs

Tabulate and plot the graphs to be added or subtracted on the same axes. Use sufficient values to enable smooth curves to be drawn and leave reasonable space above and below for the resultant graph. Calculate the value of the addition or subtraction of the graph's values at each ordinate and plot the point of the resultant curve.

12

Example 2.15. Construct the graph of $4 \sin \theta + 2 \cos 2\theta$ from $\theta = 0°$ to $180°$, Fig. 2.7(a).

Example 2.16. Construct the graph of $3 \cos \theta - 2 \sin (\theta + \pi/6)$ from $\theta = 0$ to 2π rad, Fig. 2.7(b).

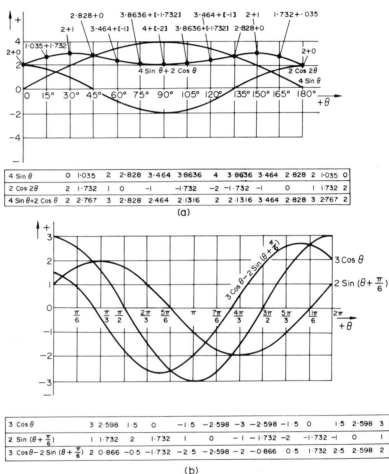

4 Sin θ	0	1·035	2	2·828	3·464	3·8636	4	3·8636	3·464	2·828	2	1·035	0
2 Cos 2θ	2	1·732	1	0	-1	-1·732	-2	-1·732	-1	0	1	1·732	2
4 Sin θ+2 Cos θ	2	2·767	3	2·828	2·464	2·1316	2	2·1316	3·464	2·828	3	2·767	2

(a)

3 Cos θ	3	2·598	1·5	0	-1·5	-2·598	-3	-2·598	-1·5	0	1·5	2·598	3
2 Sin $(\theta+\frac{\pi}{6})$	1	1·732	2	1·732	1	0	-1	-1·732	-2	-1·732	-1	0	1
3 Cosθ-2 Sin $(\theta+\frac{\pi}{6})$	2	0·866	-0·5	-1·732	-2·5	-2·598	-2	-0·866	0·5	1·732	2·5	2·598	2

(b)

Fig. 2.7. Solutions to examples 2.15 and 2.16

2.6 Phasors

Phasors are straight lines drawn to represent sinusoidal alternating quantities. They can be drawn for current or voltage, etc., and usually represent r.m.s. values. Phasors are so called since the angle at which they are drawn, measured positively anticlockwise from a given reference direction $\longrightarrow$ (usually horizontally to the right), shows their phase relationships with respect to the other alternating quantities.

They are written in the form $A \sin (\omega t + \phi)$, where A is the maximum value of the alternating quantity, I_m, V_m, etc., and ϕ is the angle at which they are drawn.

13

Example 2.17. Draw phasors to represent the following sinusoidal alternating quantities:

(a) $8 \sin(\omega t + 30°)$, (b) $240 \sin(\omega t - \pi/3)$, Fig. 2.8.

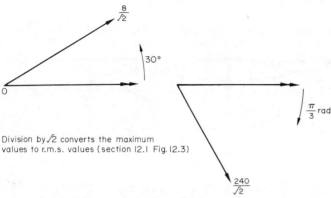

Division by $\sqrt{2}$ converts the maximum values to r.m.s. values (section 12.1 Fig. 12.3)

Fig. 2.8. Solution to example 2.17

2.7 Resolution, addition, and subtraction of phasors

Phasors can be resolved graphically or by calculation into their vertical and horizontal components, as shown in Fig. 2.9(a).

Phasors of similar quantities can be added graphically by drawing all the phasors to scale from the same pole '0' and resolving in pairs by constructing parallelograms as shown in Fig. 2.9(b) until only the resultant R remains. Subtraction of a phasor quantity is carried out by simply reversing the phasor and adding, Fig. 2.9(c).

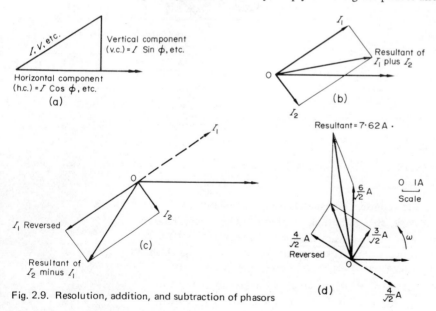

Fig. 2.9. Resolution, addition, and subtraction of phasors

14

Example 2.18. Determine graphically the resultant r.m.s. value of the following currents:

$6 \sin (\omega t + \pi/2) - 4 \sin (\omega t - \pi/6) + 3 \sin (\omega t + \pi/3)$, Fig. 2.9(d).

The resultant of several phasors can be calculated by:

(a) resolving each of the phasors into its vertical component (v.c.) and horizontal component (h.c.),

(b) tabulating these values,

(c) calculating their total effective values, and

(d) applying the formula $R = \sqrt{(\text{Total v.c.})^2 + (\text{Total h.c.})^2}$

acting at an angle ϕ whose tangent is given by $\dfrac{\text{Total v.c.}}{\text{Total h.c.}}$

Example 2.19. Calculate the r.m.s. value of the currents in example 2.18.

Current	v.c.	h.c.
$6 \sin (\omega t + \pi/2)$	$6 \sin \pi/2 = 6 \times 1$ $= 6$	$6 \cos \pi/2 = 6 \times 0$ $= 0$
$-4 \sin (\omega t - \pi/6)$ $= 4 \sin\left(\omega t + \dfrac{5\pi}{6}\right)$ refer Fig. 2.9(b)	$4 \sin \dfrac{5\pi}{6} = 4 \sin \pi/6$ $= 4 \times 0{\cdot}5 = 2$	$4 \cos\dfrac{5\pi}{6} = -4 \cos \pi/6$ $= -4 \times 0{\cdot}866 = -3{\cdot}464$
$3 \sin (\omega t + \pi/3)$	$3 \sin \pi/3 = 3 \times 0{\cdot}866$ $= 2{\cdot}598$	$3 \cos \pi/3$ $= 3 \times 0{\cdot}5 = 1{\cdot}5$
Total	$10{\cdot}598$	$-1{\cdot}964$

$I_m = \sqrt{(\text{Total v.c.})^2 + (\text{Total h.c.})^2} = \sqrt{10{\cdot}598^2 + (-1{\cdot}964)^2} = \sqrt{112{\cdot}32 + 3{\cdot}8573}$

$\quad = \sqrt{116{\cdot}18} = 10{\cdot}779$

$I = \dfrac{10{\cdot}779}{\sqrt{2}} = 7{\cdot}62$ acting at an angle whose tangent is $\dfrac{10{\cdot}598}{-1{\cdot}964} = -5{\cdot}398$

which is in the second quadrant.

Therefore, $\tan \phi = -5{\cdot}398$ and $\phi = (180° - 79° \, 30') = 100° \, 30'$.

2.8 Rates of change

When two quantities, say current and time, are related such that a given change in one produces a constant change in the other then

$$\frac{\text{change in current}}{\text{change in time}}$$

gives the rate of change of current, with respect to time.

Note: Rates of change which are not constant are beyond the scope of this course.

Example 2.20. The magnitude of the induced e.m.f. E volts in a circuit is given by the product of inductance L henrys and the rate of change of current in amperes per second. Determine the magnitude of the induced e.m.f. in a circuit having an inductance of 0·2 H in which the current changes from 4 A to 7 A in 5 s.

$$E = L \times \frac{\text{change in current}}{\text{change in time}}$$

$$= 0{\cdot}2 \times \frac{7 - 4}{5} \ \text{V} = 0{\cdot}2 \times 0{\cdot}6 \ \text{V} = \underline{0{\cdot}12 \ \text{V}}$$

2.9 Areas, volumes, mass, and weight

The diagrams in Fig. 2.12 show basic areas and volumes, with formulae for calculating their value, together with the mid-ordinate method for calculating the area of an irregular shape.

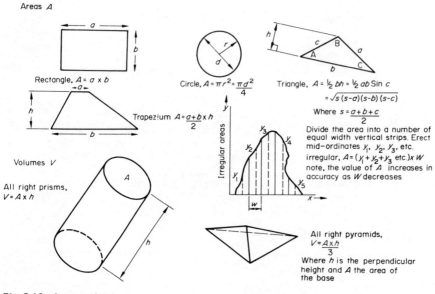

Fig. 2.10. Areas and volumes

Mass and weight. The mass of a body depends on the quantity of matter contained in the body. It is measured by comparison with a standard mass and remains constant.

Weight is the term used for the force of attraction between a mass and the planet or large body, which is near. In the past, apart from theoretical considerations this has meant the force of attraction between the earth and objects on its surface.

Today, with space travel taking place, it may be that the term weight, since it is not constant, will become obsolete and that only the mass of a body should be given. However, these problems are unlikely to affect craft students in the immediate future.

The weight of a mass on the earth's surface can be calculated using,

$$\text{weight in newtons} = \text{mass in kilogrammes} \times 9{\cdot}81$$

$$\text{or} \qquad = \text{volume} \times \text{mass per unit volume} \times 9{\cdot}81$$

however, this often gives awkward numerical values and hence in this book a multiple of 10 instead of 9·81 has usually been used to simplify calculations.

Example 2.21. Calculate the weight of an armature of length 200 mm and end-diameter 70 mm, whose average mass is 5 g/cm^3.

Length = 200 mm, area of end = $(\pi \times 70^2)/4$ mm^2 = 3849 mm^2, volume = 200 $\times$ 3849 mm^3 = 769·8 cm^3, mass = 769·8 $\times$ 5 g = 3·849 kg.

$$\text{Weight} = \text{mass (kg)} \times 10 \text{ newtons}$$

$$= 3{\cdot}849 \times 10 \text{ N} = \underline{38{\cdot}49 \text{ N}}$$

3. Levers and springs

3.1 Levers and lever linkages

A lever or system of levers enables a load force, L, to be applied at some distance from the applied effort, E. The magnitude of the load force is usually much greater than the effort, neglecting friction the ratio of their magnitudes depends on their relative distances from the fulcrum, f, Fig. 3.1.

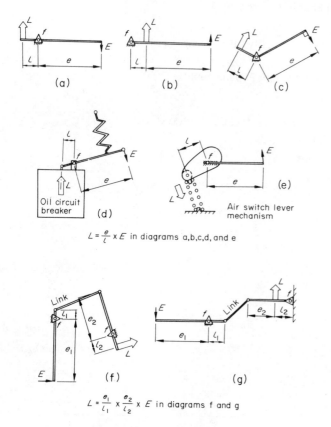

$$L = \frac{e}{l} \times E \text{ in diagrams a,b,c,d, and e}$$

$$L = \frac{e_1}{l_1} \times \frac{e_2}{l_2} \times E \text{ in diagrams f and g}$$

Fig. 3.1. Levers, lever systems, and applications

Example 3.1. During the operation of the switch mechanism, Fig. 3.1(e), the maximum force exerted by the spring is 18 N. Determine the maximum effort required at the end of a 108 mm lever. The distance from the fulcrum to the spring location pivot is 12 mm.

E_m = maximum effort, L_m = 18 N, e = 108 mm, l = 12 mm

$$L_m = \frac{e}{l} \times E_m$$

$$18 = \frac{108}{12} \times E_m$$

$$E_m = \frac{18 \times 12}{108} \text{ N} = \underline{2\text{N}}$$

3.2 Toggles

The toggle joint is a combination of levers which enable a large load force to be obtained by the application of a relatively small effort operating through a short distance, Fig. 3.2.

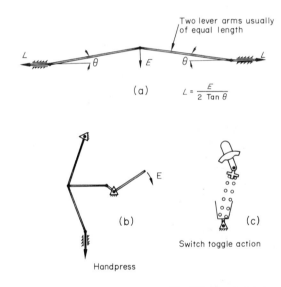

Fig. 3.2. Toggle joints

Example 3.2. The operating lever of the hand press in Fig. 3.2(b) has arm-lengths of 250 mm and 25 mm respectively. For the position shown 60% of the load force at the lever end is applied via the connecting link to the toggle joint. Calculate the force exerted by the press, when the angle between the toggle links and the vertical is 15°, for an effort of 20 N:

For the lever:

L = load force at lever end, E = 20 N, l = 25 mm, e = 250 mm

$$L = \frac{e}{l} \times E$$

$$= \frac{250}{25} \times 20 \text{ N} = \underline{200 \text{ N}}$$

For the toggle:

L = force exerted by the press, E = force applied to the toggle joint = $200 \times \dfrac{60}{100}$ N

= 120 N, $\theta = 15°$

$$L = \frac{E}{2 \tan \theta}$$

$$= \frac{120}{2 \tan 15°} \text{ N} = \frac{120}{2 \times 0.2679} \text{ N} = \underline{224 \text{ N}}$$

3.3 Eccentric cams

An eccentric cam is a component mounted off centre onto a shaft to convert the rotational movement of the shaft into a linear movement, Fig. 3.3(a). Several cams can be attached to a shaft or the shaft itself can be eccentrically shaped in order to perform a sequence of operations such as the operation of the inlet and exhaust valves in a car engine. Cams can also have shaped faces as well as shaped contours, Fig. 3.3(d).

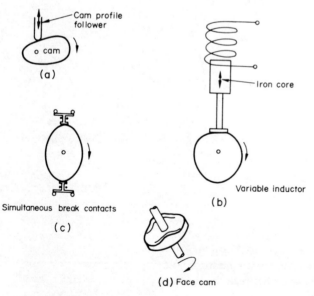

Fig. 3.3. Cam and cam mechanisms

Example 3.3. Sketch a cam mechanism suitable for operating two switches simultaneously twice every revolution of a shaft, Fig. 3.3(c).

3.4 Cranks

A crank is an arm extending from an axis used to produce rotary motion, Fig. 3.4(a). The magnitude of the rotational moment is called *torque, T,* and is given by the product of force, *F*, at right angles to the crank arm and the radius, *r*. Examples of its simplest form are that of a cranked arm used to turn over a car engine or manually wind up large oil circuit breakers.

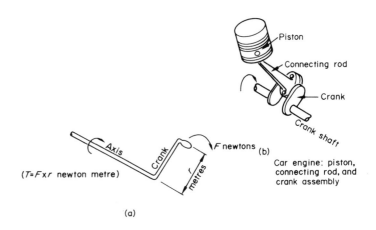

Fig. 3.4. Crank actions

Example 3.4. What is the average tangential force at the end of a 300-mm crank needed to just turn over a car engine whose average opposing torque is 15 N m.

In order to rotate the engine,

$$\text{applied torque} = \text{opposing torque}$$

$$F \times r = 15 \text{ N m}$$

$$F \times 300 \times 10^{-3} = 15 \text{ N m}$$

$$F = \frac{15}{300 \times 10^{-3}} \text{ N} = \underline{50 \text{ N}}$$

3.5 Pawl and ratchet

Pawl and ratchet wheel mechanisms are used in order to enable a shaft to either free wheel, or interlock with a fixed stop preventing counter rotation, or drive a mechanism such as another shaft, Fig. 3.5(a) and (b).

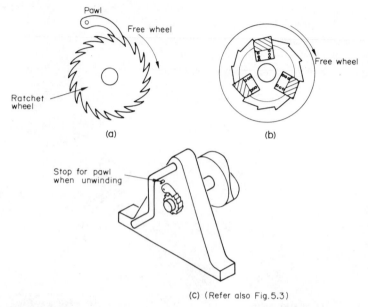

Fig. 3.5. Pawl and ratchet wheel mechanisms

Example 3.5. The simple winch shown in Fig. 5.3 is to be used as a lifting machine. Sketch a simple pawl and ratchet arrangement in order to prevent run-back while lifting, Fig. 3.5(c).

3.6 Springs

A spring is a component which makes use of the properties of some materials to regain their initial shape after being deformed providing they are not loaded beyond their elastic limit. When a force is applied so as to deform a spring, energy is expended. This energy is stored in the spring until the deforming force is removed. The energy is then released and the spring does work in regaining its initial shape. Figure 3.6 shows some of the more common spring shapes and the factors which affect the ratio (force)/(distortion), called the spring rate or stiffness.

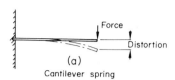

Force
Distortion

(a)

Cantilever spring

Stiffness depends upon;
(a) the material,
(b) cube of the thickness,
(c) width of the strip, and
(d) the inverse of the cube of the
distance from the clamp to the force.

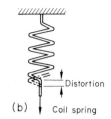

Distortion

(b)   Coil spring

Stiffness depends upon;
(a) the material,
(b) fourth power of the wire diameter,
(c) the inverse of the cube of
    the mean coil diameter,
(d) the inverse number of active turns.

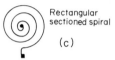

Rectangular
sectioned spiral

(c)

Distortion is produced by the
opening or closing of the spring
coils

Stiffness depends upon;
(a) the material,
(b) the width,
(c) cube of the thickness, and
(d) the inverse of the spring length.

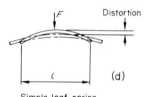

F Distortion

l (d)

Simple leaf spring

Stiffness depends upon:
(a) the material,
(b) the width of the strip,
(c) cube of the thickness, and
(d) the inverse of l^3

Fig. 3.6. Springs

Example 3.6. A simple coil spring used in a certain switch mechanism was found to need its stiffness doubling. Give three ways in which this could be effected.

Stiffness is proportional to (wire diameter)^4, inversely proportional to the number of active coils and to the cube of the mean coil diameter. Therefore,

(a) increase the wire diameter by $\sqrt[4]{2}$,

(b) halve the number of active coils,

(c) reduce the coil mean diameter $\sqrt[3]{2}$ times.

3.7 Electrical apparatus operating mechanisms

The diagrams in Fig. 3.7 show some mechanisms comprising combinations of the components previously described. Students should make a practice of sketching simple electrical mechanisms encountered in the course of their work in order to become more familiar with their operation and in order to be able to convey ideas.

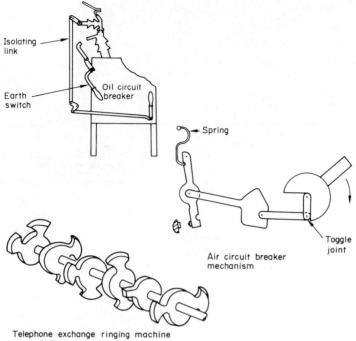

Isolating link

Oil circuit breaker

Earth switch

Spring

Toggle joint

Air circuit breaker mechanism

Telephone exchange ringing machine cam shaft

Fig. 3.7. Electrical apparatus operating mechanisms

Problems

1. A simple lever as shown in Fig. 3.1(a) is 1 metre long. How far from the load must the pivot be placed if a mass of 50 kg is to be lifted by an effort of 100 N?

2. If the lever in problem 1 has its pivot moved to the end (Fig. 3.1(b)) and the mass is positioned at the same distance from the pivot, what will be the effort required to lift the mass?

3. Calculate the largest mass that can be lifted by an effort of 80 N using the lever linkage shown in Fig. 3.1(g). The lever ratios e/l being 5:1 and 3:1 respectively.

4. Determine the lever ratios e/l for the lever linkage shown in Fig. 3.1(f) if an effort of 60 N is required to apply a load force of 600 N.

5. Make a sketch of a pair of wire strippers that use a toggle action in their operation.

6. Find the load force L that is exerted by the toggle joint shown in Fig. 3.2(a) due to an effort of 50 N applied when the angle θ is 20°.

7. Show by means of a sketch how a cam can be used to operate three switches in sequence at 0·6 s intervals by a shaft rotating at 1·8 rev/s.

8. Sketch a cam such that a profile follower will trace out a sine wave.

9. Make a sketch showing the cam shaft and valve mechanism of any car engine.

24

10. Sketch a cam-operated expanding brake mechanism, such as that used on some cars.

11. Determine the torque produced by a force of 2 kN acting on a crank arm at a radius of 60 mm.

12. Calculate the radius of a crank needed to produce a torque of $0 \cdot 6$ kN m, when the available tangential force is 12 kN.

13. Sketch a pawl and ratchet wheel arrangement suitable to prevent runback on:

(a) a small spring operated mechanism

(b) a light crane.

14. (a) Sketch the hair-spring control mechanism of an electrical indicating instrument.
(b) The hair-springs of a moving coil instrument were found to require modification in order to reduce their stiffness by 50%. Suggest two ways in which this could be done.

15. A pressure relief valve is controlled by a cantilever spring. A new design required the pressure on the valve to be doubled, give two ways in which the spring could be modified so that this can be effected.

16. A simple leaf-spring (Fig. 3.6(d)) car suspension was found to be too soft. For a given depth of spring what alterations should be made to the support distance l in order to improve the suspension.

17. What would be the effect on the stiffness of a simple coil spring due to:

(a) halving the wire diameter

(b) reducing the number of active coils by 25%.

18. Sketch three mechanisms used in electrical apparatus involving combinations of levers, cams, and springs.

Answers

1. $^{1}/_{6}$ m   2. $83^{1}/_{3}$ N
3. 120 kg   4. 5:1, 2:1 or similar to give an overall ratio of 10:1
6. $68 \cdot 7$ N   7. The cam should have a single operating point and the switches be spaced $120°$ apart.
11. 120 N m   12. 50 mm
14. Halve the spring width, double the spring length, or reduce the thickness by $\sqrt[3]{1/2}$ times.
15. Any two from
   (a) double the width of the strips
   (b) increase the thickness by $\sqrt[3]{2}$ times
   (c) reduce the distance from the orifice to the spring clamp $\sqrt[3]{2}$ times.
16. Reduce the support distance.   17. (a) $^{15}/_{16}$ reduction in stiffness
   (b) $^{4}/_{3}$ increase in stiffness

4. Work, Energy, and Power

4.1 Work, W

Work is done when a force moves through a distance against some form of resistance to movement. Work is a scalar quantity and is given by the product of the average component of force in the direction of movement, F, and the distance, l, through which the force acts:

$$W = F \times l$$

The unit of work is the joule (J) which is defined as the amount of work done when a force of 1 newton acts through a distance of 1 metre

$$1\,J = 1\,N\,m$$

Mechanical work

Example 4.1. Find the work done by a force of 12 N which moves a load through a distance of 20 m in the direction of the force:

$$W = \text{work done},\ F = 12\,N,\ l = 20\,m$$
$$W = F \times l$$
$$= 12 \times 20\,J = 240\,J$$

Work done by a force applied at an angle to the direction of motion

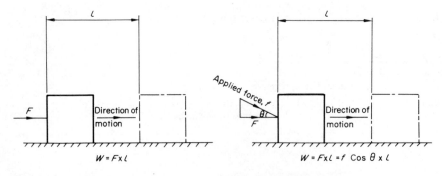

Fig. 4.1. Work done by a force applied at an angle to the direction of motion

26

Example 4.2. Calculate the work done in moving a block 40 m along a horizontal surface by a force of 400 N acting at an angle of $\boxed{30°}$ to the surface:

$W = $ work done, $F = 400\cos 30° \text{ N} = 400 \times 0\cdot866 \text{ N} = 346\cdot4 \text{ N}, l = 40 \text{ m}$

$$W = F \times l$$
$$= 346\cdot4 \times 40 \text{ J} = 13\cdot86 \text{ kJ}$$

Example 4.3. A transformer is hauled across a shop floor by a rope inclined at $\boxed{20°}$. The average rope tension is 2 kN. How far will the transformer be moved for every 10 kJ of work done?

$l = $ distance moved, $F = 2\cos 20° = 2 \times 0\cdot9397 \text{ kN} = 1\cdot879 \text{ kN}, W = 10 \times 10^3 \text{J}$

$$W = F \times l$$
$$10 \times 10^3 = 1\cdot879 \times 10^3 \times l$$
$$l = \frac{10 \times 10^3}{1\cdot879 \times 10^3} \text{ m} = 5\cdot32 \text{ m}$$

Work done in lifting. This work is the product of the weight of the body and the vertical distance moved.

Example 4.4. A mass of 20 kg is moved a distance of 60 m up a slope of 1 in 15 (rises 1 m for every 15 m along the slope) by a force of 30 N parallel to the slope. Determine:

(a) the total work done,

(b) the work done in lifting.

(a) $W = $ total work done, $F = 30 \text{ N}, l = 60 \text{ m}$

$$W = F \times l$$
$$= 30 \times 60 \text{ J} = 1\cdot8 \text{ kJ}$$

(b) $W = $ work done in lifting, $F = $ weight of the mass $= 20 \times 10 \text{ N} = 200 \text{ N}$ (refer to section 2.9), $l = 60 \times \frac{1}{15} \text{ m} = 4 \text{ m}$

$$W = F \times l$$
$$= 200 \times 4 \text{ J} = 800 \text{ J}$$

Work done by a variable force. The average force, F, is the average height of a force-distance graph. It is found by dividing the area into a number of equal width vertical strips and inserting mid-ordinates f_1, f_2, etc. (Fig. 4.2(a)).

$$F = \frac{f_1 + f_2 + f_3 \cdots}{\text{number of mid-ordinates}}$$

27

For standard shapes such as triangles the average force can be calculated from standard formulae.

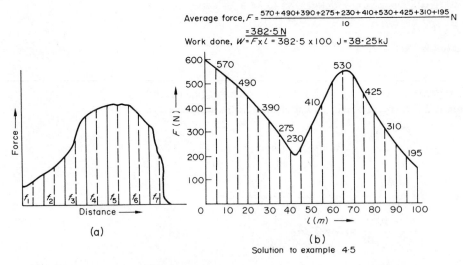

Average force, $F = \dfrac{570+490+390+275+230+410+530+425+310+195}{10}$ N

$= 382.5$ N

Work done, $W = F \times l = 382.5 \times 100$ J $= \underline{38.25\,kJ}$

Solution to example 4·5

Fig. 4.2. Work done by a variable force

Since $W = F \times l$ the area under a force-distance graph represents the work done and is therefore called a work diagram.

Example 4.5. During a towing operation the pulling force, F, between a car and breakdown truck varied with towing distance l as shown in the following table:

F (N)	600	450	220	510	380	150
l (m)	0	20	40	60	80	100

Determine the average tractive force and hence calculate the work done over the 100 m, Fig. 4.2(b).

Work done by a turning force. This is given by the product of the normal force F acting at a radius R and the length of arc l through which it moves, Fig. 4.3.

$$W = F \times l = F \times R\theta = T\theta \ (\theta \text{ in radians})$$

Work done per revolution $= 2\pi T$

Work done in n revolutions $= 2\pi n T$

Example 4.6. The force exerted by a brake shoe on a 0·4-m diameter brake drum is 300 N. What is the work done on the drum in 40 revolutions?

$W =$ work done, $F = 300$ N, $l = 2\pi n R = 2\pi \times 40 \times 0.2$ m $= 50.27$ m

$$W = F \times l = 300 \times 50.27 \text{ N m} = \underline{15.081 \text{ kN m}}$$

28

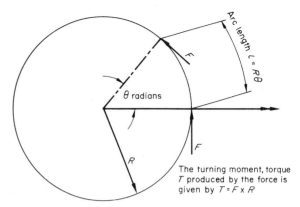

The turning moment, torque T produced by the force is given by $T = F \times R$

Fig. 4.3. Work done by a turning force

4.2 Energy, W

Energy is the ability to do work. Energy is expended when work is done. Energy is available in many forms, chemical, thermal, mechanical, electrical, etc. Units of energy and work are the same, hence the unit of all forms of energy is the joule (J).

Mechanical energy is available due to distortion, the position, or motion of a body.

Potential energy, W_p. This is the energy possessed by a body due to its position or distortion from an initial reference. The amount of potential energy possessed by a body exerting a downward force F, at a vertical height h above the reference level, is given by:

$$W_p = F \times h$$

The energy possessed by a body distorted by an amount x due to an average force F, is given by:

$$W_p = F \times x$$

Example 4.7. A mass of 60 kg is moved 1 km up a slope, the average incline of which is 30° to the horizontal. What is the increase in its potential energy?

W_p = increase in potential energy, $F = 60 \times 10$ N $= 600$ N, $h = 1000 \sin 30°$ m $= 500$ m

$$W_p = F \times h$$

$$= 600 \times 500 \text{ J} = \underline{300 \text{ kJ}}$$

29

Example 4.8. A spring which compresses 1 mm for every 0·2 N load is compressed 16 mm. How much energy is stored in the spring?

$$W_p = \text{energy stored, average force } F = \frac{0{\cdot}2 \times 16}{2} \text{ N} = 1{\cdot}6 \text{ N}, \, x = 16 \times 10^{-3} \text{ m}$$

$$W_p = F \times x$$

$$= 1{\cdot}6 \times 16 \times 10^{-3} \text{ J} = \underline{25{\cdot}6 \text{ mJ}}$$

Kinetic energy, W_k. This is the energy possessed by a body due to its motion. The amount of kinetic energy possessed by a body of mass m at a velocity v, is given by:

$$W_k = \tfrac{1}{2}mv^2$$

Example 4.9. Determine the kinetic energy of a car of mass 1000 kg when travelling at 20 m/s:

W_k = kinetic energy, $m = 1000$ kg, $v = 20$ m/s

$$W_k = \tfrac{1}{2}mv^2$$

$$= \tfrac{1}{2} \times 1000 \times 20^2 \text{ J} = \underline{200 \text{ kJ}}$$

Example 4.10. The kinetic energy possessed by each kilogramme of water at the foot of a certain water-fall was 100 J. Determine the velocity of the water:

v = velocity of the water, $W_k = 100$ J, $m = 1$ kg

$$W_k = \tfrac{1}{2}mv^2$$

$$100 = \tfrac{1}{2} \times 1 \times v^2$$

$$v^2 = 2 \times 100 \times 1 = 200$$

$$v = \underline{14{\cdot}14 \text{ m/s}}$$

Electrical energy, W. A joule of energy is expended when 1 coulomb of electricity is moved between two points having a potential difference between them of 1 volt.

If Q is the quantity of electricity in coulombs, given by the product of current I amperes, time t seconds, and potential difference V volts, then:

$$W = QV = VIt \text{ joules}$$

The kilowatt hour is also an acceptable unit where

$$W = \frac{VIt}{1000} \text{ kilowatt hours} \quad \text{where } t \text{ is the time in hours.}$$

Example 4.11. Calculate the energy in:

(a) megajoules,

(b) kilowatt hours,

expended when a current of 12 A flows through a resistance of 5 Ω for 30 min:

W = energy expended, $V = IR = 12 \times 5$ V $= 60$ V, $I = 12$ A

(a)
$$W = VIt$$
$$= 60 \times 12 \times 30 \times 60 \text{ J} = 1 \cdot 296 \text{ MJ}$$

(b)
$$W = 60 \times 12 \times 0 \cdot 5 \text{ W h} = 0 \cdot 36 \text{ kWh}$$

Example 4.12. Determine the time taken for 6 kJ of energy to be expended by a current of 4 A flowing across a potential difference of 100 V:

t = time taken, $I = 4$ A, $V = 100$ V, $W = 6$ kJ

$$W = VIt$$
$$6 \times 10^3 = 100 \times 4 \times t$$
$$t = \frac{6 \times 10^3}{100 \times 4} \text{ s} = 15 \text{ s}$$

Thermal energy, Q. Heat is a form of energy. The amount of energy required to raise the temperature of 1 kilogramme of a substance by 1 kelvin, without changing its state, is called the specific heat capacity (c). Values of specific heat capacities for different materials can be obtained from tables of physical constants; e.g., c for water = 4·18 kJ/kg K, c for aluminium = 0·385 kJ/kg K.

If m is the mass of the substance in kilogrammes, c the specific heat capacity of the substance in kilojoules per kilogramme kelvin and $\delta\theta$ is the temperature change in kelvins, then:

Quantity of sensible heat Q_s gained or lost by a substance is given by

$$Q_s = m \times c \times \delta\theta \text{ kilojoules}$$

Example 4.13. Find the quantity of sensible heat gained by 10 kg of water at a temperature of 313 K when its temperature rises to 353 K. Specific heat capacity of water is 4·18 kJ/kg K.

Q_s = quantity of sensible gained heat, $m = 10$ kg, $\delta\theta = (353 - 313)$ K $= 40$ K, $c = 4 \cdot 18$ kJ/kg K

$$Q_s = m \times c \times \delta\theta$$
$$= 10 \times 4 \cdot 18 \times 40 \text{ kJ} = 1 \cdot 672 \text{ MJ}$$

31

Example 4.14. If 8 kJ of energy are added to 2·5 kg of iron having a specific heat capacity of 0·46 kJ/kg K, what will be the temperature rise of the iron (assume no change of state)?

$\delta\theta$ = temperature rise, $c = 0\cdot46$ kJ/kg K, $m = 2\cdot5$ kg, $Q_s = 80$ kJ

$$Q_s = m \times c \times \delta\theta$$
$$80 = 2\cdot5 \times 0\cdot46 \times \delta\theta$$

$$\delta\theta = \frac{80}{2\cdot5 \times 0\cdot46} \text{ K} = \underline{69\cdot6 \text{ K}}$$

4.3 Power, P

Power is the rate at which energy is expended. If t is the time taken to expend energy W, then:

$$P = \frac{W}{t}$$

The unit for all forms of power is the watt (W), where

$$1 \text{ watt} = 1 \text{ joule per second}$$

Torque power. If a shaft produces a torque T at n revolutions per second then the torque power developed is given by:

$$P = 2\pi nT = \omega T \text{ watts}$$

where T is in newton metres and ω in radians per second.

Example 4.15. A car developing a power of 40 kW is accelerated for 20 s. Determine the energy dissipated:

W = energy dissipated, $P = 40$ kW, $t = 20$ s

$$W = P \times t$$
$$W = 40 \times 10^3 \times 20 \text{J}$$
$$= \underline{800 \text{ kJ}}$$

Example 4.16. Determine the torque produced by a belt and pulley system which transmits a power of 20 kW at an angular speed of 12 rev/s:

$$P = 2\pi nT$$
$$20 \times 10^3 = 2\pi \times 12 \times T$$
$$T = \frac{20 \times 10^3}{2\pi \times 12} \text{ N m} = \underline{264\cdot5 \text{ N m}}$$

4.4 Conservation of energy

For normal considerations all energy generated is either converted into useful energy or lost in the form of energy which does not contribute to the function of the energy transfer, e.g., in converting electrical energy into light energy by an electric light bulb some of the energy is wasted in the form of heat.

4.5 Efficiency of energy transfer η

This is the ratio of useful energy output to energy input between any two separate sections during energy transfer.

Efficiency of energy transfer $\eta = \dfrac{\text{useful energy output}}{\text{energy input}} \times 100\%$

The useful energy output = energy input − energy losses.

Energy losses arise due to energy transfer which is not available for the purpose for which the device is being used, e.g., the heat produced by the electric light bulb.

Example 4.17. A 2 kW immersion heater was found to take 10 minutes to raise the temperature of 15 kg of water, having a specific heat capacity of 4·18 kJ/kg K, by 18 K.
Calculate:
(a) the energy loss, and
(b) the efficiency of the energy transfer.

(a)
$$\text{Energy input} = P \times t$$
$$= 2 \times 10^3 \times 10 \times 60 \text{ J} = 1\cdot2 \text{ MJ}$$

$$\text{Useful energy output} = m \times c \times \delta\theta$$
$$= 15 \times 4\cdot18 \times 18 \text{ kJ} = 1\cdot129 \text{ MJ}$$

$$\text{Energy loss} = (1\cdot2 - 1\cdot129) \text{ MJ} = \underline{71 \text{ kJ}}$$

(b)
$$\eta = \frac{\text{useful energy output}}{\text{energy input}} \times 100\%$$

$$= \frac{1\cdot129}{1\cdot2} \times 100\% = \underline{94\%}$$

Example 4.18. An electric motor rotating at 30 rev/s raises a load of 100 N by means of a cord passing round a 0·1 m diameter pulley mounted on the motor shaft. If the overall efficiency is 80%, what is the power taken from the supply?

W_I = work input, W_O = useful work output = $F \times l = 100 \times 0\cdot1 \times \pi$ J/rev = 10π J/rev,

$$\eta = \frac{80}{100}$$

$$\eta = \frac{W_O}{W_I}$$

$$\frac{80}{100} = \frac{10\pi}{W_I}$$

$$W_I = 10\pi \times \frac{100}{80} \text{ J/rev} = \underline{39\cdot27 \text{ J/rev}}$$

33

P = power taken, t = time per revolution = $\frac{1}{30}$ s

$$P = \frac{W_1}{t}$$

$$= \frac{39\cdot27}{\frac{1}{30}} \ W = 1178\cdot1 \ W = \underline{1\cdot178 \ kW}$$

Example 4.19. The output of a gas engine was found to be 4·75 kW. A dynamometer, used to check the output, contained 20 kg of water of specific heat capacity 4·18 kJ/kg K. Calculate by how much the temperature of the water rose during a 20-minute running period. Neglect losses.

$P = 4\cdot75$ kW, $t = 20 \times 60$ s $= 1200$ s

$$\text{Energy output of gas engine} = P \times t$$

$$= 4\cdot75 \times 1200 \ kJ = 5700 \ kJ$$

$\delta\theta$ = temperature rise, $m = 20$ kg, $c = 4\cdot18$ kJ/kg K

Quantity of sensible heat energy gained by the water $Q_s = m \times c \times \delta\theta$

$$= 20 \times 4\cdot18 \times \delta\theta \ kJ$$

$$= 83\cdot6 \ \delta\theta \ kJ$$

Therefore, neglecting losses $83\cdot6 \ \delta\theta = 5700$

$$\delta\theta = \frac{5700}{83\cdot6} \ K = \underline{68\cdot18 \ K}$$

Problems

1.   The work done per stroke of a horizontal shaper in machining a block of metal 0·3 m long is 600 J. What is the force exerted on the tool tip?

2.   Explain what is meant by the terms work, energy, and power, and define the unit in which each of these quantities may be measured. State the principle of conservation of energy.

3.   150 J of energy are used in moving a load a distance of 12 m in the direction of the applied force. What is the magnitude of the applied force?

4.   A man drags a sack of coal at a uniform speed along a horizontal floor by exerting a constant force of 150 N, the angle between his arm and the floor being 45°. How much work does he perform in moving the sack a distance of 10 m?

5.   A bucket of water of mass 8 kg is pulled up a well by means of a rope 20 m long. The rope has a mass of 0·4 kg/m and is completely wound up when the bucket reaches the surface. Calculate:

(a) the work done in raising the bucket to the surface
(b) the power required if the task took 40 s.

6. A heavy cable being pulled through a length of underground pipe 15 m long has the following forces exerted on it at various distances:

Distance (m)	1	2	3	4	6	8	10	12	13
Force (N)	400	450	600	720	800	890	1000	1200	1350

Distance (m)	14	15
Force (N)	1400	1500

Find the work done in pulling the cable through the pipe.

7. What quantities are measured in newtons, joules, and watts? Give a definition of each of these three units. A car of mass 1000 kg is driven at a steady speed of 45 km/h up a gradient of 1 in 20 (i.e., rising 1 m in a slope distance of 20 m). Find the power used in overcoming the force of gravity and the work done against gravity in driving the car a distance of 1 km. The acceleration due to gravity may be taken as 10 m/s^2.   (C.G.L.I.)

8. Determine the amount a coiled spring, which extends 1 mm for every 0·6 N load, will extend when 54 mJ of energy are expended in stretching it.

9. Explain the terms work and power and define the unit in which each may be measured. A pump having an efficiency of 85% takes 30 min to raise 10 m^3 of water through a vertical height of 20 m. Find the amount of work done on the water, the output power of the pump, and the amount of energy wasted in the process. The acceleration due to gravity may be taken as 10 m/s^2 (1 m3 of water has a mass of 1000 kg).   (C.G.L.I.)

10. Define the newton, the joule, and the watt. Water is pumped upward at a uniform rate through a vertical distance of 50 m into a storage tank having a capacity of 30 m^3. The power input to the pumping system is 10 kW. If the overall efficiency is 65%, find the time taken to fill the tank.   (C.G.L.I.)

11. An inclined pit shaft is 0·5 km long. At the bottom of the shaft is a skip of mass 400 kg, supported by a chain having a mass of 0·6 kg/m. If the incline is 0·15 m rise per 2 m of slope, calculate the total work done against gravity in raising the skip up the shaft.

12. A drill is sharpened on a 100 mm diameter grinding wheel rotating at 7 rev/s. The tangential pressure exerted on the drill is 15 N, calculate the work done on the drill in 30 s. What is the power input to the grinder motor if losses amount to 10%?

13. A belt-driven pulley 0·4 m in diameter rotates at 4 rev/s. The tension in the tight side of the belt is 420 N and in the slackside 80 N. Calculate:

(a) the torque on the pulley
(b) the work done in 500 revolutions
(c) the power developed.

Note: The net turning force is the difference in tensions between the two sides of the belt.

14. A belt brake is used in a test on an induction motor. The load on the 80 mm diameter brake is 40 N and the average spring balance reading 5 N. Determine the power output of the motor when the motor is rotating at 3 rev/s.
Note: The effective braking force is the difference between the load and spring balance reading.

15. Calculate the torque in N m at the output shaft of a motor developing 20 kW at 5 rev/s.

35

16. Explain the terms potential energy and kinetic energy. A force of 20 N acts on a body of mass 2 kg, initially at rest, until it has moved a distance of 4 m. Calculate the work done by the force in joules. Assuming that all the work done is used in producing kinetic energy, what is the velocity of the body? If the velocity were halved, what would be its new value of kinetic energy.

17. A pile driver of mass 600 kg is raised to a height of 6 m. Determine:

(a) the potential energy of the driver
(b) its velocity just before it hits the pile.

18. A 1·5-kW kettle operates on a 240-V supply for 10 min. What is the energy expended in kJ and the current taken from the supply?

19. Find the voltage across a circuit in which a current of 16 A expends 320 kJ of energy in 160 s.

20. Determine the quantity of heat required to raise the temperature of 0·2 kg of aluminium having a specific heat capacity of 0·385 kJ/kg K by 40 K.

21. A 100-kW electric furnace is used to raise the temperature of blocks of copper by 140 K. Specific heat capacity of copper is 0·4237 kJ/kg K. Find the mass of copper that can be handled per hour if the efficiency of heat transfer is 95%.

22. During an experiment a block of metal of mass 2 g is fired at a velocity of 400 m/s into a tank containing 5 kg of water having a specific heat capacity of 4·187 kJ/kg K. Find the temperature rise in the water due to loss of kinetic energy, assuming all the kinetic energy is dissipated in the water.

23. A 3 kW electric motor is used to drive a small hoist and is capable of lifting a mass of 210 kg through a distance of 5 m. Calculate the time taken for the lift. The efficiency of energy transfer is 0·7 per unit.

Answers

1.	2 kN	3.	12·5 N	4.	1·06 kJ
5.	2·4 kJ, 60 W	6.	13·2 kJ	7.	6·26 kW, 500 kJ
8.	13·42 mm	9.	2 MJ, 1·11 kW,	10.	37·8 min
11.	206·25 kJ		0·353 MJ	12.	989·75 J, 36·65 W
13.	68 N m, 213·8 kJ, 1·71	14.	26·4 W	15.	637 N m
	kW	16.	80 J, 8·94 m/s, 20 J	17.	36 kJ, 10·95 m/s
18.	900 kJ, 6·25 A	19.	125 V	20.	3·08 kJ
21.	5·780 t	22.	7·65 K	23.	5 s

5. Mechanical machines

A machine is a device which transfers and transforms energy. Most of the machines in this chapter are basically lifting machines which enable a large mass to be lifted with a relatively small effort. The following terms are applied to machines.

Mechanical advantage, m.a. is the number of times that the force applied to the load, L, is greater than the force of the effort, E.

$$\text{m.a.} = \frac{L}{E}$$

Velocity ratio, v.r. is the number of times that the distance moved by the effort, is greater than the distance moved by the load, during the same period of time.

$$\text{v.r.} = \frac{\text{distance moved by the effort}}{\text{distance moved by the load}}$$

Efficiency, η, is the fraction or percentage of the input that is usefully used.

$$\eta = \frac{\text{useful work performed on the load}}{\text{work input by the effort}} \times 100\%$$

$$\eta = \frac{\text{force applied to the load} \times \text{distance moved by the load}}{\text{effort} \times \text{distance moved by the effort}} \times 100\%$$

$$\eta = \frac{\text{m.a.}}{\text{v.r.}} \times 100\%$$

Ideal effort and ideal load force are the effort and load force on a machine when friction is neglected. The efficiency is 100% and m.a. = v.r.

Mass, m. The mass in kilogrammes that can be lifted by a load force, L newtons, can for most practical purposes be calculated from:

$$m = \frac{L}{10} \text{ kilogrammes}$$

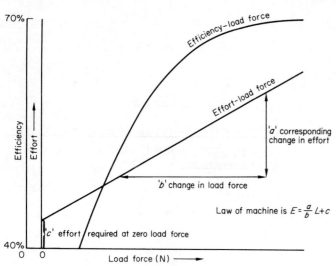

Fig. 5.1. Typical machine characteristics

The law of machine labels:

'a' corresponding change in effort

'b' change in load force

Law of machine is $E = \frac{a}{b}L + c$

'c' effort required at zero load force

5.1 Rope and pulley blocks

These are usually combined to form a lifting machine as shown in Fig. 5.2 but can be used in any position. It is a relatively cheap form of lifting gear and is easily portable, but great care must be taken to ensure the good condition of the ropes. Load forces up to about 5 times the effort can generally be obtained with this type of lifting machine. If the load is raised a distance S then each of the supporting ropes will shorten by the same amount and the effort will move a distance of $S \times$ the number of supporting ropes. For the six-wheel system shown in Fig. 5.2(a),

$$\text{v.r.} = \frac{6 \times S}{S} = 6 \quad \text{and} \quad \eta = \frac{L}{6E} \times 100\%$$

The velocity ratio depends on the number of supporting ropes, in this case 6.

Example 5.1. Draw a diagram showing a rope and pulley block system having a velocity ratio of 3. Assuming an efficiency of 80%, determine the mass in kilogrammes that can be lifted by an effort of 240 N:

$L =$ load force, effort $E = 240$ N, efficiency $\eta = 80\%$, v.r. $= 3$

$$\eta = \frac{\text{m.a.}}{\text{v.r.}} \times 100\%$$

$$80 = \frac{L}{3E} \times 100 = \frac{L}{3 \times 240} \times 100$$

$$L = \frac{3 \times 240 \times 80}{100} \text{N} = 576 \text{ N}$$

m = mass that can be lifted, L = load force = 576 N

$$m = \frac{L}{10} \text{ kilogrammes}$$

$$= \frac{576}{10} \text{ kg} = \underline{57\cdot6 \text{ kg}}$$

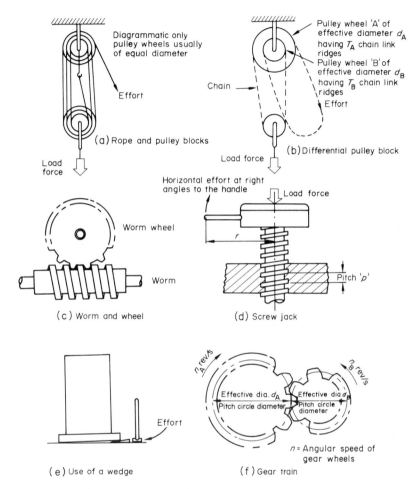

Fig. 5.2. Lifting devices and mechanisms

5.2 Differential (continuous chain) pulley block

This is a lifting machine which is more expensive and not so easily portable as the
rope and pulley blocks but is less prone to wear and deterioration. In the form shown
in Fig. 5.2 differential pulley blocks are capable of applying load forces in the region
of 40 times the effort. Load forces up to 120 times can be obtained with additional
gearing.

An effort applied to the chain as shown in Fig. 5.2(b) moves the chain and in turn the pulley wheels which are ridged to fit the links of the chain. The same length of chain is moved around all the pulleys. When wheel A turns through one revolution wheel B turns through one revolution. Therefore the chain between the upper pulley block and the load pulley will shorten by the difference between the length of chain wound onto wheel A and that wound off wheel B.

$$\text{v.r.} = \frac{d_A}{\frac{1}{2}(\pi d_A - \pi d_B)} = \frac{2d_A}{\pi(d_A - d_B)}$$

Since the diameters are proportional to the number of ridges on the pulley wheels

$$\text{v.r.} = \frac{2T_A}{T_A - T_B} \quad \text{and} \quad \eta = \frac{L}{E} \times \frac{T_A - T_B}{2T_A} \times 100\%$$

Example 5.2. A differential pulley block is required to lift a mass of 280 kg. The larger wheel has 20 ridges and the smaller 18. Calculate the effort required if the efficiency is taken as 70%:

v.r. = velocity ratio, $T_A = 20$, $T_B = 18$

$$\text{v.r.} = \frac{2T_A}{T_A - T_B}$$

$$= \frac{2 \times 20}{20 - 18} = \frac{40}{2} = 20$$

E = effort required, $L = 280 \times 10 \text{ N} = 2800 \text{ N}$, $\eta = 70\%$

$$\eta = \frac{L}{E} \times \frac{T_A - T_B}{2T_A} \times 100\%$$

$$70 = \frac{2800}{E} \times \frac{20 - 18}{2 \times 20} \times 100\%$$

$$E = \frac{2800}{70} \times \frac{1}{20} \times 100 \text{ N}$$

$$= \underline{200 \text{ N}}$$

5.3 Winch

This is a free-standing or floor-anchored machine, which may be used to exert a load force in any direction. Its main uses include light cranes, over trenches to pull cables, or as a direct lifting machine. Load forces in the region of 20 times the effort can be applied by this basic type of machine.

An effort applied to the handle turns the smaller gear which in turn rotates the larger gear and drum in the opposite direction. The rope anchored to the drum is wound in and the load moved towards the drum. When used as a lifting machine turning the handle in the opposite direction lowers the load.

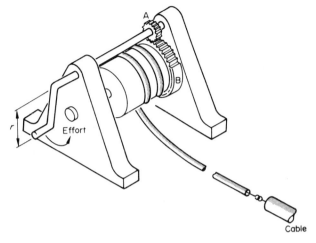

Fig. 5.3. Simple winch

In one revolution, the effort moves a distance of $2\pi r$ and the load moves a distance of $\pi d \times T_A/T_B$, where d is the mean diameter of the rope centres around the drum, Fig. 5.3.

$$\text{v.r.} = \frac{2\pi r}{\pi d \times (T_A/T_B)} = \frac{2r\,T_B}{dT_A} \quad \text{and} \quad \eta = \frac{L \times dT_A}{E \times 2rT_B} \times 100\,\%$$

Example 5.3. A single gear winch as shown in Fig. 5.3 has 14 teeth on gear A and 56 teeth on gear B. The mean diameter of the rope centres is 0·3 m. Assuming an efficiency of 85%, calculate the greatest mass that can be lifted by a man who can exert a constant effort of 200 N at a handle of radius 0·5 m. What is the mechanical advantage of the winch?

L = load force, $E = 200$ N, $r = 0·5$ m, $T_A = 14$, $T_B = 56$, $d = 0·3$ m, $\eta = 85\%$

$$\eta = \frac{L \times dT_A}{E \times 2rT_B} \times 100\%$$

$$85 = \frac{L \times 0·3 \times 14}{200 \times 2 \times 0·5 \times 56} \times 100$$

$$L = \frac{85 \times 200 \times 2 \times 0·5 \times 56}{0·3 \times 14 \times 100}\,\text{N} = \underline{2267\ \text{N}}$$

41

m = greatest mass that can be lifted, $L = 2267$ N

$$m = \frac{L}{10}$$

$$m = \frac{2267}{10}\ \text{kg} = 226 \cdot 7\ \text{kg}$$

$$\text{m.a.} = \frac{L}{E}$$

$$= \frac{2267}{200} = 11 \cdot 33$$

5.4 Worm and worm wheel

The worm and worm wheel is used to supply a rotational driving load force to the wheel at right angles to the effort applied to the worm shaft, such as the rear axle drive on trucks and relay drives from electric motors, etc.

Figure 5.2(c) shows a worm and worm wheel drive, one revolution of the worm advances the worm wheel one tooth.

$$\text{v.r.} = \frac{\text{number of teeth on the worm wheel}}{1}$$

The velocity ratio and the $90°$-change in the direction of the applied force are the important features of this machine, the former acting as a reduction gear.

Example 5.4. A worm and worm wheel is used as an 18:1 reduction drive. The efficiency of the drive at normal load is 76%. What is the mechanical advantage of the drive?

m.a. = mechanical advantage, $\eta = 76\%$, v.r. = 18

$$\eta = \frac{\text{m.a.}}{\text{v.r.}} \times 100\ \%$$

$$76 = \frac{\text{m.a.}}{18} \times 100$$

$$\text{m.a.} = \frac{76 \times 18}{100} = 13 \cdot 68$$

Note: In order to prevent run-back on high efficiency lifting machines, locking or friction devices are often fitted.

5.5 Screw jack

This is a lifting machine used between the load and some fixed platform or the ground. It is easily portable, strong, and capable of giving a very high mechanical advantage, but has a low efficiency. A horizontal effort applied to the handle turns the load platform and the screw of the jack. For simple single-start screws each revolution raises the platform and load one screw-thread pitch p, Fig. 5.2(d).

$$\text{v.r.} = \frac{2\pi r}{p} \quad \text{and} \quad \eta = \frac{L \times p}{E \times 2\pi r} \times 100\%$$

Example 5.5. A simple single-start screw jack has a thread-pitch of 10 mm. What effort would be required at a radius of 0·3 m to lift a mass of 120 kg?; the efficiency of the jack at this load is 30%.

$E =$ effort required, $\eta = 30\%$, $L = 120 \times 10$ N $= 1200$ N, $r = 0\cdot3$ m $= 300$ mm, $p = 10$ mm

$$\eta = \frac{L \times p}{E \times 2\pi r} \times 100\%$$

$$30 = \frac{1200 \times 10}{E \times 2\pi \times 300} \times 100$$

$$E = \frac{1200 \times 10}{2\pi \times 300} \times \frac{100}{30} \text{ N} = \underline{21\cdot22 \text{ N}}$$

5.6 The wedge

Wedges may be made of wood or metal, they are used to force a gap between two surfaces. They are easily made or relatively cheap to purchase and can therefore be left in position without concern for capital costs. Figure 5.2(e) shows a wedge being used to lift one end of a transformer tank. A force must be applied sufficient to overcome friction and to raise the load up the slope of the wedge. The greater the slope of the wedge the lower the velocity ratio and the greater the applied force required.

5.7 Gear trains

Gears are used to transmit greater power than belt drives, Fig. 5.2(f). They have a high efficiency and no slip. Where only two gears are used direction of rotation is reversed, but direction of rotation can be maintained by the insertion of an idling wheel between the driving and the transmitting gears. The gears can be considered as smooth wheels having effective diameters d_A and d_B running at the same rim speed. Since the diameters are proportional to the number of gear teeth T_A and T_B:

$$\frac{n_A}{n_B} = \frac{d_B}{d_A} = \frac{T_B}{T_A}$$

Example 5.6. A driving wheel has 40 teeth and rotates at 6 rev/s, it is required to drive a transmitting gear at 8 rev/s in the same direction. To do this an idling gear having 24 teeth is placed between the two gears. Determine the number of teeth on the transmitting gear:

T_C = number of teeth on transmitting gear, $T_A = 40$, $T_B = 24$, $n_A = 6$ rev/s, $n_C = 8$ rev/s

$$\frac{n_A}{n_B} = \frac{T_B}{T_A} \,(1) \quad \text{and} \quad \frac{n_B}{n_C} = \frac{T_C}{T_B} \,(2)$$

from (2)

$$T_C = \frac{n_B}{n_C} \times T_B$$

from (1)

$$n_B = n_A \times \frac{T_A}{T_B}$$

therefore,

$$T_C = n_A \times \frac{T_A}{T_B} \times \frac{T_B}{n_C} = n_A \times \frac{T_A}{n_C}$$

$$= 6 \times \frac{40}{8} = \underline{30 \text{ teeth}}$$

This example shows that idling gears can be ignored in the calculations of the speed of gears.

Problems

1.   Make a list showing which of the machines described in this chapter would be suitable to lift the following loads:
(a) 160-kg oil circuit-breaker
(b) 4-t transformer
(c) the rear end of a 400 kg electric truck.

2.   Make a sketch of a rope and pulley block having a velocity ratio of 5. What effort will be needed to raise a mass of 180 kg, assuming an efficiency of 60% at this load?

3.   The pulley system in Fig. 5.2(a) is required to lift a heavier load with the same effort. A spare pulley wheel is available. Make a sketch showing the modified pulley system, and state the effect on the velocity ratio and efficiency.

4.   A rope and pulley block system has a velocity ratio of 7. What would be the efficiency of the system when an effort of 360 N just lifts a mass of 196 kg?

5.   A differential pulley block was found to require an effort of 280 N to raise a mass of 285·6 kg. 17 chain links pass over the larger pulley while 15 links pass over the smaller pulley. Find:
(a) the mechanical advantage
(b) the velocity ratio
(c) the efficiency at this load.

6.   Make a sketch of a simple winch having an operating handle of radius r and a drum of diameter D round which a rope of diameter d is wound. Establish for the winch a formula for its velocity ratio. A simple winch has a drum of diameter 200 mm and is operated by a handle at a radius of 450 mm; it is used to lift a load of 80 kg by means of a 25 mm diameter rope. Determine the effort required at the handle if the efficiency of the winch at this load is 75%.

7. An experiment carried out on a single-gear winch gave the following results:

Load force (kN)	4	6	8	10
Effort (kN)	1	1·3	1·6	1·9

(a) Construct an effort-load force graph.
(b) Estimate the probable effort at a load force of 50 N.
(c) If the machine has a velocity ratio of 12, estimate the efficiency at the 50 N load force.

8. A rotary oil starter is operated by a worm and wheel drive. An effort of 15 N applied at a radius of 0·4 m from the worm axle is just sufficient to provide a force of 300 N at a switching stop on the worm wheel at a radius of 0·1 m. If the number of teeth on the worm wheel is 18, calculate the efficiency of the starter.

9. Describe two ways of modifying the winch in problem 6 in order to lift heavier loads with the same effort.

10. A screw jack has a screw-pitch of 10 mm and the effort is applied at a radius of 200 mm. The jack has a mechanical advantage of 50 when the mass being raised is 100 kg. Determine:
(a) the velocity ratio of the jack
(b) the effort required
(c) the efficiency at this load.

11. A switchgear cubicle is to be levelled by raising one end by means of a wedge, of what material would the wedge normally be made. If the first wedge used could not be driven under the cubicle, what factors will decide the selection of another wedge?

12. Give a practical application for each of the lifting devices in this chapter, preferably in connection with the lifting of electrical apparatus.

Answers

2. 600 N
3. The velocity ratio would increase to 7 and the efficiency would decrease.
4. efficiency = 77·8%
5. m.a. = 10·2, v.r. = 17, efficiency = 60%
6. v.r. = $2r/(D + d)$, effort = 266·7 N
7. Probable effort = 11 N, efficiency = 36·3%
8. 27·78%
9. Increase the length of the operating handle, decrease the drum diameter, increase the velocity ratio between the gears by adjusting the ratio T_A/T_B.
10. v.r. = 125·7, effort = 20 N, efficiency = 39·8%

6. Velocity and acceleration

6.1 Linear motion

This is the motion of a body in a straight line.

Average speed (v_{av}). Speed is the magnitude of velocity, which has both direction and magnitude. The average speed of a moving body between any two positions is given by:

$$v_{av} = \frac{\text{distance moved}}{\text{time taken}}$$

Units. Metre per second, (m/s), kilometre per hour, (km/h), etc.

Acceleration (a). For a body moving with constant acceleration, its acceleration (a) between any two positions is given by:

$$a = \frac{\text{change in speed}}{\text{time taken}}$$

Units. Metre per second squared, (m/s^2), kilometre per hour squared, (km/h^2), etc.

6.2 Basic relationships

For bodies having an initial speed u and final speed v in moving a distance l in time t with a constant acceleration a then

$$l = \frac{u + v}{2} \times t \quad \text{and} \quad v = u + at$$

Note:

(a) Deceleration is $-a$.

(b) Acceleration due to gravitational force is g (9·81 m/s^2).

(c) Units must be complementary, i.e., metre (m), metre per second (m/s), metre per second squared (m/s^2), and second (s).

Example 6.1. Find the average speed of an electric truck which travels a distance of 12 m in 4 s:

$$v_{av} = \frac{\text{distance moved}}{\text{time taken}} = \frac{12}{4} \text{ m/s} = \underline{3 \text{ m/s}}$$

46

Example 6.2. Calculate the acceleration of a linear motor whose initial speed was 14 m/s and after 11 s was travelling at 36 m/s:

$$a = \frac{\text{change in speed}}{\text{time taken}} = \frac{36 - 14}{11} \text{ m/s}^2 = \frac{22}{11} \text{ m/s}^2 = 2 \text{ m/s}^2$$

Example 6.3. An electric train starting from rest accelerates uniformly at 2 m/s^2. Calculate.

(a) its speed after 15 s,
(b) the time taken to reach 40 m/s.

(a) $v = $ velocity at the end of 15 s, $u = 0$, $a = 2 \text{ m/s}^2$, $t = 15$ s

$$v = u + at$$
$$v = (0 + 2 \times 15) \text{ m/s} = 30 \text{ m/s}$$

(b) $t = $ time taken to reach 40 m/s, $v = 40$ m/s, $a = 2 \text{ m/s}^2$

$$v = u + at$$
$$40 = 0 + 2 \times t$$
$$t = \frac{40}{2} \text{ s} = 20 \text{ s}$$

Example 6.4. An electrician working on pit-head gear drops his pliers down a mine shaft. The pliers took 12 s to reach the bottom. Calculate the depth of the shaft ($g = 9 \cdot 81 \text{ m/s}^2$):

It is first necessary to find the final velocity:

$v = $ final velocity, $u = 0$, $a = g = 9 \cdot 81 \text{ m/s}^2$, $t = 12$ s

$$v = u + at$$
$$v = (0 + 9 \cdot 81 \times 12) \text{ m/s} = 117 \cdot 72 \text{ m/s}$$

$l = $ depth of shaft

$$l = \frac{u + v}{2} \times t$$
$$= \frac{0 + 117 \cdot 72}{2} \times 12 \text{ m} = 706 \cdot 3 \text{ m}$$

Example 6.5. A model electric racing car crosses the finishing line at 6 km/h and slows down to 2 km/h in 3 m. Calculate its average retardation during this time:

$t = $ time taken, $u = 6$ km/h $= 1 \cdot 667$ m/s, $v = 2$ km/h $= 0 \cdot 555$ m/s, $l = 3$ m

$$l = \frac{u + v}{2} \times t$$
$$3 = \frac{1 \cdot 667 + 0 \cdot 555}{2} \times t$$
$$t = \frac{3 \times 2}{1 \cdot 667 + 0 \cdot 555} \text{ s} = 2 \cdot 7 \text{ s}$$

$-a$ = retardation

$$v = u + at$$

$$0{\cdot}555 = 1{\cdot}667 + a \times 2{\cdot}7$$

$$-a = \frac{1{\cdot}667 - 0{\cdot}555}{2{\cdot}7} \ \text{m/s}^2 = 0{\cdot}412 \ \text{m/s}^2$$

Example 6.6. During a rally a cyclist passes two check points A and B, 750 m apart. He passes A at 4·5 m/s then accelerates uniformly to pass B 2 min later. Calculate:

(a) the speed at which he passes B

(b) his acceleration.

(a) v = speed at B, $l = 750$ m, $u = 4{\cdot}5$ m/s, $t = 2$ min $= 120$ s

$$l = \frac{u + v}{2} \times t$$

$$750 = \frac{4{\cdot}5 + v}{2} \times 120$$

$$\frac{750}{60} = 4{\cdot}5 + v$$

$$v = \left(\frac{750}{60} - 4{\cdot}5\right) \text{m/s} = 8 \ \text{m/s}$$

(b) a = acceleration

$$v = u + at$$

$$8 = 4{\cdot}5 + a \times 120$$

$$a = \left(\frac{8 - 4{\cdot}5}{120}\right) \text{m/s}^2 = 29{\cdot}2 \ \text{mm/s}^2$$

6.3 Distance–time and speed–time graphs

The slope of the distance–time graph (Fig. 6.1) at any such point as A, B, C, etc., gives the speed at that point, which can be calculated approximately by constructing a small triangle, as shown, and applying:

$$v \text{ at A} = \frac{\text{change in distance}}{\text{time taken}}$$

This procedure can be repeated for a number of points, the results tabulated and a speed–time graph constructed. The slope of this graph at any point gives the acceleration at that point. A linear graph indicates that the motion takes place with constant acceleration, which can be calculated by constructing a triangle as shown (Fig. 6.1), and applying:

$$a = \frac{\text{change in speed}}{\text{time taken}}$$

The area under a speed–time graph at any time t gives the distance travelled at that time.

Example 6.7. The following table gives the corresponding distance travelled against time taken by an electric train moving from rest.

Distance, l (m)	50	200	450	800	1250	1800
Time, t (s)	5	10	15	20	25	30

Draw a distance–time graph and from it a speed–time graph. Hence find the acceleration of the train.

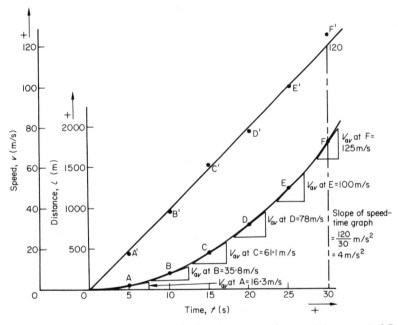

Fig. 6.1. Speed, distance–time graph for example 6.7

6.4 Angular motion

This is the motion of a body at a constant radius r about an axis of rotation O (Fig. 6.2(a))
The position of a point P after time t is given in terms of its radius and displacement θ radians from an initial axis OA.

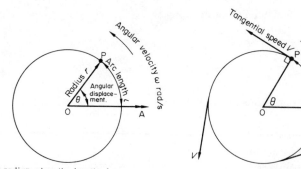

$\theta = 1$ radian when the length of arc ℓ is equal to the radius r
$\therefore 2\pi$ radians = 1 revolution and $\ell = r \times \theta$

NOTE: If the angular velocity ω is constant then the tangential speed V is constant but since its direction is always changing its velocity is not, therefore any point P is accelerating.

(a)   (b)

Fig. 6.2. Angular and angular-linear motion

6.5 Basic relationships

Angular motion relationships are similar to those for linear motion, in that, for bodies having an initial angular velocity ω_0 and final angular velocity ω_t when displaced through an angular displacement θ in time t with a constant angular acceleration α,

$$\theta = \frac{\omega_0 + \omega_t}{2} \times t \quad \text{and} \quad \omega_t = \omega_0 + \alpha t$$

Units. The units of time are usually seconds (s), but may be expressed in minutes (min) or hours (h). Angular speeds n revolutions per second (rev/s), can also be used since:

$$\text{Magnitude of } \omega = 2\pi n \text{ rad/s, therefore, } n = \frac{\omega}{2\pi}$$

If the angular speed is below 1 rev/s, n may be expressed in revolutions per minute. It is important to ensure that the units used are complementary to each other, i.e., rad/s, rad/s^2, s; rev/min, rev/min^2, min, etc.

6.6 Angular—linear relationships

For motion with constant angular velocity ω (Fig. 6.2(b))

$$\omega = \frac{v}{r}$$

where v is the linear speed of the point P.

Example 6.8. The armature of an electric motor accelerates uniformly from 10 rad/s to 40 rad/s in 3 s. Calculate:

(a) its angular displacement in this time,

50

(b) the angular acceleration.

θ = angular displacement, $\omega_0 = 10$ rad/s, $\omega_t = 40$ rad/s, $t = 3$ s

$$\theta = \frac{\omega_0 + \omega_t}{2} \times t$$

$$= \frac{10 + 40}{2} \times 3 \text{ rad} = \underline{75 \text{ rad}}$$

α = angular acceleration

$$\omega_t = \omega_0 + \alpha t$$

$$40 = 10 + \alpha \times 3$$

$$\alpha = \frac{40 - 10}{3} \text{ rad/s}^2 = \underline{10 \text{ rad/s}^2}$$

Example 6.9. A pulley 0·8 m diameter rotates at 8 rev/s. Calculate:

(a) its angular velocity in radians per second,

(b) the linear speed of its driving belt.

ω = angular velocity, $n = 8$ rev/s

$$\omega = 2\pi n \text{ rad/s}$$

$$= 2\pi \times 8 \text{ rad/s} = \underline{16\pi \text{ rad/s}}$$

v = linear speed of driving belt, $r = 0·4$ m

$$\omega = \frac{v}{r}$$

$$16\pi = \frac{v}{0·4}$$

$$v = 16\pi \times 0·4 \text{ m/s} = \underline{20·11 \text{ m/s}}$$

Example 6.10. A cyclist is riding at 16 km/h. The wheels of his cycle are 650 mm diameter. What will be the angular velocity of the wheels in rad/s? If he pulls up uniformly in 10 m what will be the angular retardation of the wheels?

ω = angular velocity, $v = 16$ km/h $= \dfrac{16\,000}{60 \times 60}$ m/s $= 4·445$ m/s, $r = 325$ mm $=$ 0·325 m

$$\omega = \frac{v}{r}$$

$$\omega = \frac{4·445}{0·325} \text{ rad/s} = \underline{13·68 \text{ rad/s}}$$

t = time taken, $\omega_0 = 13{\cdot}68$ rad/s, $\omega_t = 0$, $\theta = \dfrac{l}{r} = \dfrac{10}{0{\cdot}325} = 30{\cdot}77$ rad

$$\theta = \frac{\omega_0 + \omega_t}{2} \times t$$

$$30{\cdot}77 = \frac{13{\cdot}68 + 0}{2} \times t$$

$$t = \frac{61{\cdot}54}{13{\cdot}68}\ \text{s} = 4{\cdot}5\ \text{s}$$

$-\alpha$ = angular retardation,

$$\omega_t = \omega_0 + \alpha t$$

$$0 = 13{\cdot}68 + \alpha \times 4{\cdot}5$$

$$-\alpha = \frac{13{\cdot}68}{4{\cdot}5}\ \text{rad/s}^2 = 3{\cdot}04\ \text{rad/s}^2$$

Problems

1. Calculate the time taken by a vehicle in acquiring an average increase in velocity of 16 m/s in a distance of 8 m.

2. A particle is accelerated at 180 m/s² for 0·2 s. What is the change in speed of the particle?

3. Find the acceleration of a pile-driver falling freely from rest and reaching a velocity of 7·848 m/s after 0·8 s.

4. A car travelling at 90 km/h pulls up uniformly in 300 m. Calculate its deceleration.

5. An electric train reduces speed uniformly from 160 km/h to 40 km/h in 0·8 km. Determine how much further it will travel with the same deceleration before coming to rest, and the time taken.

6. A cyclist moving at 10 m/s decelerates at 1·2 m/s². Calculate his speed after 3 s and the time taken to come to rest.

7. A body moving with uniform acceleration has a velocity of 10 m/s at a point A and a velocity of 30 m/s at a point B, 80 m distance from A. Determine its acceleration and its velocity 4 s after leaving B.

8. A vehicle initially moving at 40 km/h is accelerated uniformly at 2 m/s². How long under these conditions does it take to travel 0·2 km?

9. A rocket fired vertically upward has an initial velocity of 3 km/s. Calculate, the height to which it will rise, and the time taken to reach this height ($g = 9{\cdot}81$ m/s²).

10. Determine the velocity at which supplies will strike the ground when dropped from a helicopter hovering at a height of 0·15 km ($g = 9{\cdot}81$ m/s²).

11.   During a linear motion experiment a ball is allowed to roll down a 'vee' section channel. The following table gives the displacement l and corresponding time t:

l (m)	0	0·5	1	1·5	2	2·5	3
t (s)	0	0·5	0·75	0·87	1	1·12	1·23

Plot the displacement–time graph. Use the graph to construct a speed–time graph, hence determine if the acceleration is uniform and if so calculate its value.

12.   A moving coal truck is uniformly decelerated. In the initial 40 s it covers 120 m and comes to rest in a total time of 80 s. Calculate the speed at 20 s, from the average speed in the first 40 s. Draw a speed–time graph and determine:

(a) its initial speed
(b) the total deceleration distance
(c) the rate of deceleration.

13.   A hovercraft starting from rest accelerates uniformly to a speed of 20 m/s at 0·16 m/s^2. It then travels at this speed for 600 s then decelerates to rest at 0·1 m/s^2. Draw a speed–time graph and determine the total distance travelled and the time taken.

14.   A flywheel, 3 m in diameter, rotates at 3 rev/s. Find the tangential speed of the rim in m/s.

15.   An alternator rotor takes 4 min to run up from rest to its normal speed of 20 rev/s. What is its angular acceleration?

16.   A pulley accelerates uniformly from rest to 400π rad/s in 2 s, it then decelerates uniformly to half this speed in 4 s, it remains at this speed for 3 s, then decelerates to rest in 0·5 s. Determine the total number of revolutions made by the pulley.

17.   A flywheel revolving at 4 rev/s has its angular speed reduced to 1 rev/s in 30 s. Find:

(a) the angular retardation in rad/s^2
(b) the number of revolutions made in the 30 s
(c) the linear speed of a point on the rim at a radius of 200 mm at 4 rev/s and 1 rev/s.

Answers

1.   0·5 s
2.   36 m/s
3.   9·81 m/s^2
4.   1·042 m/s^2
5.   53·3 m, 9·6 s
6.   6·4 m/s, 8·33 s
7.   5 m/s^2, 50 m/s
8.   9·64 s
9.   459 km, 306 s
10.   54·25 m/s
11.   4 m/s^2
12.   4 m/s, 160 m, 50 mm/s^2
13.   15·25 km, 15·4 min
14.   28·28 m/s
15. $^1/_{12}$ rev/s^2
16.   1125 rev
17.   (a) 0·6284 rad/s^2, (b) 75 revolutions
        (c) 5·027 m/s, 1·257 m/s

7. Direct current circuits

A direct current circuit is one in which the movement of electrons—or flow of current—takes place in one direction only. The following terms and units are used in d.c. circuits.

Electric current, I. The unit of electric current, called the ampere (A), is that constant current which, if maintained in two parallel rectilinear conductors of infinite length, of negligible circular cross-section, and placed at a distance of 1 metre apart in a vacuum, would produce between these conductors a force equal to 0.2 micro-newtons per metre length.

Quantity, Q. The unit of quantity of electricity, called the coulomb (C), is the quantity of electricity transported in 1 second by a current of 1 ampere.

Energy, W. The unit of energy, called the joule (J), is the work done when the point of application of a force of 1 newton is displaced through a distance of 1 metre in the direction of the force.

Power, P. The unit of power is 1 joule per second which is called the watt (W).

Resistance, R. The unit of electric resistance, called the ohm (Ω), is the resistance between two points of a conductor when a constant difference of potential of 1 volt, applied between these two points, produces in this conductor a current of 1 ampere, this conductor not being the source of any electromotive force.

Electric potential, p.d. The unit of electric potential, called the volt (V), is the difference of potential between two points of a conducting wire carrying a constant current of 1 ampere, when the power dissipated between these two points is equal to 1 watt.

7.1 Ohm's law

The current, I, flowing in a d.c. circuit depends on the circuit resistance, R, and the applied potential, V. These are related by Ohm's law which is usually stated as follows:

The current flowing in a circuit is directly proportional to the applied potential and inversely proportional to the resistance.

$$I \propto \frac{V}{R}$$

If I is in amperes, V in volts, and R in ohms then

$$I = \frac{V}{R}$$

Example 7.1. An electric heating element has a resistance of 25 Ω and is to operate on a 200-V supply. Determine the current taken by the heater:

I = heater current, $V = 200\ V$, $R = 25\ \Omega$

$$I = \frac{V}{R}$$

$$= \frac{200}{25}\ A = 8A$$

Example 7.2. What must be the resistance of an electric fire element which is designed to take a current of 4·5 A from a 200-V supply?

R = element resistance, $V = 200\ V$, $I = 4\cdot5\ A$

$$R = \frac{V}{I}$$

$$= \frac{200}{4\cdot5}\ \Omega = 44\cdot44\ \Omega$$

Example 7.3. The insulation resistance between the windings and the frame of an electric motor is 20 MΩ. Calculate the leakage current that will flow to earth when the motor is connected to a 400-V supply.

I = leakage current, $R = 20\ M\Omega = 20 \times 10^6\ \Omega$, $V = 400\ V$

$$I = \frac{V}{R}$$

$$= \frac{400}{20 \times 10^6}\ A = 20\ \mu A$$

7.2 Effect of material and dimensions on resistance

The resistance of any conductor or insulator depends on the material from which it is made, the cross-sectional area, A, and the length, l. The material determines the resistivity, ρ, which is defined as the resistance between opposite faces of a unit cube of the material.

If ρ is in ohm millimetres, l in millimetres, and A in square millimetres then:

$$R = \frac{\rho l}{A}\ \text{ohms}$$

Example 7.4. Calculate the resistance of 40 m of aluminium wire, of 2·9-mm² cross-sectional area, if the resistivity of the aluminium is 29 $\mu\Omega$ mm:

R = resistance of wire, $\rho = 29\ \mu\Omega$ mm $= 29 \times 10^{-6}\ \Omega$ mm, $l = 40$ m $= 40 \times 10^3$ mm, $A = 2\cdot9$ mm²

$$R = \frac{\rho l}{A}$$

$$= \frac{29 \times 10^{-6} \times 40 \times 10^3}{2\cdot9} \Omega = \underline{0\cdot4\ \Omega}$$

Example 7.5. A 100-m coil of copper wire of cross-sectional area 6 mm² has a resistance of 0·283 Ω. Calculate the resistivity of the copper:

ρ = resistivity of the copper, $R = 0\cdot283\ \Omega$, $l = 100$ m $= 100 \times 10^3$ mm, $A = 6$ mm²

$$R = \frac{\rho l}{A}$$

$$0\cdot283 = \frac{\rho \times 100 \times 10^3}{6}$$

$$\rho = \frac{0\cdot283 \times 6}{100 \times 10^3}\ \Omega\ \text{mm} = 0\cdot00001698\ \Omega\ \text{mm}$$

$$= \underline{16\cdot98\ \mu\Omega\ \text{mm}}$$

Example 7.6. A coil of copper wire 0·17-mm² cross-sectional area is connected to a 50-V d.c. supply and a current of 2·5 A flows. Calculate the length of wire on the coil if the resistivity of copper is 17 $\mu\Omega$ mm:

R = resistance of wire, $I = 2\cdot5$ A, $V = 50$ V

$$R = \frac{V}{I}$$

$$= \frac{50}{2\cdot5}\ \Omega = 20\ \Omega$$

l = length of wire, $A = 0\cdot17$ mm², $R = 20\ \Omega$, $\rho = 17\ \mu\Omega$ mm $= 17 \times 10^{-6}\ \Omega$ mm

$$R = \frac{\rho l}{A}$$

$$20 = \frac{17 \times 10^{-6} \times l}{0\cdot17}$$

$$l = \frac{20 \times 0\cdot17}{17 \times 10^{-6}}\ \text{mm} = 200\,000\ \text{mm} = \underline{200\ \text{m}}$$

7.3 Effect of temperature on resistance

There are a few materials such as Constantan, Eureka, and Minalpha whose resistances remain constant over normal ranges of temperature change. These are used in manufacturing such components as resistance boxes and instrument shunts.

The resistance of most other materials changes with a change in temperature. For a temperature increase, the resistance of:

pure metals   will increase, e.g., copper, iron
electrolytes   will decrease, e.g., sulphuric acid
insulators   will decrease, e.g., rubber, glass
carbon   will decrease

For most materials the resistance change will be uniform over their normal range of working temperature.

Temperature coefficient of resistance, α (units-per degree celsius, $/°C$). This is the ratio of the average change in resistance from $0°C$ for each degree change in temperature, to the resistance at $0°C$.

If the resistance at $0°C$ is known the resistance at any other temperature can be found from:

$$R_1 = R_0(1 + \alpha t_1)$$

where R_0 = resistance at $0°C$

R_1 = resistance at temperature $t_1 °C$

If the resistance at $0°C$ is not known, but is known at some other temperature, then the resistance at any temperature can be found by using the formula twice. The two formulae:

$$R_1 = R_0(1 + \alpha t_1) \quad \text{and} \quad R_2 = R_0(1 + \alpha t_2)$$

are usually combined together to give

$$\frac{R_1}{R_2} = \frac{(1 + \alpha t_1)}{(1 + \alpha t_2)}$$

where R_2 = resistance at temperature $t_2 °C$.

Example 7.7. The resistance of a relay coil used in a cold room test was 20 Ω at $0°C$. What would be its resistance when operating at a mean temperature of $20°C$, the temperature coefficient of resistance of the coil winding being $0.0043/°C$ at $0°C$?

Let R_1 be the resistance at $20°C$, $t_1 = 20°C$, $R_0 = 20\ \Omega$, $\alpha = 0.0043/°C$ at $0°C$

$$R_1 = R_0(1 + \alpha t_1)$$

$$= 20(1 + 0.0043 \times 20)\ \Omega$$

$$= 20(1.086)\ \Omega$$

$$R_1 = \underline{21.72\ \Omega}$$

Example 7.8. During a test on a d.c. generator the temperature of the field coils rose from 20°C to 50°C. If the resistance of the coils at the end of the test was 24 Ω, determine their initial resistance ($\alpha = 0.004/$°C at 0°C).

$R_1 =$ the initial resistance, $R_2 = 24 \Omega$, $t_1 = 20$°C, $\alpha = 0.004/$°C at 0°C.

$$\frac{R_1}{R_2} = \frac{1 + \alpha t_1}{1 + \alpha t_2}$$

$$\frac{R_1}{24} = \frac{1 + 0.004 \times 20}{1 + 0.004 \times 50} = \frac{1.08}{1.2}$$

$$R_1 = 24 \times \frac{1.08}{1.2} \; \Omega = \underline{21.6 \; \Omega}$$

Example 7.9. A carbon resistor has a resistance of 100 Ω at 30°C and 98·95 Ω at 70°C. Determine the average temperature coefficient of resistance of carbon over this temperature range:

$\alpha =$ average temperature coefficient of resistance, $R_1 = 100 \; \Omega$, $t_1 = 30$°C, $R_2 = 98.95 \; \Omega$, $t_2 = 70$°C.

$$\frac{R_1}{R_2} = \frac{(1 + \alpha t_1)}{(1 + \alpha t_2)}$$

$$\frac{100}{98.95} = \frac{(1 + 30\alpha)}{(1 + 70\alpha)}$$

$$100(1 + 70\alpha) = 98.95(1 + 30\alpha)$$

$$100 + 7000\alpha = 98.95 + 2968.5\alpha$$

$$7000\alpha - 2968.5\alpha = 98.95 - 100$$

$$4031.5\alpha = -1.05$$

$$\alpha = -\frac{1.05}{4031.5} /°C \text{ at } 0°C$$

$$= \underline{-0.00026/°C \text{ at } 0°C}$$

Example 7.10. The following corresponding values of resistance and temperature were obtained in an experiment on an energizing coil:

Resistance R (Ω)	10·3	10·83	11·22	11·57	12	12·42	12·67	13·25	13·6
Temperature t (°C)	8	20	30	40	50	60	70	80	90

Plot a graph of R against t and use it to determine the temperature coefficient of resistance of the coil.

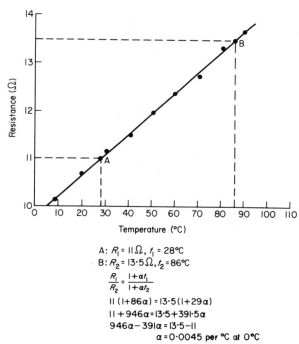

A: $R_1 = 11\,\Omega$, $t_1 = 28°C$
B: $R_2 = 13.5\,\Omega$, $t_2 = 86°C$

$$\frac{R_1}{R_2} = \frac{1+\alpha t_1}{1+\alpha t_2}$$

$11(1+86\alpha) = 13.5(1+29\alpha)$
$11+946\alpha = 13.5+391.5\alpha$
$946\alpha - 391\alpha = 13.5-11$
$\alpha = 0.0045$ per °C at 0°C

Fig. 7.1. Graph for example 7.10

7.4 Resistors in series and parallel

Resistors are said to be connected in series when the same current flows through each resistor. When resistors are connected in series the equivalent resistance is increased. The equivalent resistance R of a number of resistors R_1, R_2, R_3, etc., connected in series is given by:

$$R = R_1 + R_2 + R_3 + \text{etc.}$$

Resistors are said to be connected in parallel when the current divides, part of the current flowing through each resistor. When resistors are connected in parallel the equivalent resistance is decreased. The equivalent resistance R of a number of resistors R_1, R_2, R_3, etc., connected in parallel is given by:

$$\frac{1}{R} = \frac{1}{R_1} + \frac{1}{R_2} + \frac{1}{R_3} + \text{etc.}$$

Example 7.11. Calculate the equivalent resistance of three resistors of 17 Ω, 25 Ω, and 8 Ω connected in series:

$R =$ equivalent resistance, $R_1 = 17\,\Omega$, $R_2 = 25\,\Omega$, $R_3 = 8\,\Omega$

$$R = R_1 + R_2 + R_3$$
$$R = (17 + 25 + 8)\,\Omega = \underline{50\,\Omega}$$

Example 7.12. A circuit has four resistors connected in series. Three of the resistors have values of 2 Ω, 4 Ω, and 10 Ω. What must be the value of the fourth resistor so that the equivalent resistance of the circuit is 20 Ω?

R_4 = unknown resistance, $R_1 = 2\,\Omega$, $R_2 = 4\,\Omega$, $R_3 = 10\Omega$, $R = 20\,\Omega$.

$$R = R_1 + R_2 + R_3 + R_4$$

$$20 = 2 + 4 + 10 + R_4$$

$$R_4 = (20 - 2 - 4 - 10)\,\Omega = 4\,\Omega$$

Example 7.13. A circuit has three resistors of 10 Ω, 20 Ω, and 40 Ω connected in parallel. Calculate the equivalent resistance of the circuit:

R = equivalent resistance, $R_1 = 10\,\Omega$, $R_2 = 20\,\Omega$, $R_3 = 40\,\Omega$

$$\frac{1}{R} = \frac{1}{R_1} + \frac{1}{R_2} + \frac{1}{R_3}$$

$$\frac{1}{R} = \frac{1}{10} + \frac{1}{20} + \frac{1}{40} = \frac{4 + 2 + 1}{40} = \frac{7}{40}$$

$$R = \frac{40}{7}\,\Omega = 5{\cdot}71\,\Omega$$

There is an alternative method of calculation using reciprocal tables. This is the easiest method when a common denominator cannot easily be obtained.

$$\frac{1}{R} = \frac{1}{10} + \frac{1}{20} + \frac{1}{40}$$

$$\frac{1}{R} = 0{\cdot}1 + 0{\cdot}05 + 0{\cdot}025 = 0{\cdot}175$$

$$R = \frac{1}{0{\cdot}175}\,\Omega = 5{\cdot}71\,\Omega$$

Example 7.14. Two resistors in parallel have an equivalent resistance of 6 Ω. Calculate the value of a third resistor, which, when connected in parallel with this group, will reduce the equivalent resistance to 2·4 Ω.

R_2 = unknown resistor, R = total equivalent resistance = 2·4 Ω, R_1 = equivalent resistance of parallel group = 6 Ω

$$\frac{1}{R} = \frac{1}{R_1} + \frac{1}{R_2}$$

$$\frac{1}{2{\cdot}4} = \frac{1}{6} + \frac{1}{R_2}$$

$$\frac{1}{R_2} = \frac{1}{2{\cdot}4} - \frac{1}{6}$$

$$R_2 = 4\,\Omega$$

When there are series and parallel connections in the same circuit reduce each parallel group to its equivalent resistance, then treat it as a series circuit.

Example 7.15. Calculate the equivalent resistance of the circuit shown in Fig. 7.2(a):

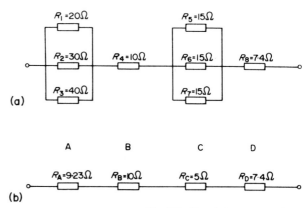

(a)

(b)

Fig. 7.2. Circuit for example 7.15

Equivalent resistance of group A:

$$\frac{1}{R} = \frac{1}{R_1} + \frac{1}{R_2} + \frac{1}{R_3}$$

$$\frac{1}{R} = \frac{1}{20} + \frac{1}{30} + \frac{1}{40} = \frac{6+4+3}{120} = \frac{13}{120}$$

$$R = \frac{120}{13}\ \Omega = \underline{9 \cdot 23\ \Omega}$$

Equivalent resistance of group C:

$$R = \frac{15}{3}\ \Omega = \underline{5\ \Omega}$$

The circuit is now equivalent to Fig. 7.2(b).
Equivalent resistance:

$$R = R_A + R_B + R_C + R_D$$

$$R = (9 \cdot 23 + 10 + 5 + 7 \cdot 4)\ \Omega = \underline{31 \cdot 63\ \Omega}$$

7.5 Electrical energy and power

Energy, W. The unit of energy is the joule (J). If a p.d. of 1 volt causes a current of 1 ampere to flow for 1 second the energy dissipated is 1 joule (refer also section 4.2).

$$W = VIt \text{ joules}$$

For commercial work this would involve very large quantities, so the commercial unit adopted is the kilowatt hour (kW h)

$$1 \text{ kW h} = 1000 \times 60 \times 60 \text{ J} = 3\,600\,000 \text{ J} = 3 \cdot 6 \text{ MJ}$$

Power, *P*. The unit of power is the watt (W), 1 watt is energy being expended at the rate of 1 joule per second (refer also to section 4.3).

$$\text{Therefore,} \quad P = \frac{VIt \text{ joules}}{t \text{ seconds}} = VI \text{ watts}$$

By substitution from Ohm's law two other useful formulae for power are obtained:

$$P = I^2 R \quad \text{and} \quad P = \frac{V^2}{R}$$

Example 7.16. An electric fire element has a resistance of 60 Ω and works off a 240-V supply. Calculate:

(a) the power input, and

(b) the energy supplied in kilowatt hours if the fire is used for 6 h.

(a) P = power, V = 240 V, $I = V/R = 240/60$ A = 4 A, $R = 60$ Ω

$$P = I^2 R$$
$$= 4^2 \times 60 \text{ W} = \underline{960 \text{ W}}$$

(b) W = energy supplied, P = 960 W, t = 6 h

$$W = P \times t$$
$$= (960 \times 6) \text{ W h} = \underline{5\cdot76 \text{ kW h}}$$

7.6 Heating effect of a current

The heat produced by an electric current is proportional to:

(a) the square of the current,

(b) the resistance of the wire in which the current flows, and

(c) the time for which the current flows.

If the current (I) is measured in amperes, the resistance (R) in ohms, and the time (t) in seconds, then:

$$\text{heat energy} = I^2 Rt \text{ joules}$$

The heat required to raise 1 kilogramme of a substance through a temperature rise of 1 degree Celsius is called the specific heat capacity of the substance and is measured in kilojoules per kilogramme kelvin.

Note: Specific heat capacity temperature change is always expressed in Kelvins, but for a **temperature change** 1 degree on the Celsius scale is equal to 1 degree on the Kelvin scale. For example, the heat required to raise 1 kg of water by 1°C is 4·187 kJ which is usually expressed as, 'The specific heat capacity of water is 4·187 kJ/kg K'.

Example 7.17. An electric water heater contains 200 kg of water at 20°C. The element has a resistance of 12 Ω and is connected to a 240-V supply. Assuming no heat loss, what will be the temperature of the water after the heater has been working for 1 hour?

Q = heat energy input, $I = 240/12$ A $= 20$ A, $R = 12\ \Omega$, $t = 60 \times 60$ s $= 3600$ s

$$Q = I^2 R t$$
$$= 20 \times 20 \times 12 \times 3600 \text{ J}$$
$$= 17\,280\,000 \text{ J}$$

$\delta\theta$ = temperature rise, $m = 200$ kg, $c = 4\cdot187$ kJ/kg K, $Q = Q_s = 17\,280$ kJ (refer section 4.2)

$$Q_s = m \times c \times \delta\theta$$
$$17\,280 = 200 \times 4\cdot187 \times \delta\theta$$
$$\delta\theta = \frac{17\,280}{200 \times 4\cdot187}\,°\text{C}$$
$$= 20\cdot6°\text{C}$$

Final water temperature $= 20 + 20\cdot6 = \underline{40\cdot6°\text{C}}$.

Example 7.18. A 3 kW immersion heater working on an 'off peak' tariff, is fitted to a water tank to raise the temperature of the water from 20°C to 80°C. How many kilogrammes of water can be heated during the 3-h afternoon boost period? The efficiency of the heater is 90%.

Q = heat given to water, $P = 3$ kW $= 3000$ W, $t = 3$ h $= 3 \times 60 \times 60 = 10\,800$ s, $\eta = 90\%$

$$Q = P \times t \times \eta$$
$$= 3000 \times 10\,800 \times \frac{90}{100} \text{ J}$$
$$= 29\,160 \text{ kJ}$$

m = mass (in kg) of water heated, $c = 4\cdot187$ kJ/kg K, $\delta\theta = 60°$K, $Q_s = 29\,160$ kJ

$$Q_s = m \times c \times \delta\theta$$
$$29\,160 = m \times 4\cdot187 \times 60$$
$$m = \frac{29\,160}{4\cdot187 \times 60} \text{ kg}$$
$$= \underline{116 \text{ kg}}$$

7.7 Series and parallel circuits

Series circuits
(a) The current is the same at any point in the circuit.
(b) The potential difference, or volt drop across any resistor R, is calculated from:

$$V = IR$$

Hence, in Fig. 7.3(a):

$$V_1 = IR_1, \ V_2 = IR_2, \ V_3 = IR_3$$

(c) The sum of the potential differences or volt drops, across all the resistors, is equal to the supply voltage.

$$V = V_1 + V_2 + V_3$$

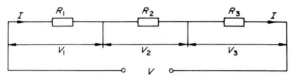

(a) Resistors connected in series

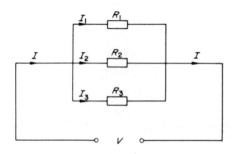

(b) Resistors connected in parallel

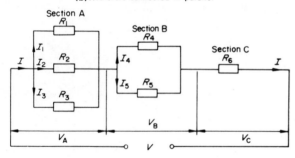

(c) Resistors connected in series – parallel

Fig. 7.3. Series and parallel connections

Example 7.19. Three resistors of 8 Ω, 4 Ω, and 12 Ω are connected in series across a 12-V supply. Calculate:

(a) the current taken from the supply,

(b) the p.d. across each resistor,

(c) the power dissipated in each resistor,

(d) the total power supplied.

Referring to Fig. 7.3(a), I = current from supply, V_1, V_2, and V_3 are potential differences across resistors, P = power dissipated, V = 12 V.

Total circuit resistance $R = R_1 + R_2 + R_3 = (8 + 4 + 12)\ \Omega = 24\ \Omega$.

(a) $$I = \frac{V}{R} = \frac{12}{24}\ \text{A} = \underline{0 \cdot 5\ \text{A}}$$

(b) p.d. across 8-Ω resistor $= IR_1 = 0 \cdot 5 \times 8\ \text{V} = \underline{4V}$

p.d. across 4-Ω resistor $= IR_2 = 0 \cdot 5 \times 4\ \text{V} = \underline{2\ \text{V}}$

p.d. across 12-Ω resistor $= IR_3 = 0 \cdot 5 \times 12\ \text{V} = \underline{6\ \text{V}}$

Check: $V_1 + V_2 + V_3$ must equal V: $(4 + 2 + 6)\ V = 12\ \text{V}$.

(c) Power dissipated in 8-Ω resistor, $P_1 = V_1 I = 4 \times 0 \cdot 5\ \text{W} = \underline{2\ \text{W}}$

Power dissipated in 4-Ω resistor, $P_2 = I^2 R_2 = 0 \cdot 5^2 \times 4\ \text{W} = \underline{1\ \text{W}}$

Power dissipated in 12-Ω resistor, $P_3 = \dfrac{V^2}{R_3} = \dfrac{6^2}{12}\ \text{W} = \underline{3\ \text{W}}$

Note: The three methods of calculating power are shown here for comparison.

(d) total power $= (2 + 1 + 3)\ \text{W} = \underline{6\ \text{W}}$

Check: total power, $P, = VI = 12 \times 0 \cdot 5\ \text{W} = \overline{\underline{6}}\ \text{W}$.

Example 7.20. Four similar indicator filament lamps, each rated at 5-W, 50-V, are connected in series across a 200-V supply. What is the total current taken from the supply? After a period of operation, one of the lamps fails and becomes open circuited. Explain how a voltmeter may be used to find which lamp has failed, stating clearly what readings would be expected on the voltmeter. The only replacement lamp available is one rated at 2·5-W, 50-V. What would be the voltages across this lamp and each of the other lamps if this replacement were used in the circuit, and what would be the probable result?   (C.G.L.I.)

$I =$ supply current, $P =$ power of each lamp $= 5$ W, $V =$ p.d. across each lamp $= 50$ V

Current taken by one lamp $I = \dfrac{P}{V} = \dfrac{5}{50}\ \text{A} = 0 \cdot 1\ \text{A}$

Since this is a series circuit, supply current $= \underline{0 \cdot 1\ \text{A}}$

Testing: voltmeter reads 0 across good lamp.

voltmeter reads 200 V across faulty lamp.

Replacement lamp.

Resistance of 5-W lamp, $R_1 = \dfrac{V}{I} = \dfrac{50}{0 \cdot 1}\ \Omega = 500\ \Omega$

Resistance of 2·5-W lamp, $R_2 = \dfrac{V^2}{P} = \dfrac{50^2}{2 \cdot 5}\ \Omega = 1000\ \Omega$

Resistance of circuit, $R = [(3 \times 500) + 1000]\ \Omega = 2500\ \Omega$

Current taken, $I = \dfrac{V}{R} = \dfrac{200}{2500}\ \text{A} = 0 \cdot 08\ \text{A}$

p.d. across 5-W lamps $= IR_1 = 0\cdot08 \times 500$ V $= 40$ V

p.d. across 2·5-W lamp $= IR_2 = 0\cdot08 \times 1000$ V $= 80$ V

Probable result—the 2·5-W lamp would burn out.

Parallel circuits

(a) The sum of the currents in the parallel branches is equal to the supply current. Referring to Fig. 7.3(b):

$$I = I_1 + I_2 + I_3$$

(b) The p.d. applied across each resistor is the same. Referring to Fig. 7.3(b):

$$V = I_1 R_1 = I_2 R_2 = I_3 R_3$$

Example 7.21. Three resistors of 8 Ω, 16 Ω, and 32 Ω are connected in parallel across a 16-V supply. Calculate:

(a) the current through each resistor,

(b) the current taken from the supply.

$I =$ current through resistor, $V = 16$ V, $R_1 = 8 \Omega, R_2 = 16 \Omega, R_3 = 32 \Omega$

(a) Current through 8-Ω resistor $= I_1 = \dfrac{V}{R_1} = \dfrac{16}{8}$ A $= 2$ A

Current through 16-Ω resistor $= I_2 = \dfrac{V}{R_2} = \dfrac{16}{16}$ A $= 1$ A

Current through 32-Ω resistor $= I_3 = \dfrac{V}{R_3} = \dfrac{16}{32}$ A $= 0\cdot5$ A

(b) Total current from supply $I = I_1 + I_2 + I_3$

$$I = (2 + 1 + 0\cdot5) \text{ A} = 3\cdot5 \text{ A}$$

Alternative method for total current $\dfrac{1}{R} = \dfrac{1}{8} + \dfrac{1}{16} + \dfrac{1}{32} = \dfrac{7}{32}$

$$R = \dfrac{32}{7} \ \Omega$$

Total current $I = \dfrac{V}{R} = 16 \times \dfrac{7}{32}$ A $= 3\cdot5$ A

Combined series and parallel circuits

These circuits can be dealt with in sections using the previous rules. Referring to Fig. 7.3(c):

$$I = I_1 + I_2 + I_3 = I_4 + I_5$$
$$V = V_A + V_B + V_{C\cdot}$$

$V_A = IR_A$, where R_A is equivalent resistance of section A, or

$$V_A = I_1 R_1 = I_2 R_2 = I_3 R_3$$

$V_B = IR_B$, where R_B is equivalent resistance of section B, or

$$V_B = I_4 R_4 = I_5 R_5$$
$$V_C = IR_6$$

Example 7.22. Six resistors are connected as shown in Fig. 7.3(c). The resistor values are $R_1 = 4\ \Omega, R_2 = 12\ \Omega, R_3 = 6\ \Omega, R_4 = 10\ \Omega, R_5 = 40\ \Omega$ and $R_6 = 5\ \Omega$. Calculate:

(a) the equivalent resistance of the complete circuit,

(b) the current taken by the circuit from a 60-V d.c. supply.

(a) Equivalent resistance of section A:

R_A = equivalent resistance, $R_1 = 4\ \Omega, R_2 = 12\ \Omega, R_3 = 6\ \Omega$

$$\frac{1}{R_A} = \frac{1}{4} + \frac{1}{12} + \frac{1}{6} = \frac{6}{12}$$

$$R_A = \frac{12}{6}\ \Omega = 2\ \Omega$$

Equivalent resistance of section B:

R_B = equivalent resistance, $R_4 = 10\ \Omega, R_5 = 40\ \Omega$

$$\frac{1}{R_B} = \frac{1}{10} + \frac{1}{40} = \frac{5}{40}$$

$$R_B = \frac{40}{5}\ \Omega = 8\ \Omega$$

Total circuit resistance: $= R_A + R_B + R_6$
$$= (2 + 8 + 5)\ \Omega = \underline{15\ \Omega}$$

(b) Current taken from 60-V supply:

I = current, $V = 60$ V, $R = 15\ \Omega$.

$$I = \frac{V}{R}$$

$$= \frac{60}{15}\ A = \underline{4\ A}$$

Example 7.23. An electric circuit has three terminals A, B, and C. Between A and B is connected a 1·9-Ω resistor; between B and C are connected a 7-Ω resistor and a 3-Ω resistor in parallel; between A and C is connected a 1-Ω resistor. A 10-V supply is then connected between terminals A and C. Make a sketch of this arrangement and calculate:

(a) the total current drawn from the supply,
(b) the p.d. across the 1·9-Ω resistor,
(c) the current in the 3-Ω resistor,
(d) the power dissipated in the 1-Ω resistor.   (C.G.L.I.)

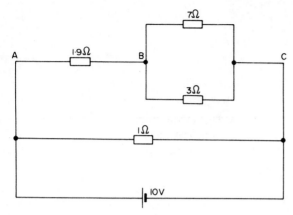

Fig. 7.4. Circuit for example 7.23

$$\text{Current through 1-}\Omega\text{ resistor, } I = \frac{V}{R} = \frac{10}{1} \text{ A} = 10 \text{ A}$$

$$\text{Resistance between BC } \frac{1}{R} = \frac{1}{7} + \frac{1}{3} = \frac{10}{21}$$

$$R = 2\cdot 1 \ \Omega$$

$$\text{Resistance between AC } = (1\cdot 9 + 2\cdot 1) \ \Omega = 4 \ \Omega$$

$$\text{Current in branch AC } = I = \frac{V}{R} = \frac{10}{4} \text{ A} = 2\cdot 5 \text{ A}$$

(a) Total current drawn from battery $= (10 + 2\cdot 5)$ A $= \underline{12\cdot 5 \text{ A}}$

(b) p.d. across 1·9-Ω resistor $= IR = 2\cdot 5 \times 1\cdot 9$ V $= \underline{4\cdot 75 \text{ V}}$

(c) p.d. across 3-Ω resistor $= (10 - 4\cdot 75)$ V $= 5\cdot 25 \text{ V}$

$$\text{therefore current through 3-}\Omega\text{ resistor} = I = \frac{V}{R} = \frac{5\cdot 25}{3} \text{ A} = \underline{1\cdot 75 \text{ A}}$$

(d) Power in 1-Ω resistor $= I^2 R = 10^2 \times 1$ W $= \underline{100 \text{ W}}$

7.8 Two-wire distribution

The volt drop in a two-wire distribution cable can be found by either of the following methods:

Method A
The resistance of the distribution cable can be calculated from the cable dimensions (refer section 7.2) and the volt drop calculated from:

$$\text{Volt drop} = IR$$

Note: The resistance of the cable depends on the total length of conductor which is twice the cable length.

Example 7.24. A twin copper cable 100 m long supplies a load of 50 A. If the voltage drop in the cable must not exceed 5 V, calculate the minimum cross-sectional area of conductor required. Resistivity of copper may be taken as 17 $\mu\Omega$ mm. Calculate also the power loss in the cable.

R = cable resistance, volt drop $V = 5$ V, $I = 50$ A

$$V = IR$$
$$5 = 50 \times R$$
$$R = 0\cdot 1 \ \Omega$$

A = cross-sectional area of cable, $R = 0\cdot 1 \ \Omega$, $l = 2 \times 100 \times 10^3$ mm, $\rho = 17 \ \mu\Omega$ mm
$= 17 \times 10^{-6} \ \Omega$ mm

$$R = \rho \frac{l}{A}$$
$$0\cdot 1 = \frac{17 \times 10^{-6} \times 2 \times 100 \times 10^3}{A}$$
$$A = \frac{17 \times 10^{-6} \times 200 \times 10^3}{0\cdot 1} \ \text{mm}^2$$
$$= 34 \ \text{mm}^2 \simeq 19/1\cdot 53 \ \text{cable}$$

P = power loss, $I = 50$ A, $R = 0\cdot 1 \ \Omega$

$$P = I^2 R$$
$$= 50^2 \times 0\cdot 1 \ \text{W} = 250 \ \text{W}$$

Method B
By the use of tables of volt drops in cables.

The tables of volt drops for metric sized cables usually give the volt drop in millivolts per ampere per metre. To find the volt drop in a given length of cable it is necessary to multiply the figure obtained from the tables by the current flowing in the cable in amperes and by the length of the cable in metres.

Total volt drop = volt drop per ampere per metre x current in cable x length of cable.

Example 7.25. A cable 30 m long supplies a load of 40 A. The cable is a twin 7/1·35 copper core, P.V.C. insulated and sheathed. Calculate the volt drop in the cable.

Referring to Table 1.M in the metric supplement to the 14th edition of the I.E.E. Regulations for the electrical equipment of buildings, the volt drop per ampere per metre for a twin 7/1·35 cable is 4 mV.

$$\text{Volt drop} = \text{volt drop per ampere per metre} \times I \times l$$
$$= 4 \times 10^{-3} \times 40 \times 30 \ \text{V}$$
$$= 4\cdot 8 \ \text{V}$$

Example 7.26. A twin 19/1·53 copper cable supplies two loads X and Y. Load X takes 30 A and is 25 m from the supply end, load Y takes 40 A and is a further 50 m from X. If the p.d. at the supply end is 240 V calculate:

(a) the p.d. at each load,

(b) the power loss in the cable.

Referring to Table 1.M in the I.E.E. Regulations, volt drop per ampere per metre for 19/1·53 twin cable is 1·2 mV.

$$\text{Volt drop between supply and } X = 1 \cdot 2 \times 10^{-3} \times (40 + 30) \times 25 \text{ V}$$

$$= 2 \cdot 1 \text{ V}$$

$$\text{Volt drop between } X \text{ and } Y = 1 \cdot 2 \times 10^{-3} \times 40 \times 50 \text{ V}$$

$$= 2 \cdot 4 \text{ V}$$

p.d. at load $X = (240 - 2 \cdot 1)$ V $= 237 \cdot 9$ V

p.d. at load $Y = (237 \cdot 9 - 2 \cdot 4)$ V $= 235 \cdot 5$ V

$$\text{Total power loss} = (\text{volt drop to } X \times I) + (\text{volt drop } X \text{ to } Y \times I)$$

$$= [(2 \cdot 1 \times 70) + (2 \cdot 4 \times 40)] \text{ W}$$

$$= (147 + 96) \text{ W}$$

$$= 243 \text{ W}$$

7.9 Tariffs and costing

The commercial unit of electrical energy is the kilowatt hour (kW h) and all charges for electrical energy are based on this unit.

$$1 \text{ kW h} = 3\,600\,000 \text{ J} = 3 \cdot 6 \text{ MJ}$$

Example 7.27. A consumer has the following electrical equipment installed: forty 100-W lamps, sixty 200-W lamps and six 4-kW electric heaters. The average use of the equipment during the year is: lamps 20 h each week, heaters 24 h each week. If the tariff is 1p/kW h, what is the cost of running the equipment for a 50-week working year?

$$\text{Total lighting load} = [(40 \times 100) + (60 \times 200)] \text{ W} = 16\,000 \text{ W} = 16 \text{ kW}$$
$$\text{Energy used per year} = 16 \times 20 \times 50 \text{ kW h} = 16000 \text{ kW h}$$
$$\text{Total heating load} = 6 \times 4 \text{ kW} = 24 \text{ kW}$$
$$\text{Energy used per year} = 24 \times 24 \times 50 \text{ kW h} = 28\,800 \text{ kW h}$$
$$\text{Total energy per year} = (16\,000 + 28\,800) \text{ kW h} = 44\,800 \text{ kW h}$$
$$\text{Cost} = 44\,800 \times 1 \text{ p} = £448$$

Example 7.28. Calculate the cost of raising 10 kg of water from 16°C to 94°C by means of an 80% efficient electrical heating appliance. Electrical energy costs 1·75 p/kW h.

$m = 10$ kg, $c = 4·187$ kJ/kg K, $\delta\theta = (94 - 16)$ K $= 78$ K

Heat energy given to water $= m.c.\ \delta\theta$

$$= 10 \times 4·187 \times 78 \text{ kJ}$$

$$= 3265·86 \text{ kJ}$$

Electrical energy supplied $= 3265·86 \times \dfrac{100}{80}$ kJ

$$= 4082·3 \text{ kJ}$$

$$= \frac{4082·3}{3600} \text{ kW h}$$

$$= 1·134 \text{ kW h}$$

$$\text{Cost} = 1·134 \times 1·75\text{p} = \underline{1·98\text{p}}$$

7.10 Mechanical-electrical relationships

Mechanical work is calculated from:

Force (newtons) x distance (metres) = work (joules)
1 newton metre = 1 joule

Note: The joule is the unit of both mechanical and electrical work or energy. Power is the rate of doing work:

1 newton metre per second = 1 joule per second = 1 watt

Note: The watt is the unit of both mechanical and electrical power.

Example 7.29. Explain the difference between power and energy and name their units. A pump is used for 6 h to lift 100 kg of water per minute to a height of 15 m. If the overall efficiency of the pump and motor is 75% calculate the power input required and the total energy dissipated.

(C.G.L.I.)

Power is the rate of doing work, or expending energy. The unit of power is the watt which is equal to 1 joule per second.

Energy is the ability to do work. The unit of energy is the joule which is equal to 1 newton metre.

Note: The gravitational force on a 1 kg mass is taken as $\simeq$ 10 N (refer to section 2.9).

P = power required, F = force required to lift the mass of water = 100×10 N = 1000 N, $h = 15$ m.

$$W = F \times h$$
$$= 1000 \times 15 \text{ N m} = 15\,000 \text{ N m}$$
$$\text{Output power} = \frac{15\,000}{60} \text{ N m/s} = \frac{15\,000}{60} \text{ J/s} = 250 \text{ W}$$
$$\text{Input power} = 250 \times \frac{100}{75} \text{ W} = \underline{333 \text{ W}}$$

$$\text{Total energy dissipated} = \text{power} \times \text{time}$$
$$= \frac{333}{1000} \times 6 \text{ kW h} = \underline{2 \text{ kW h}}$$

Example 7.30. Explain what is meant by power and energy. A crane motor takes an average current of 10 A from a 200-V d.c. supply when raising a load of 2 tonne through a height of 6 m in 1·5 min. Calculate:

(a) the power input to the motor,
(b) the potential energy gained by the load,
(c) the electrical energy delivered to the motor,
(d) the overall efficiency of the crane.

(C.G.L.I.)

(For definitions of power and energy see example 7.29.)

(a) P = input power to motor, $V = 200$ V, $I = 10$ A

$$P = V \times I = 10 \times 200 \text{ W} = 2000 \text{ W} = \underline{2 \text{ kW}}$$

(b) W = potential energy, $F \simeq 2 \times 10^3 \times 10$ N = 20 000 N, (*Note:* that 1000 kg = 1 tonne), $h = 6$ m

$$W = F \times h$$
$$= 20\,000 \times 6 \text{ N m}$$
$$= 120\,000 \text{ J} = \underline{120 \text{ kJ}}$$

(c) W = electrical energy, $P = 2000$ W, $t = 1\cdot5 \times 60$ s

$$W = Pt$$
$$= 2000 \times 1\cdot5 \times 60 \text{ J}$$
$$= 180\,000 \text{ J} = \underline{180 \text{ kJ}}$$

(d) η = efficiency, output = 120 kJ, input = 180 kJ

$$\eta = \frac{\text{output}}{\text{input}} = \frac{120}{180} \times 100\% = \underline{66{\cdot}7\%}$$

Problems

1.   An electric kettle element has a resistance of 30 Ω. What current will flow when it is connected to a 240-V supply?

2.   Determine the current flowing when a 12-V supply is connected across a 5-kΩ resistor.

3.   Calculate the resistance of a relay coil that takes 5 mA from a 40-V supply.

4.   What must be the minimum insulation resistance of an electric motor if the leakage current must not exceed 8 μA when connected to a 400-V supply?

5.   What potential difference must be applied across a 5-kΩ resistor to pass a current of 20 mA?

6.   What is the maximum potential difference that can be applied to a 15-Ω resistor if the current must not exceed 16 A?

7.   Determine the resistance of 25 m of copper wire, 1 mm^2 cross-sectional area if the resistivity of copper is 17 $\mu\Omega$ mm.

8.   Calculate the resistance of 200 m of aluminium wire, 1$\cdot$5 mm^2 in cross-sectional area if the resistivity of aluminium is 28 $\mu\Omega$ mm.

9.   What length of copper wire, 2$\cdot$5 mm^2 cross-sectional area, will have a resistance of 1$\cdot$7 Ω? Resistivity of the copper is 17 $\mu\Omega$ mm.

10.   Calculate the cross-sectional area of an aluminium conductor 500 m long if the resistance is 3$\cdot$5 Ω. Resistivity of the aluminium is 28 $\mu\Omega$ mm.

11.   Calculate the cross-sectional area of a copper conductor 200 m long, if the voltage drop across the ends of the conductor is 6 V when it is carrying a current of 240 A. Resistivity of the copper is 17 $\mu\Omega$ mm.

12.   100 m of copper wire, 2 mm diameter, has a resistance of 6$\cdot$7 Ω. Calculate the resistance of 200 m of the same type of wire 1$\cdot$5 mm diameter.

13.   A length of copper wire, 10 μm diameter, has a resistance of 0$\cdot$1 Ω. What would be the resistance after each of the following changes?
(a) the diameter decreased to 5 μm, same length;
(b) the length reduced to one-eighth, same diameter:
(c) the original piece of wire bent back at its mid-point, the two ends joined, and the two-strand result used.

(C.G.L.I.)

14.   A coil of insulated wire, 80 m long, has an insulation resistance of 55 GΩ, and a conductor resistance of 0$\cdot$3 Ω. Find:
(a) the insulation resistance of the coil per 1000 m
(b) the resistance of 1000 m of the conductor.

15.   A lamp filament has a resistance of 27 Ω at 20°C. What is its resistance when operating at 2000°C? Average temperature coefficient of resistance of tungsten may be taken as 0$\cdot$005/°C at 0°C.

16.   An aluminium conductor has a resistance of 16 Ω at 10°C. What will be its resistance at 65°C if the temperature coefficient of resistance of the aluminium is 0·003 53/°C at 0°C?

17.   The resistance of an armature winding is found to be 80 mΩ at 15°C. What will be its resistance at 50°C? Temperature coefficient of resistance is 0·004/°C at 0°C.

18.   The operating current of a 200-V lamp is 0·5 A at 2000°C. Calculate the current at the instant of switching on the lamp at a room temperature of 20°C. Temperature coefficient of resistance is 0·005/°C at 0°C.

19.   A p.d. of 240 V is applied to a field coil at 16°C and the current is 6 A. Calculate the temperature of the coil when the current has fallen to 5 A, if the p.d. remains the same. Temperature coefficient of resistance is 0·004 28/°C at 0°C.

20.   What is meant by the temperature coefficient of resistance of a material? Name one material that has a positive temperature coefficient and one material that has a negative temperature coefficient. A coil of wire has a resistance of 50 Ω at 0°C. Calculate its resistance when it is cooled to − 18°C. The temperature coefficient of resistance is 0·004/°C at 0°C.

21.   What is the equivalent resistance of a circuit containing three resistors of 7 Ω, 20 Ω, and 46 Ω connected in series?

22.   A circuit consists of three resistors in series and has an equivalent resistance of 96 μΩ. Two of the resistors each have a resistance of 25 μΩ. What is the value of the third resistor?

23.   Three resistors of 16 MΩ, 25 MΩ, and 41 MΩ are connected in series. What is the equivalent resistance?

24.   Four resistors are connected in parallel. Two of the resistors each have a resistance of 10 Ω and the other two resistors each have a resistance of 40 Ω. Calculate the equivalent resistance of the circuit.

25.   How many 1-MΩ resistors must be connected in parallel to give an equivalent resistance of 0·25 MΩ?

26.   Four resistors of 16 Ω, 25 Ω, 42 Ω, and 15 Ω are connected in parallel. Using reciprocal tables find the equivalent resistance of the group.

27.   The four field coils of an electric motor each have a resistance of 200 Ω and are connected in parallel. What value of resistor is required in series with this group to give a total resistance of 56 Ω?

28.   Two resistors A and B, each having a resistance of 16 Ω, are connected in parallel. This group is then joined in series with a further group of two resistors C and D also connected in parallel. If the value of C is 20 Ω and D is 100 Ω, calculate the equivalent resistance of the circuit.

29.   A circuit has two resistors of 20 Ω and 30 Ω connected in parallel. This group is then joined in series with a third resistor of 15 Ω. Calculate the equivalent resistance of the circuit and the current taken when the circuit is connected to a 30-V supply.

30.   The heating element of an electric kettle has a resistance of 25 Ω and works off a 250-V supply. If the kettle efficiency is 80% calculate the time taken to raise 2 litres of water from 15°C to boiling point (1 litre of water has a mass of 1 kg).

31.   An electric kettle takes 8 min to raise the temperature of 1·15 kg of water from 10°C to 90°C. If the efficiency of the kettle is 90% what current does it take from the supply?

(C.G.L.I.)

32.   An immersion heater element has a resistance of 20 Ω and works off a 240-V supply. How long will it take to raise 150 kg of water from 10°C to 90°C? Assume that the losses are 5% of the input.

33.   An electric kettle contains 3 litres of water at 16°C. What current will be taken from a 240-V supply if the water is brought to boiling point in 6 min? (neglect losses).

34.   Explain the difference between power and energy and state the units in which each is measured. An immersion heater for a water tank, has an element resistance of 80 Ω and is connected across a 400-V supply. The tank contains 15 kg of water. For how long must the current flow in order that the water be raised from its initial temperature of 12°C to its final temperature of 72°C if the efficiency is 90%?

35.   An automatic electric bedside tea-maker sounds an alarm when the water in the kettle boils. If the alarm is to ring at 0630 hours, at what time must the kettle switch on? The kettle contains 1 litre of water at 10°C, has an efficiency of 84%, and is fitted with a 750-W element.

36.   Three resistors, 2 Ω, 6 Ω, and x Ω are connected in series across a 128-V supply. The volt drop across the 2-Ω resistor is 16 V. Find;

(a) the current flowing
(b) the voltage drop across the x-Ω resistor
(c) the ohmic value of resistor x.   (U.L.C.I.)

37.   Three resistors of 16 Ω, 20 Ω, and 44 Ω are connected in series across a 10-V supply. Calculate:

(a) the current taken from the supply
(b) the p.d. across the 16-Ω resistor
(c) the energy dissipated in 2 min in the 20-Ω resistor.

38.   How many 20-V, 3-W christmas-tree lamps must be connected in series to operate satisfactorily off a 240-V supply? What would be:

(a) the total power, and
(b) the current, when this set of lamps was operating?

39.   Two resistors, A of 30 Ω and B of 60 Ω, are connected in parallel across a 12-V supply. What current would flow in each resistor and what would be the equivalent resistance of the circuit?

40.   Three resistors of 4 Ω, 10 Ω, and 40 Ω are connected in parallel. If the supply voltage is 10 V calculate:

(a) the current through each resistor
(b) the current taken from the supply.

41.   Two coils of resistance 10 Ω and 2·5 Ω are joined in parallel and the group thus formed is joined in series to a third coil of 8 Ω resistance. The complete circuit is connected to a 200-V supply. What energy (in kW h) is expended in the circuit in 8 h? What must be the resistance of a further coil to be connected in parallel with the complete circuit in order to increase the power consumed to 5 kW?
                                                                        (U.L.C.I.)

42.   Three resistors of 4 Ω, 6 Ω, and 12 Ω are connected in parallel and the group thus formed is connected in series to a second group which consists of two resistors of 5 Ω and r Ω connected in parallel. When the complete circuit is connected to the terminals of a 12-V battery 1·2 kJ are dissipated in 5 min in the 4-Ω resistor. Calculate the value of r.
                                                                        (U.L.C.I.)

43.   A circuit consists of two resistors, of 10 Ω and 2·5 Ω, connected in parallel, this group being joined in series to a second group of two resistors of, $6\frac{2}{3}$ Ω and R Ω, connected in parallel. When the complete circuit is connected across a 210-V supply 360 W are dissipated in the 10-Ω resistor. Calculate the total current, the value of R and the power dissipated in R.

(U.L.C.I.)

44.   Three coils of resistance 3 Ω, 4 Ω, and 6 Ω are connected in parallel. This group is then joined in series with a single coil of $2\frac{2}{3}$ Ω resistance. Find the equivalent resistance of the whole circuit and the current flowing through the 4-Ω coil when the circuit is connected to a 6-V supply. What must be the resistance of a further coil to be connected in parallel with the $2\frac{2}{3}$-Ω coil so that the total power dissipated in the circuit is doubled when connected to the same supply?

45.   It is desired to use a 75-W, 110-V lamp in series with a 40-W, 100-V lamp on a 210-V mains. A variable resistor is available capable of giving a continuous series of resistances between 300 Ω and 400 Ω. Explain how the circuit could be arranged so that the lamps took their normal current at the correct voltage. Calculate the value of the resistor. What would be the power wastage in the resistor?

(U.L.C.I.)

46.   A two-core cable supplies two loads from a 230-V supply. The first load is 70 m from the supply end and takes a current of 40 A, the second load is 100 m from the supply end and takes 20 A. Draw a circuit diagram and find the voltage applied across the second load if each core of the cable has a cross-sectional area of 25 mm². Assume the resistivity is 17 $\mu\Omega$ mm at the working temperature.

47.   Why is a cable with large cross-sectional area used to supply heavy current? A 12-V battery supplies five outlets at 10-m spacing. The distance between battery and first outlet is 10 m. The resistance of the whole cable is 0·01 Ω, go and return. If each outlet supplies 10 A, calculate the voltage at the last outlet.

(C.G.L.I.)

48.   A 200-V d.c. supply supplies three loads: load A, 100 m from the supply point, takes 20 A; load B 175 m from the supply point, takes 12 A; and load C, 300 m from the supply point, takes 10 A. Determine:

(a) the voltages at the load points

(b) the power lost in the cable.

The resistance of each core of the cable is 0·05 Ω per 100-m length.

(C.G.L.I.)

49.   A two-core d.c. cable ABCD is supplied at end A at 200 V, and loads are taken as follows: 10 A at point B; 20 A at point C; 10 A at point D. Each core of the cable has a resistance of 0·02 Ω/100 m and there is a length of two-core cable of 200 m between A and B, 100 m between B and C, and 300 m between C and D. Draw a diagram showing the current in each section of the distributor, and calculate:

(a) the voltage at each load point (B, C, and D)

(b) the power lost in the cable.

(C.G.L.I.)

50.   A 10-kw d.c. load is supplied at 200 V by two 170-m long 7/2·14 P.V.C. insulated non-armoured cables enclosed in conduit. Calculate the voltage drop and power loss in the cable.

51.   A 40-A load is to be supplied by two P.V.C. insulated non-armoured copper cables 50 m long enclosed in conduit. Calculate the minimum standard size of cable required if the supply voltage is 250 V.

52.   Calculate the cost of raising the temperature of 500 kg of water by 90°C if the heating unit is 90% efficient. Electrical energy costs 0·5p/kW h.

53.   A 60-W electric soldering iron is used in a repair shop. It is left connected to the supply for 8 h each day, five days a week. Find the cost of running the soldering iron for 48 weeks if electrical energy costs 1p/kW h.

54.   A 10-kW electric motor is 80% efficient. What will be the running cost per hour if electrical energy costs 1·6p/kW h?

55.   Calculate the cost of running six 3-kW convector heaters for 8 h if electrical energy costs 1·25p/kW h.

56.   An installation comprises the following: two 3-kW electric fires, eight 75-W lamps and ten 100-W lamps. It is estimated that the average use of both fires will be two hours daily for 365 days each year and that the average use of the lamps will be 25 h weekly for 52 weeks. The consumer has a choice of two tariffs:

(a) £5 per annum plus 1p/kW h.
(b) The first 60 units each quarter at 3p/kW h, each additional unit 0·9p/kW h.

Which will be the cheaper tariff and by how much?

57.   A domestic consumer has four 3-kW storage heaters and two 2-kW storage heaters installed. Calculate the weekly cost of running the heaters if each heater accepts a full 8-h charge each day. The off peak tariff is 0·4p/kW h.

58.   (a) What is the difference between electrical power and electrical energy? Name the units in which each is measured.
(b) A 250-V d.c. electric motor operates a lift that raises a load of 1000 kg through a vertical distance of 15 m in 8 s. If the overall efficiency of the motor and lift mechanism together is 64%, calculate the current taken by the motor.
(c) If the lift makes 400 ascents during a period of 8 h, calculate the cost of the electrical energy used at 0·5p per unit. Assume that no electrical energy is used during descent.

(C.G.L.I.)

59.   Write down the units in the SI system for each of the quantities:
work, energy, power, potential energy, kinetic energy.
A motor exerts a force of 40 N through a distance of 2·4 km for 2 min. The supply is 200 V and the motor is 80% efficient. Calculate the current taken by the motor.

(U.L.C.I.)

60.   A crane motor takes 15 A from a 200-V supply when raising a mass of 120 kg. The load is raised 100 m in 50 s. Calculate:

(a) the input power to the motor
(b) the electrical energy delivered to the motor
(c) the efficiency of the crane
(d) the cost of lifting the load at 2p/kW h.

61.   A 12-tonne mass is raised vertically at 7 m/min. Calculate the power of the driving motor and its input power in kW. The efficiency of the gearing is 90%, and of the motor 88%.

Answers

1.	8 A		2.	2·4 mA
3.	8 kΩ		4.	50 MΩ
5.	100 V		6.	240 V
7.	0·425 Ω		8.	3·73 Ω
9.	250 m		10.	4 mm²
11.	136 mm²		12.	23·8 Ω

13. (a) 0·4 Ω   (b) 0·0125 Ω   (c) 0·025 Ω
14. (a) 4·4 GΩ   (b) 3·75 Ω
15. 270 Ω
16. 19 Ω
17. 90·5 mΩ
18. 5 A
19. 65·9°C
20. 46·4 Ω
21. 73 Ω
22. 46 μΩ
23. 82 MΩ
24. 4 Ω
25. 4
26. 5·181 Ω
27. 6 Ω
28. 24·66 Ω
29. 27 Ω, 1·11 A
30. 5·9 min
31. 3·87 A
32. 5·1 h
33. 12·2 A
34. 34·8 min
35. 0620 hours
36. (a) 8 A   (b) 64 V   (c) 8 Ω
37. (a) 0·125 A   (b) 2 V   (c) 37·5 J
38. 12; (a) 36 W   (b) 0·15 A
39. A = 0·4 A; B = 0·2 A; 20 Ω
40. 2·5 A; 1 A; 0·25 A; 3·75 A
41. 32 kW h; 40 Ω
42. 20
43. 30 A; 20 Ω; 1125 W
44. 4 Ω, 0·5 A, 0·89 Ω
45. 357 Ω, 28·1 W
46. 223·5
47. 11·7 V
48. (a) 195·8 V; 194·15 V; 192·9 V (b) 225·3 W
49. (a) 196·8 V; 195·6 V; 194·4 V   (b) 176 W
50. 13·6 V; 680 W
51. 7/1·70
52. 29·1p
53. £1·15
54. 20p
55. £1·8
56. £6·42
57. £3·58
58. (b) 114·9 A   (c) 12·75p
59. 5 A
60. (a) 3 kW   (b) 0·0416 kW h   (c) 78·6%   (d) 0·083p
61. 15·26 kW; 17·34 kW

8. Electrostatics

8.1 Capacitors

A capacitor consists basically of two metal plates, separated by a layer of insulating material called the dielectric. It has the ability to store a quantity of static electricity. If electrons are taken away from one plate and added to the other plate, the capacitor is said to possess an electric charge. The method of producing this charge is to apply a potential difference between the plates.

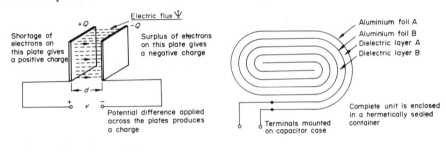

(a) Charged capacitor   (b) Foil type capacitor

Fig. 8.1. Capacitors

Electric field is the space round a charged body where another charged body would have a force exerted upon it. In a similar manner to magnetic fields the shape and distribution of the electric field can be represented by lines of electric flux, (Ψ). One unit of electric flux is produced between a positive charge of 1 coulomb and a negative charge of 1 coulomb.

Electric flux Ψ = charge Q (in coulombs)

Note: The charge Q is the same as the quantity of electricity Q required to produce the charge, since both represent the displacement of a given number of electrons.

Electric flux density, D, is the flux per square metre measured at right angles to the direction of the electric flux:

$$D = \frac{Q}{A} \text{ coulombs/square metre (C/m}^2\text{)}$$

Electric field strength, E. When a potential difference is applied between two conductors, separated by a layer of insulation, a state of electric stress is established in the dielectric. This state of electric stress tends to break down the insulation and cause a spark to pass between the conductors. The electric field strength is the potential drop per metre thickness of insulation. If a p.d. of V volts is applied between two conductors d metres apart:

$$E = \frac{V}{d} \text{ volts per metre (V/m)}$$

79

Example 8.1. Two parallel metal plates, each 600 cm^2 in area, are spaced 2 mm apart. A p.d. of 200 V is applied between the plates and a current of 0·54 μA flows for 10 s. Calculate:

(a) the electric flux,
(b) the electric flux density,
(c) the electric field strength between the plates.

(a) Q = charge, I = 0·54 μA, t = 10 s

$$Q = I \times t$$
$$= 0·54 \times 10 \ \mu C = \underline{5·4 \ \mu C}$$

Since charge and electric flux are equal to each other:

$$\Psi = \underline{5·4 \ \mu C}$$

(b) D = electric flux density, Q = 5·4 μC, A = 600 cm^2 = 0·06 m^2

$$D = \frac{Q}{A}$$
$$= \frac{5·4}{0·06} \ \mu C/m^2 = \underline{90 \ \mu C/m^2}$$

Note: The area A is the area of one plate.

(c) E = electric field strength, V = 200 V, d = 2 mm = 0·002 m

$$E = \frac{V}{d}$$
$$= \frac{200}{0·002} \ V/m = 100000 \ V/m = \underline{100 \ kV/m}$$

Capacitance, C, is the property of a capacitor to store an electric charge when a potential difference is applied. The unit is the farad, F. If a capacitor requires a p.d. of 1 volt to maintain a charge of 1 coulomb then its capacitance is 1 farad.

$$Q = CV$$

where Q is in coulombs, C is in farads, and V is in volts.

Example 8.2. A capacitor has a capacitance of 100 μF and is connected across a 400-V d.c. supply. Calculate the charge on the capacitor:

Q = charge, C = 100 μF = 100 × 10^{-6} F, V = 400 V

$$Q = CV$$
$$= 100 \times 10^{-6} \times 400 \ C = 0·04 \ C = \underline{40 \ mC}$$

Example 8.3. A 20-μF capacitor is given a charge of 400 μC. The capacitor consists of two parallel aluminium plates each 400 cm^2 in area and separated by a distance of 2·5 mm, calculate:

(a) the p.d. across the plates,

(b) the electric flux density,

(c) the electric field strength between the plates.

(a) V = p.d. across plates, Q = 400 μC = 400 $\times$ 10^{-6}C, C = 20 μF = 20 $\times$ 10^{-6} F

$$Q = CV$$

$$400 \times 10^{-6} = 20 \times 10^{-6} \times V$$

$$V = \frac{400 \times 10^{-6}}{20 \times 10^{-6}} \quad V = \underline{20 \text{ V}}$$

(b) D = electric flux density, A = 400 cm^2 = 0·04 m^2

$$D = \frac{Q}{A}$$

$$= \frac{400 \times 10^{-6}}{0 \cdot 04} \text{ C/m}^2 = \underline{10 \text{ mC/m}^2}$$

(c) E = electric field strength, V = 20 V, d = 2·5 mm = 2·5 $\times$ 10^{-3} m

$$E = \frac{V}{d}$$

$$= \frac{20}{2 \cdot 5 \times 10^{-3}} \text{ V/m} = 8000 \text{ V/m} = \underline{8 \text{ kV/m}}$$

8.2 Types of capacitors

The following dielectric materials are in common use for capacitors:

(a) **Air dielectric**: usually used for variable capacitors where the plates consist of rigid aluminium sheets separated by air.

(b) **Mica dielectric**: usually consist of thin aluminium foils separated by a layer of mica. Usually used only on high frequency circuits.

(c) **Paper dielectric**: usually consist of thin aluminium foils separated by a layer of waxed paper. These are often rolled together to form a compact unit (Fig. 8.1(b)).

(d) Ceramic dielectric: for some high frequency applications thin layers of metal are deposited on the opposite faces of a thin layer of ceramic material.

(e) Plastic dielectric: some modern plastic materials can be used as dielectrics. The construction is similar to that of a paper dielectric capacitor but using plastic film instead of paper.

(f) Aluminium oxide and tantalum oxide: these are normally termed electrolytic capacitors. They have a relatively low insulation value and can only be used on circuits where the direction of the voltage applied to the capacitor is never reversed. Care must therefore be taken that they are never inadvertently connected with the wrong polarity. The commonest type consists of two aluminium or tantalum foils, one of which has an oxide coating. The two foils are separated by an absorbent film saturated with a suitable electrolyte. The oxide film acts as the dielectric and since it is very thin very large capacitances can be obtained in a small volume. The whole unit is enclosed in a hermetically sealed container.

8.3 Capacitors in parallel and series

Parallel

When a number of capacitors, C_1, C_2, C_3, etc., are connected in parallel (Fig. 8.2(a)), the resultant capacitance is increased and is calculated from:

$$C = C_1 + C_2 + C_3 + \text{etc.}$$

The charge on each capacitor is calculated from:

$$Q_1 = C_1 V, \quad Q_2 = C_2 V, \quad Q_3 = C_3 V, \text{etc.}$$

The p.d. across each capacitor is the same.

Series

When a number of capacitors, C_1, C_2, C_3, etc. are connected in series (Fig. 8.2(b)) the resultant capacitance is decreased and is calculated from:

$$\frac{1}{C} = \frac{1}{C_1} + \frac{1}{C_2} + \frac{1}{C_3} + \text{etc.}$$

The charge on each capacitor is the same:

$$Q = C_1 V_1 = C_2 V_2 = C_3 V_3 = CV$$

The sum of the voltages across the capacitors is equal to the applied voltage:

$$V = V_1 + V_2 + V_3$$

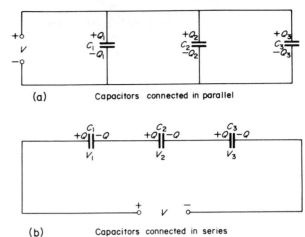

(a)   Capacitors connected in parallel

(b)   Capacitors connected in series

Fig. 8.2. Capacitors connected in parallel and series

Example 8.4. Three capacitors have capacitances of 4 μF, 8 μF, and 10 μF. Find the resultant capacitance when they are connected:

(a) In parallel,

(b) In series.

C = resultant capacitance, $C_1 = 4\ \mu$F, $C_2 = 8\ \mu$F, $C_3 = 10\ \mu$F

(a) In parallel:

$$C = C_1 + C_2 + C_3$$
$$= (4 + 8 + 10)\ \mu\text{F} = \underline{22\ \mu\text{F}}$$

(b) In series:

$$\frac{1}{C} = \frac{1}{C_1} + \frac{1}{C_2} + \frac{1}{C_3}$$

$$\frac{1}{C} = \frac{1}{4} + \frac{1}{8} + \frac{1}{10}$$

$$\frac{1}{C} = 0\cdot 25 + 0\cdot 125 + 0\cdot 1$$

$$\frac{1}{C} = 0\cdot 475$$

$$C = \underline{2\cdot 11\ \mu\text{F}}$$

Note: Calculations are worked throughout in μF. It is not necessary to insert the 10^{-6} at each stage.

Example 8.5. Two capacitors of 12 μF and 20 μF are connected in series across a 200-V d.c. supply. Calculate:
(a) the resultant capacitance,
(b) the charge on each capacitor,
(c) the p.d. across each capacitor.

(a) C = resultant capacitance, V = 200 V, C_1 = 12 μF, C_2 = 20 μF

$$\frac{1}{C} = \frac{1}{C_1} + \frac{1}{C_2}$$

$$= \frac{1}{12} + \frac{1}{20}$$

$$= \frac{8}{60}$$

$$C = 7 \cdot 5 \ \mu\text{F}$$

(b) Charge on C_1 = charge on C_2 = Q

$$Q = CV$$

$$= 7 \cdot 5 \times 200 \ \mu C = 1500 \ \mu C = 1 \cdot 5 \ \text{mC}$$

(c) V_1 = p.d. across C_1, V_2 = p.d. across C_2, Q = 1·5 mC

$$V_1 = \frac{Q}{C_1}$$

$$= \frac{1 \cdot 5 \times 10^{-3}}{12 \times 10^{-6}} \ V = 125 \ \text{V}$$

$$V_2 = \frac{Q}{C_2}$$

$$= \frac{1 \cdot 5 \times 10^{-3}}{20 \times 10^{-6}} \ V = 75 \ \text{V}$$

Example 8.6. Two capacitors having capacitance of 20 μF and 30 μF are connected in parallel. Calculate the value of a third capacitor connected to this group to give a resultant capacitance of 25 μF.

The third capacitor must be connected in series since the addition of any more capacitors in parallel would increase the total capacitance.

C_p = capacitance of parallel group, C_1 = 20 μF, C_2 = 30 μF

$$C_p = C_1 + C_2$$

$$= (20 + 30) \ \mu F = 50 \ \mu F$$

C = resultant capacitance = 25 μF, C_p = 50 μF, C_3 = unknown capacitance

$$\frac{1}{C} = \frac{1}{C_p} + \frac{1}{C_3}$$

$$\frac{1}{C_3} = \frac{1}{C} - \frac{1}{C_p} = \frac{1}{25} - \frac{1}{50} = \frac{1}{50}$$

$$C_3 = 50\ \mu F$$

8.4 Energy stored in a capacitor, W

If a capacitor of C farads is charged to a voltage of V volts, the energy stored is found from:

$$\text{Energy stored } W = \tfrac{1}{2}CV^2 \text{ joules}$$

Example 8.7. A 200-μF capacitor is charged from a 200-V d.c. supply. Calculate the charge on the capacitor and the energy stored in the capacitor:

Q = charge on capacitor, $C = 200 \times 10^{-6}$ F, $V = 200$ V

$$Q = CV$$

$$= 200 \times 10^{-6} \times 200 \text{ C} = 0.04 \text{ C} = 40 \text{ mC}$$

$$\text{Energy stored} = \tfrac{1}{2}CV^2$$

$$= \frac{200 \times 10^{-6} \times 200^2}{2} \text{ J} = 4 \text{ J}$$

8.5 Working voltage

The maximum working voltage of a capacitor is governed by the type and thickness of the dielectric. A given type of dielectric material will have a maximum value of electric field strength to which it can be subjected without electrical breakdown occurring. From this value, and knowing the working voltage of the capacitor, the required dielectric thickness can be calculated. When subjected to alternating voltages the dielectric must be capable of withstanding the **maximum** value of voltage without breakdown occurring.

Example 8.8. The dielectric material used in a certain capacitor can withstand a maximum electric field strength of 8 MV/m. What is the minimum thickness of the dielectric material required in a capacitor to operate on a 400-V d.c. supply?

d = dielectric thickness, $V = 400$ V, $E = 8$ MV/m $= 8 \times 10^6$ V/m

$$E = \frac{V}{d}$$

$$8 \times 10^6 = \frac{400}{d}$$

$$d = \frac{400}{8 \times 10^6} \text{ m} = 50\ \mu\text{m}$$

8.6 Variable capacitors

Air spaced

Normally consists of alternate fixed and moveable aluminium blades. Since the capacitance of a capacitor depends on the area of plates opposite to each other, if the moveable blades are rotated between the fixed blades the capacitance can be increased or decreased.

Fixed

By varying the pressure between the plates and the dielectric of a capacitor with a solid dielectric, usually mica, the capacitance can be varied over a limited range.

8.7 Safety precautions

When a capacitor has been disconnected from the supply it may still be charged, and it may retain this charge for some considerable time. If the capacitor forms part of a piece of equipment that may be handled by unskilled persons, e.g., a discharge lamp circuit, precautions must be taken to ensure that the capacitor is automatically discharged after the supply is switched off (I.E.E. Regulations 14th Edition, Regulation C 35). This is done by connecting a high value resistor across the capacitor terminals. This resistor is usually mounted within the metal casing of the capacitor.

Problems

$V = E \times d$ thus E

1.   A potential difference of 100 V is maintained across two parallel metal plates each 0·2 m² in area, and spaced 1 mm apart. What is the electric field strength in the dielectric and the electric flux density when the capacitor is given a charge of 200 pC?

2.   Two metal plates, each 0·1 m² in area, are placed parallel to each other 2 mm apart. A 200-V d.c. supply is connected across the plates. If the capacitor is given a charge of 400 pC, calculate:

(a) the electric flux density

(b) the electric field strength.

3.   What charge must be applied to a capacitor consisting of two parallel plates, each of 50 cm² area, to produce an electric flux density of 50 μC/m²?

4.   Calculate the electric field strength between two parallel metal plates situated in air when the potential difference between the plates is 200 V and the distance between the plates is 5 mm.

5.   A capacitor consists of two parallel rectangular metal plates each 50 mm x 60 mm spaced 0·2 mm apart. When a p.d. of 1000 V is applied between the plates an average current of 10 mA flows for 5 s. Calculate:

(a) the charge on the capacitor

(b) the electric flux density

(c) the electric field strength in the dielectric.

6.   A capacitor consisting of two parallel metal plates each 8·4 m² in area is given a charge of 200 μC. The electric field strength must not exceed 100 kV/m. If the supply p.d. is 200 V, calculate:

(a) the distance between the plates

(b) the electric flux density.

7.   Calculate the charge on an 8-μF capacitor when connected to:

(a) a 500-V d.c. supply

(b) a 100-V d.c. supply.

8.   What voltage must be applied across the plates of a 20-μF capacitor to produce a charge on the capacitor of 100 μC?

9.   What is the capacitance of a capacitor if a 250-V potential difference across the plates produces a charge on the capacitor of 20 μC?

10.   A 10-μF capacitor is given a charge of 50 μC. If the capacitor consists of two sheets of aluminium foil each 500 cm^2 in area separated by a layer of paper 1·5 mm thick, calculate:

(a) the p.d. across the plates

(b) the electric field strength in the paper

(c) the electric flux density.

11.   A 10-μF capacitor consists of two metal plates 0·1 mm apart and is connected to a 15-V d.c. supply. Calculate:

(a) the charge on the capacitor

(b) the electric field strength.

12.   A 500-μF capacitor is to be given a charge of 400 mC. Calculate the d.c. voltage required:

13.   Three capacitors of 16 μF, 20 μF, and 48 μF are connected

(a) in series, and

(b) in parallel.

Calculate the resultant capacitance in each case.

14.   A circuit has a capacitance of 50 μF which is to be reduced to 30 μF. What additional value of capacitor is required, and how is it connected?

15.   Two capacitors of 14 μF and 26 μF are connected in parallel. What value of capacitor must be connected in series with this group to give a total capacitance of 10 μF?

16.   Two capacitors of 16 μF and 32 μF are connected in series across a 100-V d.c. supply. Calculate:

(a) the charge on each capacitor.

(b) the p.d. across each capacitor

(c) the resultant capacitance of the two in series.

17.   Two capacitors of 25 μF and 40 μF are connected in series. What is the value of a third capacitor required to give a total capacitance of 10 μF and how is it connected?

18.   Calculate the total capacitance of the following capacitors which are connected in parallel:

10 μF, 0·6 μF, 16 μF, 4·5 μF, and 8·2 μF.

19.   A 100-μF capacitor is charged from a 200-V supply. What is the energy stored in the capacitor?

20. A 16-μF capacitor is required to store 2 J of energy. To what voltage must it be charged?

21. A circuit operating on 800 V requires a stored energy of 16 J. What capacitance of capacitor should be used?

22. The electric field strength in the dielectric of a capacitor must not exceed 250 kV/m. What is the maximum working voltage of a capacitor with a dielectric thickness of 0·2 mm?

Answers

1. 100 kV/m; 1 nC/m^2
2. (a) 4 nC/m^2 (b) 100 kV/m
3. 0·25 μC   4.   40 kV/m
5. (a) 50 mC   (b) 16·66 C/m^2 (c) 5 MV/m
6. (a) 2 mm   (b) 23·81 μC/m^2
7. (a) 4 mC   (b) 0·8 mC
8. 5 V   9.   80 nF
10. (a) 5 V   (b) 3·33 kV/m   (c) 1 mC/m^2
11. (a) 150 μC   (b) 150 kV/m
12. 800 V   13.   (a) 7·5 μF   (b) 84 μF
14. 75 μF in series   15.   13·33 μF
16. (a) 1·067 mC   (b) 66·7 V; 33·3 V   (c) 10·67 μF
17. 28·57 μF connected in series   18.   39·3 μF
19. 2 J   20.   500 V
21. 50 μF   22.   50 V

9. Magnetism and electromagnetism

Magnetic field is the area round a magnet where the effects of the magnetic force produced can be detected.

Magnetic flux, Φ (Webers, Wb) is the flux which, linking a circuit of 1 turn produces in it an electromotive force of 1 volt as it is reduced to zero at a uniform rate in 1 second.

Magnetic flux density, B (tesla, T, = Wb/m^2)

$$B = \frac{\text{magnetic flux}}{\text{area (at right angles to flux)}} = \frac{\Phi}{A} \text{ teslas}$$

Example 9.1. A magnetic pole face has a rectangular section 0·2 m x 0·1 m. The total flux on the pole is 0·2 mWb. Calculate the average flux density:

B = flux density, $\Phi = 0\cdot2$ mWb $= 0\cdot2 \times 10^{-3}$ Wb, $A = 0\cdot2 \times 0\cdot1$ m$^2 = 0\cdot02$ m^2

$$B = \frac{\Phi}{A} = \frac{0\cdot2 \times 10^{-3}}{0\cdot02} \text{ T} = \underline{10 \text{ mT}}$$

Permanent magnets are now usually made from alloys of nickel, cobalt, aluminium, copper, and iron. They require a strong magnetizing force to initially magnetize them, but are then capable of retaining their magnetism for very long periods of time.

Anisotropic magnets are permanent magnets which, after casting, are allowed to cool under the influence of a very strong magnetic field.

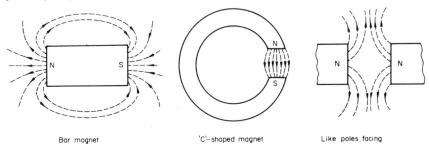

Bar magnet   'C'-shaped magnet   Like poles facing

Fig. 9.1. Magnetic fields round permanent magnets

9.1 Magnetic field round permanent magnets

The shape of the magnetic field between the poles of a permanent magnet depends mainly on the shape and position of the magnetic poles, but is similar to the patterns shown in Fig. 9.1. The flux direction is always considered to be from the N-pole of the magnet, through the surrounding medium to the S-pole of the magnet, and each line of magnetic flux forms a closed loop. Lines of magnetic flux never join or cross each other and can be considered like stretched elastic threads, always trying to shorten themselves.

Electromagnets. Whenever an electric current flows in a conductor a magnetic field is formed round the conductor. The shape and strength of the magnetic field will depend on:

(a) the way in which the conductor is coiled,

(b) the dimensions and material of the core on which the coil is wound,

(c) the current flowing in the coil.

9.2 Magnetic field round straight conductor

The shape of the field round a straight conductor is in the form of concentric cylinders, as shown in Fig. 9.2(a) and (b). The direction of the magnetic field depends on the direction of current flow.

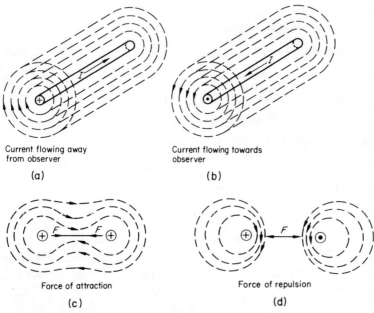

Current flowing away
from observer

(a)

Current flowing towards
observer

(b)

Force of attraction

(c)

Force of repulsion

(d)

Fig. 9.2. Magnetic fields

9.3 Magnetic field round adjacent parallel conductors

The shape of the field for conductors carrying current in the same direction is shown in Fig. 9.2(c). A force of attraction will be exerted between the conductors. The shape of the field for conductors carrying current in opposite directions is shown in Fig. 9.2(d). A force of repulsion will be exerted between the conductors.

9.4 Magnetic field round solenoid

This is as shown in Fig. 9.3. The strength of the magnetic field inside the solenoid can be increased by inserting an iron core in the coil.

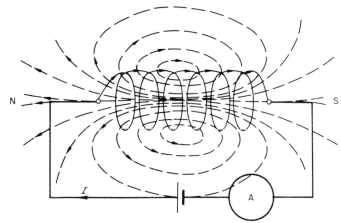

Fig. 9.3. Magnetic field round solenoid

Electromagnet cores are made from soft alloy steels which are easily magnetized, and once the magnetizing force is removed they tend to lose the majority of their magnetism. These materials are used for the cores of relays, motors, generators, transformers, etc.

Magnetization curves for magnetic materials show the relationship between flux density B and magnetic field strength H for a particular sample of material, and are often referred to as B/H curves. These curves are essential in the designing of any electrical equipment that depends for its operation on a magnetic field being produced. Typical curves for permanent and electromagnetic materials are shown in Fig. 9.4. Magnetization curves are all similar in shape, rising steeply at first until saturation point is reached, beyond which point a large increase in magnetic field strength only produces a small increase in flux density.

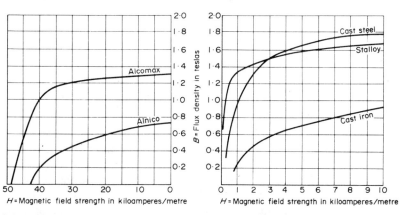

(a) Permanent magnet materials: Demagnetizing curve

(b) Electro-magnet materials: Magnetizing curve

Fig. 9.4. Magnetization curves

9.5 Force on conductor carrying current across a magnetic field

When an electric current flows in a conductor which is situated in a magnetic field, a force will be exerted on the conductor. The direction in which the force acts can be reversed by reversing either the direction of the magnetic field or reversing the direction of the current flowing in the conductor.

Conductor at right angles to magnetic field
The magnitude of the force (F) exerted at right angles to the magnetic field is directly proportional to:

(a) the magnetic flux density, B teslas,

(b) the length of the conductor in the magnetic field, l metres, and

(c) the magnitude of the current flowing in the conductor, I amperes.

If the units given above are used then:

$$F = BlI \text{ newtons}$$

Example 9.2. A conductor 0·5 m long carries a current of 25 A and lies at right angles to a magnetic field of flux density 0·25 T. Determine the force exerted on the conductor:

F = force on conductor, B = 0·25 T, l = 0·5 m, I = 25 A

$$F = BlI$$

$$= 0{\cdot}25 \times 0{\cdot}5 \times 25 \text{ N} = \underline{3{\cdot}125 \text{ N}}$$

Example 9.3. Determine the current required in a conductor 0·2 m long situated at right angles to a magnetic field of flux density 0·55 T, if a force of 0·5 N is to be exerted on the conductor:

I = current in conductor, F = 0·5 N, l = 0·2 m, B = 0·55 T

$$F = BlI$$

$$0{\cdot}5 = 0{\cdot}55 \times 0{\cdot}2 \times I$$

$$I = \frac{0{\cdot}5}{0{\cdot}55 \times 0{\cdot}2} \text{ A} = \underline{4{\cdot}55 \text{ A}}$$

Direction of force
The direction of the force exerted on the conductor depends on the relative directions of the magnetic flux and the current in the conductor. The direction of the force can be determined by drawing the magnetic field of the permanent or electromagnet and the field surrounding the current-carrying conductor. If the two fields are then superimposed upon each other, as in Fig. 9.5, the resultant magnetic field distribution can be determined and from this the direction of the force can be derived. Reversal of either the permanent flux or the current in the conductor will cause a reversal in the direction of the force.

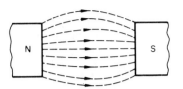

Flux distribution due to magnet

Flux distribution round current carrying conductor

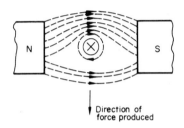

Direction of
force produced

Field strengthened on one side of conductor and weakened on other side

Fig. 9.5. Direction of force produced on current-carrying conductor situated in a magnetic field

9.6 E.M.F. induced by a conductor cutting magnetic flux

If a conductor cuts a magnetic flux, or a magnetic flux cuts a conductor, an e.m.f. will be induced in the conductor. The value of the e.m.f. induced depends on the rate of cutting the magnetic flux. If there is a complete circuit the induced e.m.f. will cause a current to flow. For a conductor moving at right angles to the magnetic field the magnitude of the induced e.m.f. will be directly proportional to the flux density, B teslas, the length of conductor, l metres, and the velocity of the conductor, v metres/second.

If the units given above are used then:

$$E = Blv \text{ volts}$$

Example 9.4. A 0·5-m long conductor moves at right angles to a magnetic field of flux density 0·4 T at a velocity of 25 m/s. Calculate the e.m.f. induced in the conductor:

E = induced e.m.f., B = 0·4 T, l = 0·5 m, v = 25 m/s

$$E = Blv$$
$$= 0·4 \times 0·5 \times 25 \text{ V} = \underline{5 \text{ V}}$$

Direction of induced e.m.f.

The direction of the induced e.m.f. can be determined from either:

(a) Lenz's law, or

(b) Fleming's right-hand rule.

Lenz's law. The direction of the induced e.m.f. is such that it will tend to establish a current which will oppose the motion or change of flux inducing the e.m.f.

Fleming's right-hand rule. If the thumb, forefinger, and second finger of the right hand are held at right angles to each other, so that the thumb indicates the direction of motion of the conductor, and the forefinger indicates the direction of the flux, then the second finger will indicate the direction of the induced e.m.f.

Conductor moving at an angle θ to magnetic field

If the conductor is moving at an angle θ to the magnetic field then for a given linear velocity, if the angle θ is less than $90°$, the rate of cutting the flux will be less, and the induced e.m.f. is calculated from:

$$E = Blv \sin \theta \text{ volts}$$

where θ is the angle between the direction of the flux and the direction of movement.

Example 9.5. A conductor 0·7 m long moves with a velocity of 16 m/s at an angle of $40°$ to a magnetic field of flux density 0·3 T. Calculate the induced e.m.f. in the conductor:

E = induced e.m.f., $B = 0\cdot3$ T, $l = 0\cdot7$ m, $v = 16$ m/s, $\theta = 40°$, $\sin \theta = 0\cdot6428$

$$E = Blv \sin \theta$$

$$= 0\cdot3 \times 0\cdot7 \times 16 \times 0\cdot6428 \text{ V} = \underline{2\cdot16 \text{ V}}$$

Example 9.6. A 0·25-m long conductor moves at 40 m/s at an angle of $45°$ to a magnetic field produced by two square-faced poles of side length 0·25 m. The flux on the pole face is 4 mWb. Calculate the induced e.m.f. in the conductor:

B = flux density, $\Phi = 0\cdot004$ Wb, $A = 0\cdot25 \times 0\cdot25$ m^2 = 0·0625 m^2

$$B = \frac{\Phi}{A}$$

$$= \frac{0\cdot004}{0\cdot0625} \text{ T} = 0\cdot064 \text{ T}$$

E = induced e.m.f., $B = 0\cdot064$ T, $l = 0\cdot25$ m, $v = 40$ m/s, $\sin \theta = 0\cdot7071$

$$E = Blv \sin \theta$$

$$= 0\cdot064 \times 0\cdot25 \times 40 \times 0\cdot7071 \text{ V} = \underline{0\cdot45 \text{ V}}$$

9.7 Induced e.m.f. due to flux change

If a coil of wire is linked with a changing magnetic flux an e.m.f. will be induced in the coil. The value of the induced e.m.f. depends on the rate of change of flux linkages, the direction in which the e.m.f. acts being in accordance with Lenz's law. For a uniform change of flux,

e.m.f. $\propto$ rate of change of flux $\dfrac{(\Phi_2 - \Phi_1)}{t}$ $\times$ number of turns on coil, N.

If flux Φ is in webers and time t in seconds then:

$$\text{e.m.f.} = -\frac{(\Phi_2 - \Phi_1)}{t} \times N \text{ volts}$$

Example 9.7. A coil of 10 000 turns is linked with a magnetic flux which changes from 30 mWb to 10 mWb in 0·5 s. Calculate the induced e.m.f.:

E = induced e.m.f., $\Phi_2 = 0\cdot03$ Wb, $\Phi_1 = 0\cdot01$ Wb, $t = 0\cdot5$ s, $N = 10000$

$$E = \frac{\Phi_2 - \Phi_1}{t} \times N$$

$$= \frac{(0\cdot03 - 0\cdot01)}{0\cdot5} \times 10000 \text{ V} = \underline{400 \text{ V}}$$

Example 9.8. What rate of change of flux is required to induce an e.m.f. of 15 kV in an ignition coil consisting of 12 000 turns?

$E = 15$ kV $= 15000$ V, $N = 12000$ turns

$$E = N \times (\text{rate of change of flux})$$

$$15000 = 12000 \times (\text{rate of change of flux})$$

$$\text{Rate of change of flux} = \frac{15000}{12000} \text{ Wb/s} = \underline{1\cdot25 \text{ Wb/s}}$$

9.8 Self inductance, L

Any circuit in which a change of current produces a change of flux and therefore produces an induced e.m.f. is said to possess self inductance, or just inductance. The unit of electric inductance, called the henry (H), is the inductance of a closed circuit in which an e.m.f. of 1 volt is produced when the electric current in the circuit varies uniformly at the rate of 1 ampere per second. Hence:

$$\text{Induced e.m.f.} = -L \times \frac{(I_2 - I_1)}{t} \text{ volts}$$

The negative sign indicates that the induced e.m.f. opposes the current change.

If a current of I amperes flowing in a coil of N turns establishes a flux of Φ webers, then the inductance can be calculated from:

$$L = \frac{N\Phi}{I} \text{ henrys}$$

Example 9.9. If the current through a coil of inductance 0·7 H is increased from 2 A to 10 A in 40 ms, calculate the average value of the induced e.m.f.:

$E = $ induced e.m.f., $I_1 = 2$ A, $I_2 = 10$ A, $t = 0·04$ s, $L = 0·7$ H

$$E = -L \times \frac{(I_2 - I_1)}{t}$$

$$= -0·7 \times \frac{(10-2)}{0·04} \text{ V} = \underline{-140 \text{ V}}$$

9.9 Mutual inductance, M

If a current change in one coil induces an e.m.f. in a second coil then the coils are said to possess mutual inductance. Two coils have a mutual inductance of 1 henry when the current in one coil, varying uniformly at 1 ampere/second, induces an e.m.f. of 1 volt in the second coil.

If E is the average e.m.f. induced in the second coil and $(I_2 - I_1)$ the current change in the first coil:

$$E = -M\frac{(I_2 - I_1)}{t} \text{ volts}$$

But

$$E = -\frac{(\Phi_2 - \Phi_1)}{t} \times N \text{ volts}$$

therefore,

$$M\frac{(I_2 - I_1)}{t} = \frac{(\Phi_2 - \Phi_1)}{t} \times N$$

$$M = \frac{(\Phi_2 - \Phi_1)}{(I_2 - I_1)} \times N \text{ henry}$$

Example 9.10. Two coils have a mutual inductance of 0·5 H. If the current in one coil is varied from 5 A to 1 A in 0·3 s. Calculate:

(a) the average induced e.m.f. in the second coil, and

(b) the change of flux linked with the second coil if it is wound with 400 turns.

(a) $E = $ induced e.m.f. in second coil, $M = 0·5$ H, $I_2 = 5$ A, $I_1 = 1$ A, $t = 0·3$ s

$$E = -M\frac{(I_2 - I_1)}{t}$$

$$= -0·5\frac{(5-1)}{0·3} \text{ V} = \underline{-6·66 \text{ V}}$$

(b) Φ = change of flux, $E = 6.66$ V, $N = 400$ turns, $t = 0.3$ s

$$E = \frac{\Phi}{t} N$$

$$6.66 = \frac{\Phi}{0.3} \times 400$$

$$\Phi = 0.005 \text{ Wb} = \underline{5 \text{ mWb}}$$

9.10 Energy stored in a magnetic field

When an inductive circuit is opened, the current that was flowing in the circuit has to die away and the magnetic energy has to be dissipated (refer to section 11.1). If there is a resistor in parallel with the circuit the stored energy will be dissipated as heat in the resistor and the inductive coil. If there is no resistor in parallel the energy will be mainly dissipated as heat in an arc at the switch contacts. The energy stored in a coil having a constant inductance of L henrys and carrying a current of I amperes, is calculated from:

$$\text{Energy stored, } W = \tfrac{1}{2} \times LI^2 \text{ Joules}$$

Example 9.11. A coil has a resistance of 16 Ω and an inductance of 3 H. It is connected to a 40-V d.c. supply. Calculate the energy stored in the magnetic field when the current has reached a steady value:

$W =$ energy stored, $L = 3$ H, $R = 16\ \Omega$, $V = 40$ V

$$\text{Final value of current, } I = \frac{V}{R}$$

$$= \frac{40}{16} \text{ A} = 2.5 \text{ A}$$

$$\text{Energy stored, } W = \tfrac{1}{2}LI^2$$

$$= \frac{1 \times 3 \times 2.5^2}{2} \text{ J} = \underline{9.375 \text{ J}}$$

9.11 Energy loss

Energy is lost due to flux reversals in magnetic materials and rotation of magnetic components in magnetic fields. These losses are usually divided into hysteresis and eddy-current losses.

Hysteresis loss
If a sample of iron or steel is subjected to one complete reversal of magnetic field strength the graph of B/H will be as shown in Fig. 9.6(a). When the magnetic field strength is reduced to zero there is a residual flux density O-R which is known as the the remanent flux density. Before the material can be magnetized in the opposite direction.this remanent flux density must be destroyed. The magnetic field strength

O-C required to collapse this flux is known as the coercive force. This process occurs every half-cycle of the magnetic field strength. The complete loop formed by one cycle of the magnetic field strength is referred to as a hysteresis loop. The area of the loop enables the hysteresis loss per cycle to be determined for a given specimen of steel. Typical loops for materials with high and low hysteresis losses are given in Fig. 9.6(b).

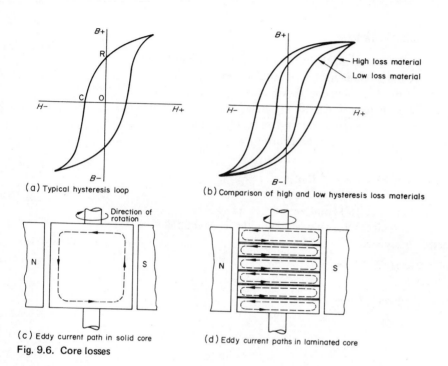

(a) Typical hysteresis loop

(b) Comparison of high and low hysteresis loss materials

(c) Eddy current path in solid core

(d) Eddy current paths in laminated core

Fig. 9.6. Core losses

Eddy current loss

In many electrical components such as motors and generators where the rotating steel cores cut the magnetic flux, or in components such as transformers and relays where the cores are subjected to an alternating flux, an e.m.f. will be induced not only in the conductors and coils but also in the steel cores. These induced e.m.f.s set up circulating currents in the cores which produce heating of the core and consequential lowering of efficiency. These circulating currents are termed eddy-currents. They can be reduced by laminating the core and inserting a very thin layer of insulating material between each pair of laminations. It is not usual to produce laminations thinner than 0·4 mm since the savings produced by thinner laminations do not warrant the extra manufacturing cost. The insulation layers are usually about 0·025 mm thick. Eddy currents are also reduced by using a silicon-iron alloy for the cores which has good magnetic properties but offers a high resistance to the electrical currents produced, Fig. 9.6(c) and (d).

9.12 Magnetic shielding

If a component is required to be shielded from surrounding magnetic fields it can be placed in a soft iron cylinder as shown in Fig. 9.7. The inside of the cylinder only has a very weak magnetic field passing through it since the majority of the flux will pass through the ring as shown.

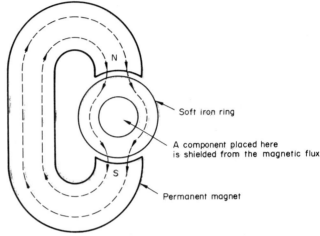

Fig. 9.7. Principle of magnetic shielding

Problems

1.   Calculate the total flux on a magnet pole-face 80 mm x 100 mm if the flux density is 0·4 T.

2.   A circular magnetic pole-face is 0·2 m diameter. Calculate the flux density if the total flux on the pole-face is 25 mWb.

3.   If the maximum flux density in a particular sample of steel must not exceed 0·8 T, what area of pole-face is required if the working flux is to be 0·16 Wb?

4.   Calculate the force exerted on a conductor 0·8 m long carrying a current of 30 A at right angles to a magnetic field of flux density of 0·08 T.

5.   A conductor 0·33 m long is situated at right angles to a magnetic field. Determine the strength of the magnetic field if a current of 10 A in the conductor produces a force on it of 4 N.

6.   A conductor 0·3 m long is situated at right angles to a magnetic field of flux density 0·04 T. Calculate the current required so that a force of 1·2 N will be exerted on the conductor.

7.   (a) A single conductor carrying direct current lies at right angles to the magnetic field between the poles of a two-pole d.c. motor. Make a sketch of this arrangement and, assuming your own direction of magnetic field and current, indicate the direction in which the conductor will tend to move.
(b) A conductor 0·3 m long lies at right angles to a magnetic field of intensity 1·6 T and carries a current of 25 A. Calculate the force on the conductor.

(C.G.L.I.)

8.   A rectangular coil of 200 turns is situated with two of its sides at right angles to a magnetic field of flux density 1·2 T. If the length of a coil side is 0·25 m, calculate the force on one coil side for a current of 16 A in the coil.

9.   A 0·2-m long copper conductor is situated in a magnetic field of flux density 25 mT. The current flowing in the conductor is 40 A. Calculate the force on the conductor:

(a) at right angles to the field

(b) at an angle of 40° to the magnetic field.

10.   A moving-coil loudspeaker has a circular coil of 30 mm diameter which is situated in a radial magnetic field of flux density 0·3 T. If the coil has 1000 turns calculate the force exerted when a current of 8 mA flows in the coil.

11.   The coil of a moving coil instrument is wound with $60\frac{1}{2}$ turns and carries a current of 15 mA. The flux density in the gap is 25 mT. Calculate the torque if the coil is wound on a square former having sides 15 mm long.

12.   The armature of a motor is 0·4 m diameter and 0·25 m long. There are 400 conductors on it. The flux density in the air gap is 0·8 T and it may be assumed that 70% of the conductors lie in this field. If the current per conductor is 20 A, find the torque exerted by the armature.

(U.L.C.I.)

13.   Determine the speed at which a conductor 0·5 m long must move at right angles to a uniform magnetic field of intensity 0·25 T in order that an e.m.f. of 2 V is induced in the conductor.

14.   A wire 0·3 m long moves at right angles to a magnetic field with a velocity of 5 m/s. If the intensity of the field is 0·6 T calculate the e.m.f. induced in the conductor.

15.   A conductor 0·4 m long cuts a magnetic field at right angles at a velocity of 16 m/s. What is the intensity of the magnetic field if an e.m.f. of 5 V is induced in the conductor?

16.   The maximum flux density in the air gap of a d.c. generator is 0·9 T. The armature is 1·4 m in diameter and the active length of each armature conductor is 0·4 m. Calculate the maximum e.m.f. induced in a conductor when the armature rotates at 25 rev/s.

17.   Calculate the induced e.m.f. in a 0·2-m long conductor moving at an angle of 40° to a magnetic field at 14 m/s. The magnetic field has a flux density 0·2 T.

18.   A length of stiff copper wire is made into a rectangle measuring 0·24 m by 0·1 m. It is rotated at a uniform speed of 10 rev/s about one of its longer sides as an axis, this side lying in and at right angles to a magnetic field of 0·5 T. Calculate the average electromotive force induced in the coil.

(U.L.C.I.)

19.   An e.m.f. of 20 V is induced in a circuit of inductance 0·4 H. Calculate the rate of change of current.

20.   If the current in an inductive coil varies at the rate of 200 A/s and induces an e.m.f. of 60 V what is the inductance of the coil?

21.   What e.m.f. will be induced in a coil of inductance 60 mH if the current changes from 100 A to zero in 0·1 s?

22. Define the unit of self inductance. An air-cored coil of 500 turns carries a current of 3 A which produces a flux of 30 μWb. Calculate:

(a) the inductance of the coil

(b) the average e.m.f. induced, when the current is reduced to zero in 2 ms.

(U.L.C.I.)

23. An iron ring is wound with 50 turns and when no current flows in the coil there is a residual flux in the core of 0·1 Wb. When the current flows in the coil the flux increases to 1·25 Wb in 0·1 s. Calculate the induced e.m.f.

24. Each field coil of a 200-V four-pole motor has 500 turns and when working each pole carries a flux of 0·2 Wb. If the field circuit is opened in 0·05 s, calculate the induced e.m.f. across the coils. The coils are all connected in series and the residual magnetism is 10% of the maximum flux.

25. A four-pole d.c. generator has four field coils connected in series, each coil being wound with 600 turns. When a current of 4 A flows in the coils a magnetic flux of 0·4 mWb is produced. Calculate:

(a) the inductance of the field windings

(b) the average value of e.m.f. induced when the field switch is opened in 0·002 s.

The residual flux is 10% of the maximum flux.

26. When a current of 10 A flows in a 1000-turn coil a flux of 1·8 mWb is established. Calculate:

(a) the inductance of the coil

(b) the average e.m.f. induced when this current is reversed in 0·01 s.

27. Two coils A and B have a mutual inductance of 0·7 H and the current flowing in coil A is 5 A. Calculate the induced e.m.f. in coil B when the current in A is reversed in 0·02 s.

28. Calculate the average value of e.m.f. induced in a 1000-turn coil when the flux in the coil changes from 0·02 Wb to 0·002 Wb in 0·1 s.

29. The flux linked with a coil changes steadily from 10 mWb to 60 mWb in 10 ms. The average value of induced e.m.f. is 200 V. How many turns are there on the coil?

30. A coil of resistance 25 Ω has an inductance of 4 H. Calculate the energy stored in the coil when working off a 250-V d.c. supply.

31. A coil has an inductance of 4 H and takes a current of 16 A from an 80-V supply. Calculate:

(a) the resistance of the coil

(b) the energy stored in the coil when the current has reached a steady value.

Answers

1.	3·2 mWb		2.	0·796 T
3.	0·2 m²		4.	1·92 N
5.	1·21 T		6.	100 A
7.	(b) 12 N		8.	960 N
9.	(a) 0·2 N	(b) 0·128 N	10.	0·226 N
11.	5·1 μN m		12.	224 N m
13.	16 m/s		14.	0·9 V
15.	0·782 T		16.	39·6 V
17.	0·36 V		18.	0·754 V

19.	50 A/s		20.	0·3 H
21.	60 V		22.	(a) 5 mH (b) 7·5 V
23.	575 V		24.	7·2 kV
25.	(a) 0·24 H (b) 108 V		26.	(a) 0·18 H (b) 360 V
27.	350 V		28.	1·8 kV
29.	40		30.	200 J
31.	(a) 5 Ω (b) 512 J			

Laboratory work

1. Plotting magnetic fields round permanent and electromagnets.

(a) Place a flat bar-magnet on a level surface and cover with a piece of thin card.

(b) Place a small compass in different positions on the card to indicate the direction of the magnetic field.

(c) Indicate on the card the direction of the compass needle at each position.

(d) Remove the card and join the marked points with pencil lines to indicate the field distribution.

(e) Repeat for the following magnet arrangements:
  (i)   two bar-magnets with N and S poles adjacent
  (ii) two bar-magnets with N and N poles adjacent
  (iii) two bar-magnets with S and S poles adjacent
  (iv) a solenoid through which current is passing
  (v)   a flat coil through which current is passing.

2. Plotting the magnetization curve for a sample of steel.

(a) Demagnetize the specimen by connecting as shown in Fig. 9.8(a).

(b) Connect the demagnetized specimen as shown in the test circuit in Fig. 9.8(b).

(c) Increase the current in the magnetizing coil in equal steps from zero to maximum.

(d) Tabulate the readings of current and fluxmeter deflection obtained.

(e) Calculate the values of flux density in the core and the magnetic field strength for each step.

(f) Plot these values of flux density against magnetic field strength as shown in Fig. 9.4(b).

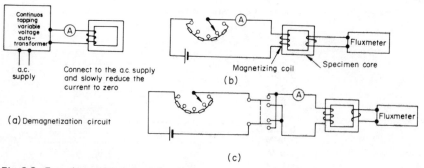

(a) Demagnetization circuit

(b)

(c)

Fig. 9.8. Experimental test circuits

102

3. Plotting the hysteresis loop for a sample of steel.

(a) The specimen does not need to be demagnetized.

(b) Connect the specimen in the test circuit as shown in Fig. 9.8(c).

(c) Set the resistor so that the maximum current will flow.

(d) Reduce the current in equal steps from maximum to zero.

(e) Reverse the current by means of the change over switch.

(f) Increase the current in equal steps from zero to maximum.

(g) Tabulate the readings of current and fluxmeter deflection obtained.

(h) Plot the values of B against H as shown in Fig. 9.6.

(i) Complete the hysteresis loop by using the same results in the reverse order.

10. Electrical machines

Electrical machines can be divided into two groups:

Generators, which convert mechanical energy into electrical energy.

Motors, which convert electrical energy into mechanical energy.

10.1 Alternating generators

When a conductor cuts a magnetic flux an e.m.f. is induced in the conductor. This principle can be applied in the following ways to produce an alternating e.m.f.:

Moving conductor–stationary magnetic flux. If a single-turn coil is rotated between the poles of a magnet, as shown in Fig. 10.1(a), the two sides of the coil will cut the

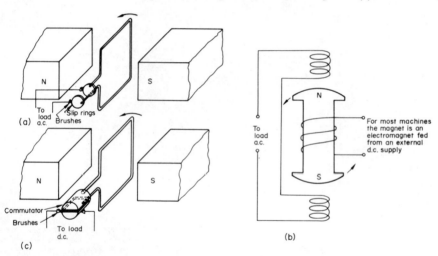

Fig. 10.1. Generation of e.m.f.

magnetic flux and an e.m.f. will be induced in the coil. The magnitude of the induced e.m.f. will depend on the rate at which the conductors cut the magnetic flux (refer to section 9.6). The direction in which the induced e.m.f. will act depends on the direction of cutting the magnetic flux (refer to section 9.6). As the coil is rotated each coil-side will move alternately past a north and south pole of the magnet, so that the induced e.m.f. will act first in one direction and then in the opposite direction, thus producing an alternating e.m.f. If connections from the coil ends are taken, via slip rings as shown in Fig. 10.1(a) to the load, then an alternating e.m.f. will be applied to the load and an alternating current will flow in the circuit.

Stationary conductor–moving magnetic flux. To avoid the necessity for excessively large slip rings and brushes on machines with large power outputs, such as power station alternators, this type of machine is designed with stationary conductors and rotating magnets, Fig. 10.1(b). As the magnet rotates between the stationary coils the magnetic flux cuts the conductors and an alternating e.m.f. is induced in the coils. This alternating e.m.f. will establish an alternating current through the load, which is fed through fixed connections from the coils. The rotating magnet is usually an electromagnet which only requires a relatively small value of current to produce the required magnetic flux.

Output waveform of alternator. The output of both types of machines described in section 10.1 can be arranged to be sinusoidal by suitable design of the shape of the magnets and the positions of the coils.

Output frequency. Every time a pair of magnetic poles pass a coil one complete cycle of e.m.f. will be induced in the coil. The frequency, f, of the output e.m.f. will therefore depend on the number of magnetic pole pairs p and the speed n at which the magnet rotates:

$f = n \cdot p$ Hertz   where n is in revolutions per second.

Example 10.1. A single-phase 16-pole alternator runs at 6·25 rev/s. What is the frequency of the output?

f = output frequency, $n = 6\cdot25$ rev/s, $p = 16 \div 2 = 8$ pairs

$$f = n \times p$$
$$= 6\cdot25 \times 8 \text{ Hz} = \underline{50 \text{ Hz}}$$

Induced e.m.f. The magnitude of the e.m.f. will depend on the rate of cutting magnetic flux (refer to section 9.6) and will therefore be proportional to the speed and the value of the magnetic flux on the poles:

$$E \propto n \times \Phi$$

Example 10.2. An alternator has an e.m.f. of 200 V, and runs at 25 rev/s.

(a) If the flux on the machine is increased by 20% what will be the new e.m.f.?

(b) If the flux remains constant at what speed must the machine be run to again generate an e.m.f. of 200 V?

(a) E_2 = new e.m.f., $E_1 = 200$ V, $n = 25$ rev/s, $\Phi_1 = \Phi$, $\Phi_2 = 1\cdot2\ \Phi$

$$E \propto n \times \Phi$$

since n is constant $E \propto \Phi$

$$\frac{E_1}{E_2} = \frac{\Phi_1}{\Phi_2}$$

$$\frac{200}{E_2} = \frac{\Phi}{1\cdot2\ \Phi}$$

$$E_2 = \frac{200 \times 1\cdot2}{1} \ V = \underline{240 \ V}$$

(b) n_2 = new speed, n_1 = 25 rev/s, E_2 = 200 V, E_1 = 240 V

since Φ is now constant $E \propto n$

$$\frac{E_1}{E_2} = \frac{n_1}{n_2}$$

$$\frac{240}{200} = \frac{25}{n_2}$$

$$n_2 = \frac{200 \times 25}{240} \ \text{rev/s} = \underline{20\tfrac{5}{6} \ \text{rev/s}}$$

10.2 Unidirectional generators

The principle is the same as shown in Fig. 10.1(a) but the slip rings are replaced by a commutator as shown in Fig. 10.1(b). The commutator reverses the connections between the coil and the load every time the e.m.f. in the coil reverses, thus applying a unidirectional (d.c.) e.m.f. to the load and causing a unidirectional current to flow in the load. D.C. generators are constructed with fixed magnet systems and moving conductors.

Induced e.m.f. As with an a.c. generator the magnitude of the e.m.f. is directly proportional to speed and magnetic flux density.

$$E \propto n \times \Phi$$

10.3 D.C. machine as a motor or generator

Most direct current machines will function either as a motor or as a generator. The various types are classified according to their field and armature connections.

Generators

(a) **Separately-excited generators.** The field winding is not connected to the armature of its own machine but receives its supply from some other d.c. source (Fig. 10.2(a)). These machines are only used when a wide variation in terminal p.d. is required or when exact control of the field current is necessary (Fig. 10.2(b)).

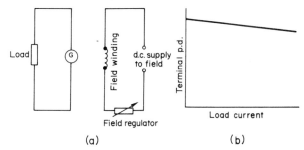

Fig. 10.2. Connections and characteristics of separately-excited d.c. generator

(b) Self-excited generators. The field winding receives its supply from the armature of its own machine. This group is subdivided into:

(*i*) *Series-wound:* the field winding is connected in series with the armature (Fig. 10.3(a)). These machines are unsuitable for use with varying loads and have a very limited use in modern applications (Fig. 10.3(b)).

(*ii*) *Shunt-wound:* the field winding is connected in parallel with the armature (Fig. 10.3(c)). These machines can be used wherever the slightly drooping characteristic will not affect the equipment supplied, e.g., supplies to machines and components in factories where rapid variations in load do not occur. They must be worked well below the maximum current value to avoid excessive drop in the terminal p.d. (Fig. 10.3(d)).

(*iii*) *Compound-wound:* the machine has a combination of series and shunt windings (Fig. 10.3(e)). A cumulative level-compounded machine will maintain an almost constant terminal p.d. under varying loads. A cumulative over-compounded machine will produce a slight rise in terminal p.d. with load which will offset the increased drop in p.d. in the cables to the load. Differential compounded machines are only used for specialist applications where a large drop in terminal p.d. with load is required, e.g., electric welding supplies (Fig. 10.3(f)).

Motors

(a) Series-wound. The field winding is in series with the armature across the supply (Fig. 10.4(a)). They are used wherever a large starting torque at slow speeds is required such as cranes, hoists, trains, etc. On light loads the speed may become excessively high and they should never be used where the load may be accidently removed, such as belt drives (Fig. 10.4(b)).

(b) Shunt-wound. The field winding is in parallel with the armature across the supply (Fig. 10.4(c)). Up to full load these machines produce a greater torque for a given

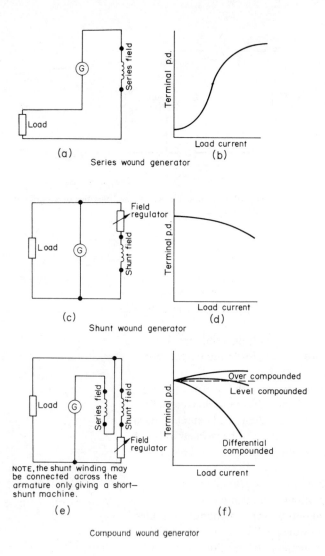

(a)
Series wound generator

(b)

Terminal p.d.

Load current

(c)
Shunt wound generator

(d)

Field regulator

Shunt field

Terminal p.d.

Load current

(e)

Series field

Shunt field

Field regulator

NOTE, the shunt winding may be connected across the armature only giving a short-shunt machine.

(f)

Terminal p.d.

Over compounded

Level compounded

Differential compounded

Load current

Compound wound generator

Fig. 10.3. Connections and characteristics of self-excited d.c. generators

armature current than the series motor. The shunt motor has an approximately constant speed over a very wide variation in load, but is not suitable for heavy overloads (Fig. 10.4(d)).

(c) **Compound-wound.** A combination of series and shunt field windings, usually connected as shown in Fig. 10.4(e). The characteristics are between those of a series-wound motor and a shunt-wound motor. The exact shape of the characteristic curve depends on the magnetomotive force produced by each winding. They are suitable for applications where a wide range of speed control is required, only requiring resistors in the field and armature circuits to produce this speed variation (Fig. 10.4(f)).

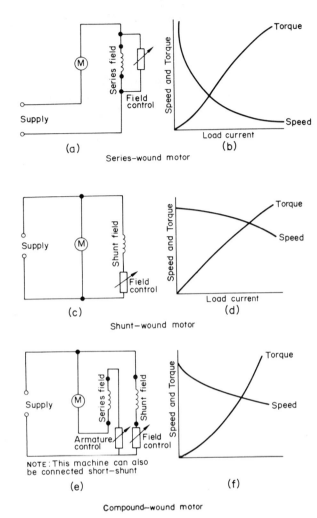

Fig. 10.4. Connections and characteristics of d.c. motors

10.4 D.C. generator

The armature conductors are made to cut the magnetic flux produced by the field coils. The e.m.f. induced in each conductor can be calculated from:

$$E = Blv \quad \text{(refer to section 9.6)}$$

This formula can be developed into the e.m.f. equation for a d.c. machine.
If in a d.c. machine: p = number of pole pairs, Φ = flux per pole (Wb), Z = number of armature conductors, C = number of parallel circuits in armature (C = 2 for wave windings, C = 2p for lap windings), n = speed in rev/s, then:

$$E = 2p \times \Phi \times \frac{Z}{C} \times n \text{ volts}$$

109

Since $(2p \times Z)/C$ is a constant for a given machine

$$E \propto \Phi \times n$$

Example 10.3. A four-pole generator has a total of 600 conductors divided into two parallel circuits. The flux per pole is 50 mWb. Calculate the induced e.m.f. when the armature is rotated at 10 rev/s:

$E =$ induced e.m.f., $2p = 4$, $\Phi = 50 \times 10^{-3}$ Wb, $Z = 600$, $C = 2$, $n = 10$

$$E = 2p \times \Phi \times \frac{Z}{C} \times n$$

$$= 4 \times 50 \times 10^{-3} \times \frac{600}{2} \times 10 \text{ V} = \underline{600 \text{ V}}$$

Example 10.4. An eight-pole generator has a lap-wound armature with 900 conductors. The useful flux per pole is 0·04 Wb. Calculate the speed at which the machine must be driven to generate an e.m.f. of 250 V:

$n =$ speed in rev/s, $E = 250$ V, $2p = 8$, $\Phi = 0·04$ Wb, $Z = 900$, $C = 2p = 8$

$$E = 2p \times \Phi \times \frac{Z}{C} \times n$$

$$250 = 8 \times 0·04 \times \frac{900}{8} \times n$$

$$n = \frac{250 \times 8}{8 \times 0·04 \times 900} \text{ rev/s} = \underline{6·95 \text{ rev/s}}$$

Example 10.5. A d.c. generator running at 25 rev/s has a generated e.m.f. of 250 V. What percentage increase in flux per pole is required to produce 300 V at 20 rev/s?

$\Phi_1 = 100\%$, $\Phi_2 =$ new flux, $n_1 = 25$ rev/s, $n_2 = 20$ rev/s, $E_1 = 250$ V, $E_2 = 300$ V

$$E \propto \Phi \times n$$

$$\frac{E_1}{E_2} = \frac{\Phi_1 \times n_1}{\Phi_2 \times n_2}$$

$$\frac{250}{300} = \frac{100 \times 25}{\Phi_2 \times 20}$$

$$\Phi_2 = \frac{300 \times 100 \times 25}{250 \times 20} \% \text{ of } \Phi_1 = 150\% \text{ of } \Phi_1$$

Increase in flux per pole $= \underline{50\%}$

Terminal p.d.

The terminal p.d. V of a generator will be slightly less than the generated e.m.f. E due to the volt drop in the armature circuit.

Armature circuit volt drop $= I_a R_a$

Therefore,
$$V = E - I_a R_a$$

Example 10.6. An armature of a shunt-wound d.c. generator has a resistance of $20\,m\Omega$ and an open circuit e.m.f. of 400 V. Calculate the terminal p.d. when the armature carries a current of 150 A:

$V =$ terminal p.d., $E = 400$ V, $I_a = 150$ A, $R_a = 20$ m $\Omega = 0.02\ \Omega$

$$V = E - I_a R_a$$
$$= [400 - (150 \times 0.02)]\ V = [400 - 3]\ V$$
$$= 397\ V$$

10.5 D.C. motor

The current flowing in the armature conductors situated in the magnetic field causes a torque to be exerted on the armature. The torque on an armature can be calculated from:

$$\text{Torque} = \frac{p \times \Phi \times Z \times I_a}{\pi \times C}\ \text{newton metres}$$

Since $(p \times Z)/(\pi \times C)$ is a constant for any given machine,

$$\text{Torque} \propto \Phi \times I_a$$

Example 10.7. A four-pole motor has a wave-wound armature with 800 conductors. The useful flux per pole is 20 mWb. Calculate the torque exerted when a current of 20 A flows in each armature conductor:

$T =$ torque, $p = 2$, $\Phi = 20$ mWb $= 0.02$ Wb, $Z = 800$, $C = 2$, $I_a = 20$ A

$$T = \frac{p \times \Phi \times Z \times I_a}{\pi \times C}$$
$$= \frac{2 \times 0.02 \times 800 \times 20}{3.142 \times 2}\ \text{N m}$$
$$= 101.76\ \text{N m}$$

Back e.m.f.

When a d.c. motor rotates, an e.m.f. is induced in the armature conductors. In accordance with Lenz's law this induced e.m.f. E opposes the supply voltage V and is called a back e.m.f. The difference between the back e.m.f. and the supply voltage is the volt drop in the armature $I_a R_a$.

$$V - E = I_a R_a$$

Example 10.8. A d.c. motor operates from a 400-V supply. The armature resistance is 0·2 Ω. Calculate the back e.m.f. when the armature current is 40 A:

E = back e.m.f., V = 400 V, I_a = 40 A, R_a = 0·2 Ω

$$E = V - I_a R_a$$
$$= [400 - (40 \times 0\cdot2)] \text{ V} = [400 - 8] \text{ V} = \underline{392 \text{ V}}$$

Example 10.9. A six-pole lap-wound motor is connected to a 240-V d.c. supply. The armature has 480 conductors and a resistance of 0·8 Ω. The flux per pole is 30 mWb. Calculate the speed when the armature current is 50 A:

E = back e.m.f., V = 240 V, I_a = 50 A, R_a = 0·8 Ω

$$E = V - I_a R_a$$
$$= [240 - (50 \times 0\cdot8)] \text{ V} = [240 - 40] \text{ V} = 200 \text{ V}$$

n = speed in rev/s, $2p$ = 6, Φ = 30 mWb = 0·03 Wb, Z = 480, $C = 2p$ = 6

$$E = 2p \times \Phi \times \frac{Z}{C} \times n$$

$$200 = 6 \times 0\cdot03 \times \frac{480}{6} \times n$$

$$200 = 14\cdot4n$$

$$n = \frac{200}{14\cdot4} \text{ rev/s} = \underline{13\cdot88 \text{ rev/s}}$$

The expression $V - E = I_a R_a$ can be used as an alternative method of determining the torque produced.

$$V = E + I_a R_a$$

If both sides of the equation are multiplied by I_a

$$VI_a = EI_a + I_a^2 R_a$$

but

$$VI_a = \text{power supplied to the armature}$$

$$I_a^2 R_a = \text{power loss in the armature}$$

therefore, $$EI_a = \text{output power from armature, } P$$

If torque T is in newton metres, mechanical power output

$$P = 2\pi nT \text{ watts}$$

therefore,

$$2\pi nT = EI_a$$

$$T = \frac{E \times I_a}{2 \times \pi \times n} \text{ newton metres}$$

Example 10.10. Calculate the torque in newton metres developed by a 400-V d.c. motor having an armature resistance of 0·25 Ω and running at 12·5 rev/s. The armature current is 50 A.

$T =$ torque, $I_a = 50$ A, $R_a = 0.25$ Ω , $V = 400$ V

$$\text{Back e.m.f., } E = V - I_a R_a$$

$$= [400 - (50 \times 0.25)] \text{ V} = 387.5 \text{ V}$$

$$T = \frac{E \times I_a}{2 \times \pi \times n}$$

$$= \frac{387.5 \times 50}{2 \times \pi \times 12.5} \text{ N m}$$

$$= 247 \text{ N m}$$

10.6 Polyphase generators

The alternator described in section 10.1 (Fig. 10.1(b)) has only one circuit and is termed a single-phase alternator. If, however, three similar coils are placed as shown in Fig. 10.5(a), and the magnet rotated, then an e.m.f. will be generated in each coil. The e.m.f. generated in each coil will have the same frequency and maximum value, but owing to the relative displacements of the coils the maximum values of the three e.m.f.s will occur at different instants. If the three coils are spaced 120° apart, as shown in Fig. 10.5(a), then the waveforms of the e.m.f.s induced in the coils will be as shown in Fig. 10.5(b). An alternator of this type is termed a three-phase alternator.

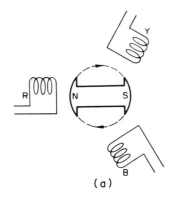

(a)

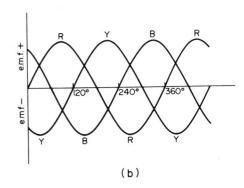

(b)

Fig. 10.5. Generation of three-phase e.m.f.

10.7 Polyphase supply systems

The standard method of generation, transmission, and distribution of electrical energy is by a three-phase system. The main advantages of a three-phase system over a single-phase system are:

(a) a reduction in the size of the alternator to produce the same power output,

(b) a reduction in the amount of copper or aluminium required to transmit the same power, and

(c) three-phase motors produce a uniform torque.

If three single-phase supplies were used to transmit the output power of the three-phase alternator, six conductors would be required. If, however, the three coils are connected as shown in Fig. 10.6(a), the whole of the output can be transmitted by three conductors, termed lines. Each winding of a three-phase alternator, transformer, or motor is termed a phase. Figure 10.6(a) shows the line and phase voltages and currents of a three-phase delta-connected supply system.

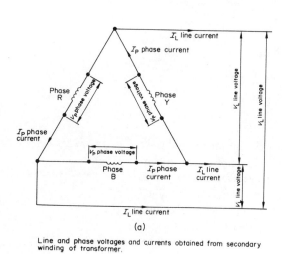

Line and phase voltages and currents obtained from secondary winding of transformer.

(a)

(b)
Star connection

(c)
Delta connection

Fig. 10.6. Three-phase connections

10.8 Star and delta connections

The two main methods of connecting the three coils of a three-phase system are as shown in Fig. 10.6(b) and (c). The relationships between the voltages and currents of a balanced system are:

Star connection: Line current I_L = phase current I_p
Line voltage $V_L = \sqrt{3}$ × phase voltage V_p

Delta connection: Line voltage V_L = phase voltage V_p
Line current $I_L = \sqrt{3}$ × phase current I_p

It is normal practice to connect the windings of three-phase alternators in star, whilst the majority of three-phase motors are connected in delta (refer to section 10.13).

10.9 Three-phase four-wire systems

The standard method of distribution of low voltage electrical energy is by a three-phase four-wire system, often called a three-phase and neutral system. To obtain a three-phase four-wire supply from the standard three-wire transmission system the secondary winding of the distribution transformer is connected in star, and a fourth conductor, called the neutral, is taken from the common, or star, point. This enables either a three-phase supply, usually at a line-voltage of 415 V to be obtained for driving electric motors (refer to section 10.13) or a single-phase supply, usually at a phase voltage of 240 V, to be obtained for lighting and heating purposes. Figure 10.7 shows the connections for a three-phase four-wire system and the various voltages normally available in Great Britain. Voltage ratios for distribution transformers are normally given as line values.

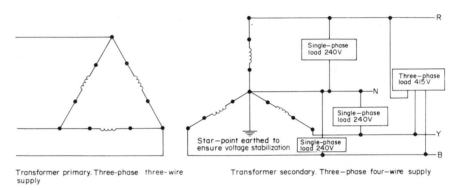

Transformer primary. Three-phase three-wire supply

Transformer secondary. Three-phase four-wire supply

Fig. 10.7. Distribution transformer connections

An advantage of this system of distribution is that the neutral conductor carries only the out of balance (or phasor sum) of the line currents. If therefore the three line currents are equal, then due to their phase displacement the neutral current will be zero. Many distribution cables therefore use a smaller cross-section conductor for the neutral.

10.10 Rotating magnetic fields

If a three-phase supply is connected to three coils, as shown in Fig. 10.8(a), the magnetic fluxes in the coils will reach maximum values in sequence. This will produce a magnetic field, of constant intensity, which will rotate between the coils. For a three-pole arrangement as shown the flux will rotate from coil R to coil Y in $\frac{1}{3}$ cycle, or rotate through one revolution in one cycle. This rotational speed is termed synchronous speed and is dependent on the supply frequency. The speed of rotation cannot be increased beyond synchronous speed but it can be reduced to one-half of synchronous speed by connecting the three-phase supply to six coils, as shown in Fig. 10.8(b).

Similarly, the speed of the rotating field can be reduced to $\frac{1}{3}$ or $\frac{1}{4}$ of synchronous speed by using nine or twelve coils respectively.

$$\text{Rotational speed} = \frac{\text{frequency}}{\text{number of poles pairs}} \text{ revolutions per second}$$

$$n = \frac{f}{p} \text{ revolutions per second}$$

The direction of rotation of the magnetic field can be reversed by interchanging any two of the supply connections to the field windings.

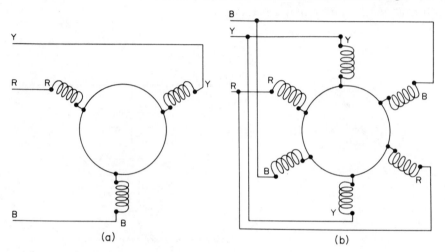

(a)   (b)

Fig. 10.8. Rotating magnetic fields

10.11 The synchronous motor

If the output windings of an alternator are connected to an alternating current supply and the field excited by a d.c. supply—as when functioning as an alternator—it can be made to run as a motor in which the rotor speed is equal to the speed of the rotating flux in the stator.

A motor of this type, where the rotor and stator speeds are synchronized, is termed a synchronous motor. Figure 10.9(a) represents a section of the rotor and stator of an a.c. machine. Since the poles on the rotor are magnetized by windings carrying direct current their polarity will remain the same, but the stator poles are fed from an alternating source so their polarity will depend on the instantaneous value of current in the stator coils. If the rotor is stationary in the position shown, with polarities as indicated, then the rotor will tend to move in a clockwise direction. Half a cycle later however, the stator polarity will have reversed so that the rotor will now tend to move in the reverse direction. Due to this alternating torque the motor is not self-starting. Consider now the case when the rotor is rotating in an anticlockwise or clockwise direction. If by the time the stator poles have reversed their polarity the rotor has moved forward exactly one pole pitch then the motion will be maintained.

A synchronous motor working on a fixed-frequency supply will only run at one particular speed given by:

$$n = \frac{f}{p} \text{ revolutions per second}$$

and will continue to run in whichever direction it is started.

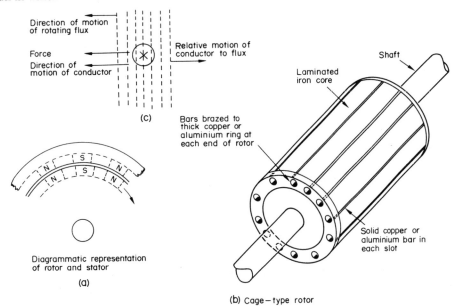

Diagrammatic representation of rotor and stator

(a)

(c)

(b) Cage–type rotor

Fig. 10.9. Alternating current motors

10.12 The asynchronous motor

A motor in which the rotor speed is not equal to the stator speed is termed an asynchronous motor. The difference between stator and rotor speeds is termed the slip and can be expressed either as a per-unit value or a percentage value of synchronous speed:

$$\text{slip} = \frac{\text{synchronous speed} - \text{rotor speed}}{\text{synchronous speed}}$$

Rotor frequency. The frequency of the e.m.f. induced in the rotor, f_r, is calculated by using the per unit, or fractional, slip s. For a supply frequency of f:

$$f_r = sf \text{ Hertz}$$

Example 10.11. An eight-pole asynchronous motor has a slip of 4% at full load. What will be its speed when running from a 50-Hz supply? Calculate also the frequency of the rotor e.m.f.:

n_r = rotor speed, n_s = synchronous speed = $50 \div 4 = 12.5$ rev/s, slip = 4/100

$$\text{slip} = \frac{n_s - n_r}{n_s}$$

$$\frac{4}{100} = \frac{12.5 - n_r}{12.5}$$

$$\frac{4 \times 12.5}{100} = 12.5 - n_r$$

$$2 = 12.5 - n_r$$

$$n_r = (12.5 - 2) \text{ rev/s} = \underline{10.5 \text{ rev/s}}$$

f_r = frequency of rotor e.m.f., $s = 4\% = 0.04$ per unit, $f = 50$ Hz

$$f_r = s f$$
$$= 0.04 \times 50 \text{ Hz} = \underline{2 \text{ Hz}}$$

10.13 Induction motor

This is the commonest type of asynchronous motor and derives its name from the fact that the current in the rotor is **induced** by the magnetic field instead of being supplied through electrical connections to the supply. The induction motor therefore does not require any electrical supply connections to the rotor during running conditions. Connections may be necessary in some types during starting (refer to section 10.14).

Stator. This is built like an alternator stator winding and usually carries a three-phase winding which is connected to the supply. Most induction motors run with the stator windings connected in delta.

Rotor. The simplest type of rotor is a cage rotor consisting of a laminated iron core with solid copper or aluminium bars in slots, the bars being connected together at each end (Fig. 10.9(b)).

Torque production. When the supply is switched on the stator field rotates at synchronous speed and the magnetic flux cuts the rotor conductors thus inducing currents in the rotor conductors. The magnetic field produced by these rotor currents reacts with the rotating field and causes the rotor to follow the rotating magnetic field (Fig. 10.9(c)). The magnitude of the induced rotor currents, and therefore the magnitude of the torque produced, depends on the relative speed of the rotating field and the rotor, hence the rotor speed must always be less than the synchronous speed. As the load on the motor increases the rotor speed drops thus increasing the relative speeds of stator and rotor. This causes larger currents to be induced in the rotor bars and thus a greater torque is produced to meet the increased load. It should be noted that even though there is no electrical connection to the rotor the rotor power is still drawn from the supply by induction.

10.14 Motor starters

When a motor is starting from rest there will be no back e.m.f. and the starting current will normally be several times greater than the full load running current. To prevent damage to the motor, and undue disturbance of the supply conditions, most motors are fitted with starting devices which limit the current on starting. As the motor speeds up and the back e.m.f. increases, the starting devices can be gradually cut out of the circuit. The motor starter normally also includes overload and low voltage protection. The type of starter used depends on the type of motor and the load conditions on starting. The following are some of the main types in use:

D.C. Motors. A resistor is normally placed in the armature circuit of the motor, arranged so that it can be gradually cut out of circuit as the motor speed increases. Figure 10.10(a) shows the connections for d.c. shunt and compound motors. The resistors can either be cut out of circuit manually or by automatic controllers when remote control is required.

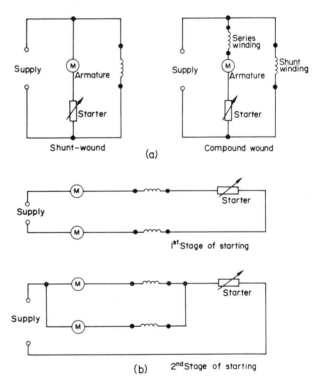

Fig. 10.10. Starting arrangements for d.c. motors

Series motors used for traction work are often worked in pairs. They are connected in series for initial starting and when the starting resistor has been cut out of circuit they are then connected in parallel and the same resistor again used to bring them up to full speed (Fig. 10.10(b)). The resistor may be used during running conditions for speed control.

119

Three-phase cage-rotor induction motor. The smaller sizes can be started by switching direct-on-line. Some machines designed to produce a higher starting torque are made as double-cage rotors with two sets of rotor bars, one of high resistance and the other in deeper slots with low resistance. The distribution of the bars is such that on starting the high resistance bars produce the majority of the torque and due to their resistance limit the starting current. As the motor speeds up the torque production is gradually transferred to the low resistance bars thus preventing overheating and reducing the losses.

For larger size machines the following methods are used:

Star-delta. Both ends of each of the three-phase windings are brought out to the terminal box. When starting, the windings are first connected in star across the supply, thus limiting the voltage applied across each winding to line voltage $\div \sqrt{3}$. When the motor has reached partial full speed the winding connections are changed to delta, thus applying full line voltage across each winding so that the motor now builds up to full speed.

Auto-transformer. By using a tapped transformer, usually an auto-transformer, the voltage applied to the windings can be gradually increased from zero to full voltage (Fig. 10.11(a)).

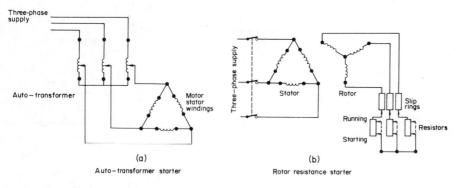

(a)
Auto–transformer starter

(b)
Rotor resistance starter

Fig. 10.11. Starting arrangements for a.c. motors

Rotor resistance. If the motor is required to start against a large starting torque it is usual to use rotor resistance starting. This requires a wound-rotor machine with the rotor connections brought out via slip rings to a resistance unit. No supply connections are made to the rotor. When starting, the resistors are fully in circuit and the full supply voltage is applied to the stator (Fig. 10.11(b)). As the motor speeds up, the resistors are gradually cut out of circuit, and when the motor attains full speed the ends of the rotor windings are connected together on the rotor and the brushes then lifted from the slip rings to prevent wear. The motor is now running as an induction motor. Care must be taken when interlocks are not fitted that no attempt is made to start the motor with the rotor resistors out of circuit.

120

Problems

1.   A single-phase alternator has twelve poles and runs at 10 rev/s. What is the output frequency?

2.   At what speed must a sixteen-pole alternator be driven to produce an output at 50 Hz?

3.   How many poles are required on an alternator which runs at 20 rev/s and has an output frequency of 80 Hz?

4.   What is the maximum speed at which an alternator can be run to produce an output at 50 Hz? How many poles will be required on this machine?

5.   An alternator runs at 40 rev/s and generates an e.m.f. of 200 V. If the speed is increased to 50 rev/s what change in flux is required so that the machine still generates an e.m.f. of 200 V?

6.   The total flux on an alternator is 0·25 Wb; the machine runs at 30 rev/s. What flux will be required to produce an increase of 10% in the generated e.m.f. at 25 rev/s?

7.   A d.c. generator running at $16\frac{2}{3}$ rev/s generates an e.m.f. of 200 V. At what speed must it be driven to generate the same e.m.f. when the flux per pole is reduced by 20%?

8.   A d.c. generator produces an e.m.f. of 250 V on open circuit. The full load current is 50 A and the armature resistance 0·2 Ω. What percentage increase in flux is required to maintain the same terminal voltage at full load if the speed remains constant?

9.   Determine the value of the back e.m.f. of a motor working from a 220-V supply when the armature current is 25 A, if the armature resistance is 0·75 Ω.

10.   A two-pole d.c. motor has a flux per pole of 0·6 Wb. There are 160 active conductors on the armature, each carrying a current of 10 A. Calculate the torque in newton metres.

11.   (a) Sketch the load characteristic of terminal voltage against load current, for the following types of d.c. generators:

(i) series connected

(ii) shunt connected

(iii) compound connected.

(b) State one purpose for which each is used.   (C.G.L.I.)

12.   (a) Show, with the aid of diagrams, three different methods of exciting a d.c. generator.

(b) A shunt-wound d.c. machine has an armature resistance of 0·3 Ω, and a shunt winding resistance of 200 Ω. Calculate the armature and field currents when it is used:

(i) as a shunt motor driving a mechanical load and taking a current of 140 A from the 460-V d.c. supply

(ii) as a generator delivering a current of 140 A to an external load at 460 V.
                                                            (C.G.L.I.)

13.   (a) Draw a circuit diagram showing the connections for a d.c. shunt generator supplying current to a bank of lamps.

(b) A d.c. shunt generator delivers 20 kW at 200 V to a resistive load. If the armature resistance is 0·12 Ω and the field resistance is 100 Ω calculate:

(i) the armature current

(ii) the generated e.m.f.

14. A d.c. generator has an armature resistance of 0·2 Ω. When driven at 16⅔ rev/s and delivering 50 A its terminal voltage is 240 V. If its speed is raised to 20 rev/s and the current delivered is raised to 100 A, the flux remaining constant, what is then its terminal voltage?

15. A shunt-wound d.c. machine has a field winding resistance of 115 Ω. The machine is used separately:

(i) as a 460-V shunt motor taking 140 A from a d.c. supply

(ii) as a 460-V shunt generator delivering a current of 140 A.

(a) For each case find the current in the armature and in the shunt field winding.

(b) If a rheostat is connected in series with the shunt winding, and varied whilst the machine is running, explain the effect on the working of the machine in each case.

(C.G.L.I.)

16. Explain the meaning of back e.m.f. in a direct-current motor. Describe how it affects the starting and running of a motor. Calculate the force acting on a single armature conductor of length 480 mm, which carries 90 A, and lies in a magnetic field of average density 1·2 T.

(C.G.L.I.)

17. With the aid of sketches and diagrams, describe how an alternating current may be generated in a simple two-pole machine. Assume that the armature consists of a single coil of wire. What are the effects of an alteration of:

(a) the driving speed

(b) the excitation?

18. Explain how a single-phase supply can be obtained from a three-phase double-wound delta/star transformer. If the transformer is a step-down with a voltage ratio of 40:1, what will be the single-phase output voltage for an input voltage of 10 kV?

19. Explain how a rotating magnetic field can be obtained from a three-phase supply.

20. A three-phase cage-rotor motor which failed to start was found to have one phase reverse connected. Illustrate by diagrams:

(a) the connections before the fault was found

(b) the correct connections.

(C.G.L.I.)

21. What is meant by the slip of an induction motor? Calculate the speed of a six-pole induction motor which has a slip of 6% at full load with a supply frequency of 50 Hz. What will be the speed of a four-pole alternator supplying the motor?

(C.G.L.I.)

22. The rotor of a four-pole induction motor rotates at 23 rev/s and the slip is 8%. Calculate the supply frequency.

23. Why cannot an induction motor run at synchronous speed? A six-pole, 50-Hz induction motor runs with a 5% slip. What is its speed? What is the frequency of the rotor current?

(C.G.L.I.)

Answers

1.	60 Hz		2.	6·25 rev/s
3.	8 poles		4.	50 rev/s; 2
5.	Reduce by 20%		6.	0·33 Wb
7.	20⅚ rev/s		8.	4%
9.	201·25 V		10.	305·3 N m

12. (i) $I_a = 137\cdot7A; I_f = 2\cdot3$ A; (ii) $I_a = 142\cdot3$ A; $I_f = 2\cdot3$ A
13. (i) 102 A (ii) 212·24 V 14. 280 V
15. (i) $I_a = 136$ A; $I_f = 4$ A (ii) $I_a = 144$ A; $I_f = 4$ A
16. 51·84 N 18. 250 V
21. $15\frac{2}{3}$ rev/s; 25 rev/s 22. 50 Hz
23. $15\frac{5}{6}$ rev/s; 2·5 Hz

Laboratory work

1. Alternator characteristics. The following tests should be carried out on a single-phase alternator driven by a variable speed motor:

(a) With the alternator field current set at a fixed value, increase the alternator speed from zero to full speed and record, over this range, the generated e.m.f. and frequency. Plot graphs of:

(i) generated e.m.f. against speed

(ii) frequency against speed.

(b) With the speed maintained constant at normal full speed increase the field current from zero to maximum and record the generated e.m.f. over this range. Plot a graph of generated e.m.f. against field current.

2. D.C. Shunt generator characteristics. The following tests should be carried out on a small shunt-wound d.c. generator driven by a variable speed motor and with a variable resistor connected in the field circuit:

(a) With the field current kept constant at normal value, increase the speed of the machine from zero to full speed and record the terminal voltage over this range. Plot a graph of terminal voltage against speed.

(*Note:* On no-load the terminal voltage is the same as the generated e.m.f.)

(b) With the speed kept constant at normal speed, vary the field current from zero to full value and record the terminal voltage over this range. Plot a graph of terminal voltage against field current. Compare the shape of this curve with a *B–H* curve for steel (section 9.4).

3. D.C. motor characteristics. The following tests should be carried out using a small d.c. compound-wound motor with either a mechanical or electrical means of loading the motor:

(a) Connect the motor as a compound-wound motor and with the supply voltage maintained constant increase the load from zero to approximately 25% overload. Record the load and speed over this range and plot a graph of load against speed.

(b) Repeat the above test but using a shunt-wound motor.

(c) Repeat the above test but using a series-wound motor ensuring that when starting the test there is a small load on the motor to prevent overspeeding.

4. Line and phase relationships

(a) Connect three similar single-phase loads across the phases and neutral of a star-connected supply as shown in Fig. 10.7. Insert an ammeter in each line and in the neutral conductor. Tabulate the ammeter readings and compare the phasor sum of the ammeter readings in the lines with the neutral ammeter reading. Measure the voltage between phases and calculate the voltage between one line and the neutral. Compare this with the measured value.

(b) Repeat the above tests and comparisons using three dissimilar loads to produce an unbalanced system.

11. D.C. Switching circuits

11.1 Effect of inductance in d.c. circuits

When the switch S in Fig. 11.1 is closed the current I_2 flowing in resistor R_2 will reach its maximum value almost immediately, whereas the current I_1, flowing in the inductive branch R_1L_1 will take some considerable time to reach its maximum value. If the growth of current in each circuit is plotted against time, the results will be similar to those shown in Fig. 11.2(a). The rate of growth of the current in the inductive circuit will depend on the relative values of L and R (refer to section 11.2).

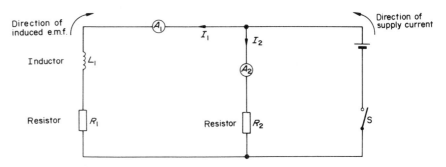

Fig. 11.1. Induced e.m.f. in an inductive circuit

The reason for the different rates of growth of the two currents is that a self-induced e.m.f. is set up in the inductor due to the change in flux produced by current I_1. The value of the induced e.m.f. will depend on the rate of change of flux (refer to section 9.7). The direction of the induced e.m.f. opposes the change in current being supplied to the circuit (Lenz's law) causing the current to be delayed in reaching its maximum value.

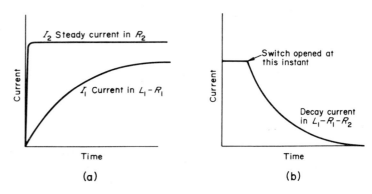

Fig. 11.2. Growth and decay of current in an inductive circuit

In a d.c. circuit containing resistance and inductance, e.g., field coils on electric motors, when steady state conditions have been established there will be no change in flux and therefore no induced e.m.f. so that the inductance will have no effect on the circuit conditions.

However when the inductive circuit is first connected to the supply, or when the current in the circuit changes in value, then the inductance of the circuit will cause an e.m.f. to be induced, which will affect the time taken for the current to reach its new value. In a circuit connected to a d.c. supply the relative values of inductance and resistance will determine the time taken for the current to reach its maximum value, whilst the resistance will determine the final value reached by the current.

11.2 Plotting curve of current growth and decay in an L-R circuit

In order to plot a curve of the growth of current in a circuit having inductance L (henrys) and resistance R (ohms) connected to a d.c. supply of V (volts), it is necessary to first calculate the maximum value of the current and the time constant. The maximum value of the current is calculated from ohm's law:

$$I = \frac{V}{R} \text{ amperes}$$

In an inductive circuit the rate of growth of current at any instant is such that if the current continued to increase at the same steady rate it would reach maximum value in a time of L/R seconds. This period of time is termed the time constant τ,

$$\tau = \frac{L}{R} \text{ seconds}$$

The current curve can now be plotted as follows:
1. Draw the axes of current and time as shown in Fig. 11.3. The length of the time axis should be approximately five times the time constant.
2. Mark on the current axis the maximum value of the current and draw in line a–b at this value.
3. Starting from O, construct a right-angled triangle OCD where OC is equal to the time constant.
4. Mark on OD point O_1 approximately 1/5 along OD.
5. Construct triangle $O_1 C_1 D_1$ where $O_1 C_1$ is again equal to the time constant.
6. Repeat this process at O_2, O_3, O_4, etc., remembering that OC, $O_1 C_1, O_2 C_2, O_3 C_3$, etc., are always equal to the time constant.
7. Join points O, O_1, O_2, O_3, O_4, etc., to produce the current curve.

When a d.c. inductive circuit is switched off, the current will fall to zero almost immediately. This may cause a very high, and possibly dangerous, e.m.f. to be induced in the circuit (refer to section 9.10). If a field discharge resistor is fitted in the position of R_2 in Fig. 11.1, then the decay in current will be as shown in Fig. 11.2(b), the energy stored in the inductive circuit being dissipated harmlessly as heat in the resistor.

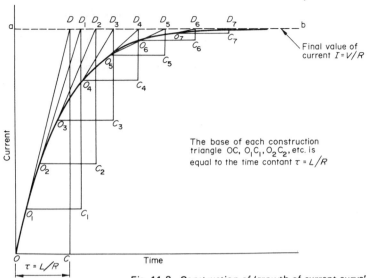

The base of each construction
triangle OC, O_1C_1, O_2C_2, etc. is
equal to the time contant $\tau = L/R$

Fig. 11.3. Construction of 'growth of current curve'

Example 11.1. A coil has an inductance of 2 H and resistance of 4 Ω. Plot a curve of the growth in current when the coil is connected to a 40-V d.c. supply. From the graph determine:

(a) the value of current 1 s after switching on,

(b) the time required for the current to reach 6 A:

τ = time constant, $L = 2$ H, $R = 4\,\Omega$

$$\tau = \frac{L}{R} = \frac{2}{4}\text{ s} = 0.5\text{ s}$$

I_{max} = maximum value attained by the current, $V = 40$ V, $R = 4\,\Omega$

$$I_{max} = \frac{V}{R} = \frac{40}{4}\text{ A} = 10\text{ A}$$

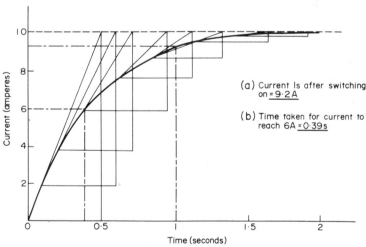

(a) Current Is after switching on = 9·2 A

(b) Time taken for current to reach 6A = 0·39s

Fig. 11.4. Solution to example 11.1

127

11.3 Effect of capacitance in d.c. circuits

When switch S in Fig. 11.5 is closed the currents I_1 and I_2 will both reach their maximum values almost immediately. As the capacitor charges the current flowing in the capacitive circuit C_1R_1 will gradually drop to zero whilst the current in R_2 will remain steady. If the change in current in each circuit is plotted against time, the results will be similar to those shown in Fig. 11.6(a).

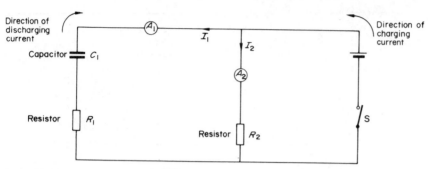

Fig. 11.5. Capacitor connected to a d.c. supply

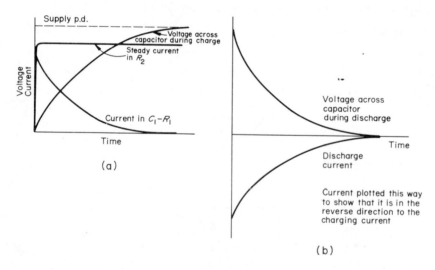

Fig. 11.6. Charge and discharge curves for capacitor

The reason for the current in R_1C_1 dropping to zero is that as the capacitor becomes charged the p.d. across it increases until it reaches the same value as the supply p.d. (Fig. 11.6(a)). The p.d. across the capacitor opposes the supply p.d. and thus limits the current flowing. When the capacitor is fully charged the p.d. across it will be equal, and opposite in polarity, to the supply p.d. and therefore no current will then flow in the circuit. If switch S is now opened the capacitor will gradually discharge through resistors R_1 and R_2. The variation in current and p.d. across the capacitor during discharging is shown in Fig. 11.6(b).

128

11.4 Plotting curves of current and voltage change in a *C-R* circuit

To plot the curves of variation in current and voltage during charging and discharging of a capacitor of capacitance C (farads) in series with a resistor of resistance R (ohms) connected across a d.c. supply of V (volts), it is necessary to calculate the initial charging or discharging current I from:

$$I = \frac{V}{R} \text{ amperes}$$

and also the time constant τ from:

$$\tau = CR \text{ seconds}$$

Using these values the curves of current and voltage can now be plotted in exactly the same manner as detailed in section 11.2.

Example 11.2. A 2-μF capacitor is connected in series with a 50-kΩ resistor across a 50-V d.c. supply. Construct a curve showing the change in current when the capacitor is disconnected from the supply and discharged through a 150-kΩ resistor:

(a) What will be the value of the current 0·5 s after starting to discharge?
(b) How long will it take for the discharge current to fall to 0·12 mA?

$\tau = $ time constant, $C = 2 \times 10^{-6}$ F, $R = [(50 \times 10^3) + (150 \times 10^3)] \, \Omega = 200 \times 10^3 \, \Omega$

$$\tau = C \times R$$
$$= 2 \times 10^{-6} \times 200 \times 10^3 \text{ s}$$
$$= 0 \cdot 4 \text{ s}$$

$I = $ initial value of discharge current, $V = 50$ V, $R = 200 \times 10^3 \, \Omega$

$$I = \frac{V}{R} = \frac{50}{200 \times 10^3} \text{ A} = 0 \cdot 25 \text{ mA}$$

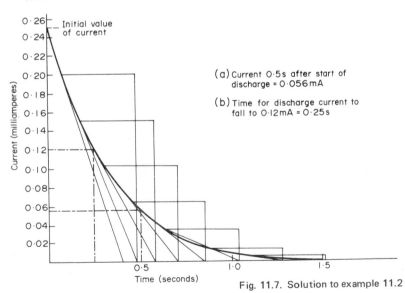

(a) Current 0·5s after start of discharge = 0·056 mA

(b) Time for discharge current to fall to 0·12mA = 0·25s

Fig. 11.7. Solution to example 11.2

Problems

1.   Explain the meaning of the term time constant when applied to an inductive circuit.

2.   A coil of resistance 25 Ω and inductance 5 H is connected to a 100-V d.c. supply. Calculate:
(a) the time constant
(b) the final value of current in the coil.

3.   The field winding of a d.c. machine has an inductance of 0·2 H and resistance of 16 Ω, and is connected to a 400-V d.c. supply. Construct a growth of current curve when the machine is switched on.

4.   A relay coil of resistance 2 kΩ and inductance 0·01 H works off a 200-V supply. Construct a growth of current curve when the coil is switched on. What will be the value of the current 5 μs after switching on?

5.   The field coil of a d.c. generator is connected across a 240-V supply. The coil has a resistance of 120 Ω and an inductance of 0·2 H. When the coil is disconnected from the supply a field discharge resistor of 120 Ω resistance is connected across the coil. Calculate:
(a) the initial value of discharge current
(b) the time constant.
Construct a curve of the discharge current.

6.   Explain what is meant by the time constant of a circuit containing capacitance and resistance in series.

7.   A 20-μF capacitor is charged from a 200-V d.c. supply through a 24-kΩ resistor. Calculate:
(a) the time constant
(b) the initial value of the charging current
(c) the final value of charging current.

8.   A capacitor and resistor are connected in series across a d.c. supply. Sketch curves to show the variation in the following quantities with time:
(a) charging current
(b) capacitor p.d.
The capacitor is now disconnected from the supply and discharged through the resistor. Sketch curves showing the variation with time of:
(a) the discharge current
(b) the discharge voltage across the capacitor.

9.   A 10-μF capacitor is charged from a 100-V d.c. supply through a 5-kΩ resistor. Construct a curve to show the variation in charging current during the time the capacitor is being charged. After what period of time will the capacitor be approximately fully charged?

10.   A 100-μF capacitor charged to a p.d. of 500 V is discharged through a 2-MΩ resistor. Construct a curve showing the variation in current with time as the capacitor discharges.

Answers

2.   (a) 0·2 s   (b) 4 A
5.   (a) 1 A   (b) 0·83 ms
9.   0·2–0·25 s

4.   0·0632 A
7.   (a) 0·48 s   (b) 8·3 mA   (c) 0

12. Alternating current circuits

Alternating current flows first in one direction and then in the reverse direction in a series of fluctuations. When a magnetic field is rotated inside a stationary coil, such that the flux cuts the axial sides of the coil, an alternating e.m.f. is induced in the coil. Alternatively, the coil can be rotated in the magnetic field (Fig. 12.1). Suitable design of the magnetic circuit enables a sinusoidal alternating e.m.f. to be produced. This is the most suitable wave shape since its rate of change is also sinusoidal, which gives smooth continuous mechanical relationships, makes calculations relatively simple and relationships between different circuit quantities easily expressible. Also, all wave shapes can be expressed as a sum of sinusoidal waves. Other wave forms, however, can be produced.

12.1 Terminology of a.c. waveforms

Cycle is a complete sequence of alternating events (Fig. 12.1).

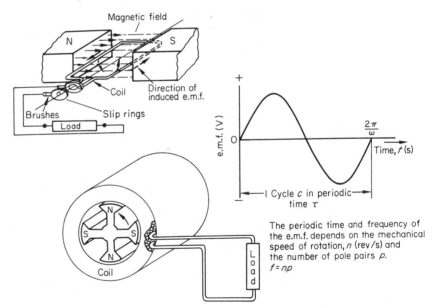

The periodic time and frequency of the e.m.f. depends on the mechanical speed of rotation, n (rev/s) and the number of pole pairs p.
$f = np$

Fig. 12.1. Generation of an e.m.f.

Frequency, f, is the number of cycles per second, the units are hertz (Hz).

Periodic time, τ, is the time taken for one cycle, the units are seconds (s).

$$\tau = \frac{1}{f} = \frac{2\pi}{\omega},$$

ω = angular speed of electrical generation
$= 2\pi f$

131

Instantaneous values are the values of the alternating quantities at any instant. They are represented by small letters, e, i, etc. (Fig. 12.2(a)).

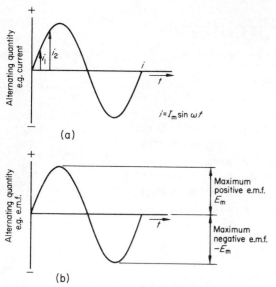

(a)

$i = I_m \sin \omega t$

(b)

Fig. 12.2. Instantaneous and maximum values

Maximum values are the values of the alternating quantities at the peaks of the waveform. They are represented by E_m, I_m, etc. (Fig. 12.2(b)).

Average values: the average value over a complete cycle of a symmetrically alternating quantity is zero: however, over half a cycle it has a value. Therefore in the case of rectified supplies the average value is that upon which the metal deposited in a plating process and the deflexion of moving coil instruments depend. The average value of a rectified wave can be calculated, using the mid-ordinate rule (refer to section 2.9) from,

$$\frac{\text{area under the curve}}{\text{length of base}}$$

For sinusoidal waveforms the average value is given in Fig. 12.3(a).

Root mean square (r.m.s.) values are the effective values of alternating quantities and are those indicated by a.c. instruments and are the values given unless otherwise specified. They are the values upon which the average power depends.

$$\text{Instantaneous power, } p = i^2 R$$

Since R is constant,

$$\text{average power, } P \propto \text{average of } i^2$$

Therefore,

$$\text{effective value of current} = \sqrt{\text{average of sum of values of } i^2},$$

132

i.e., square root of the mean of the sum of the squares of the instantaneous values. They are represented by capital letters E, I, etc. (Fig. 12.3(b)). R.M.S. values can be calculated from

$$\sqrt{\frac{\text{area under the squared waveform}}{\text{length of base}}}$$

For sinusoidal waveforms the r.m.s. value is given in Fig. 12.3(b).

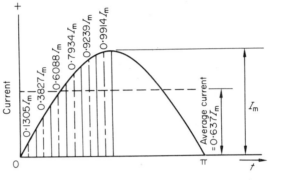

Average value $= 2 \times I_m \dfrac{(0.1305+0.3827+0.6088+0.7934+0.9239+0.9914) \times \frac{\pi}{12}}{\pi} = 0.638\, I_m$

If an infinite number of values were taken the average value would be $\dfrac{2}{\pi} I_m$

(a)

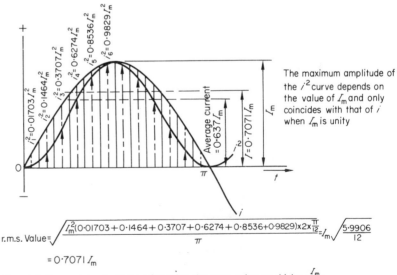

The maximum amplitude of the i^2 curve depends on the value of I_m and only coincides with that of i when I_m is unity

r.m.s. Value $= \sqrt{\dfrac{I_m^2(0.01703+0.1464+0.3707+0.6274+0.8536+0.9829) \times 2 \times \frac{\pi}{12}}{\pi}} = I_m \sqrt{\dfrac{5.9906}{12}}$

$= 0.7071\, I_m$

If an infinite number of values were taken the r.m.s. value would be $\dfrac{I_m}{\sqrt{2}}$

(b)

Fig. 12.3. Average and r.m.s. values

133

For a given waveform:

$$\text{form factor} = \frac{\text{r.m.s. value}}{\text{average value}}$$

$$\text{peak factor} = \frac{\text{maximum value}}{\text{average value}}$$

Phase is the electrical angular displacement between two alternating quantities.

Phase angle, ϕ, is the electrical angle by which the current leads or lags the voltage. If either the current or voltage is used as a reference quantity, for example the current $i = I_m \sin \omega t$, then the voltage can be written $v = V_m \sin(\omega t \pm \phi)$.

Sinusoidal alternating quantities are phasor quantities, they can be represented graphically, resolved, added, and subtracted as shown in sections 2.4 to 2.7.

Example 12.1. (a) Calculate the r.m.s. value of a sinusoidal current of maximum value 12 A:

$$I = \frac{I_m}{\sqrt{2}} = 0.7071 \times 12 \text{ A} = \underline{8.485 \text{ A}}$$

(b) What is the periodic time of a quantity which has a frequency of 50 Hz?

$$\frac{1}{f} = \frac{1}{50} \text{ s} = \underline{0.02 \text{ s}}$$

(c) Write an expression for the basic instantaneous current represented in (a) at a frequency of 50 Hz:

$$i = I_m \sin \omega t = I_m \sin 2\pi ft = 12 \sin 2\pi \times 50t = \underline{12 \sin 314 \, t}$$

(d) Calculate the value of the current in (c) when $t = 0.004$ s:
$i = 12 \sin 2\pi \times 50 \times 0.004 = 12 \sin 0.4\pi = 12 \sin 72° = 12 \times 0.9511 \text{ A} = \underline{11.41 \text{ A}}$

(e) Sketch the waveform of $i = 12 \sin 314 \, t$ and indicate on the graph the value obtained in (d), Fig. 12.4(a).

(f) Write an expression for an instantaneous voltage of maximum value 339·4 V which is out of phase with the current in (c) by $\pi/3$ radians, the current lagging the voltage:

Since the current is lagging, the voltage waveform will be in front of the current waveform.

$$v = V_m \sin(\omega t + \phi) = \underline{339.4 \sin(314t + \pi/3)}$$

(g) Calculate the value of the voltage in (f) when $t = 0.008$ s:
$v = 339.4 \sin(2\pi \times 50 \times 0.008 + \pi/3) \text{ V} = 339.4 \sin(0.8\pi + 0.333) \text{ V} = 339.4 \sin 204° \text{ V}$
$= -339.4 \sin(204° - 180°) \text{ V} = -339.4 \sin 24° \text{ V} = -339.4 \times 0.4067 \text{ V} = \underline{-138 \text{ V}}$

(h) Draw a phasor diagram showing the current $i = 12 \sin 314t$ and voltage $v = 339.4 \sin(314t + \pi/3)$. Fig. 12.4(b).

(i) Use the phasor diagram of (h) to sketch the current and voltage waveforms (Fig. 12.4(c)).

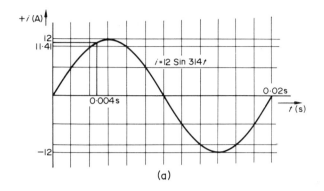

(a)

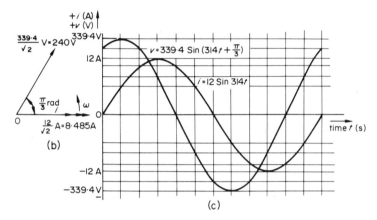

(b)

(c)

Fig. 12.4. Solution to example 12.1(e), (h), and (i)

12.2 Circuit terminology and relationships

When an alternating voltage is applied to a complete circuit an alternating current is set up. The amount of current depends on the amount of opposition to current flow. These quantities are related by.

$$\frac{V \text{ (volts)}}{I \text{ (amperes)}} = \text{opposition (ohms)}$$

Opposition to current flow occurs due to resistance, inductive reactance, and capacitive reactance. Although circuits usually consist of combinations of these quantities, their individual effects must be considered separately.

Resistance, R, (Fig. 12.5(a)) is due to $\rho l/A$ (refer to section 7.2) and since resistance does not oppose change in current, the current alternations follow those of the applied voltage.

$$\frac{V}{I} = R$$

135

Inductive reactance, X_L (Fig. 12.5(b)), arises due to the property of a circuit known as inductance, L, (refer to section 9.8) which, when the current in the circuit changes, causes an e.m.f. to be induced, the direction of which is always such as to try to prevent the change in the circuit current. The resulting steady-state conditions are such that the current lags the voltage by $90°$ ($\pi/2$ radians). The opposition to current flow is called inductive reactance, X_L.

$$\frac{V}{I} = X_L \quad \text{where } X_L = 2\pi f L \text{ ohms (}L \text{ in henrys)}$$

Capacitive reactance, X_C (Fig. 12.5(c)), arises due to the property of a circuit known as capacitance, C, (refer to section 8.1) which is a measure of the circuits ability to store electricity, and opposes the change in the voltage across the circuit. The resulting steady-state conditions are such that the current leads the voltage by $90°$. The opposition to current flow is called capacitive reactance, X_C.

$$\frac{V}{I} = X_C \quad \text{where } X_C = \frac{1}{2\pi f C} \text{ ohms (}C \text{ in farads)}$$

Impedance, Z, is the term given to the total opposition to current flow and is due to the combined effects of resistance, inductive reactance, and capacitive reactance.

$$\frac{V}{I} = Z$$

where Z is the **phasor** sum of R, X_L and X_C (section 2.7).

Power, P. The power p at any instant is given by $p = i \times v$ or $i^2 R$. Average (effective) power P is dissipated in the resistance only and is given by

$$P = I^2 R \text{ or } VI \cos \phi.$$

Units: watts, W; kilowatts, kW; etc.
Note: All formulae assume sinusoidal waveforms.

Example 12.2.

(a) Calculate the current that would flow in a purely resistive circuit of 12 Ω, when an alternating voltage of 240 V is applied:

$$I = \frac{V}{R} = \frac{240}{12} \text{ A} = \underline{20 \text{ A}}$$

(b) Calculate the inductive reactance at 40 Hz in a circuit having an inductance of 0·2 H:

$$X_L = 2\pi f L = 2\pi \times 40 \times 0\cdot2 \ \Omega = \underline{50\cdot27 \ \Omega}$$

(c) If the current in the inductance of (b) is 20 mA, calculate the p.d. across the inductance:

$$V = I \times X_L = 20 \times 10^{-3} \times 50\cdot27 \text{ V} = \underline{1\cdot005 \text{ V}}$$

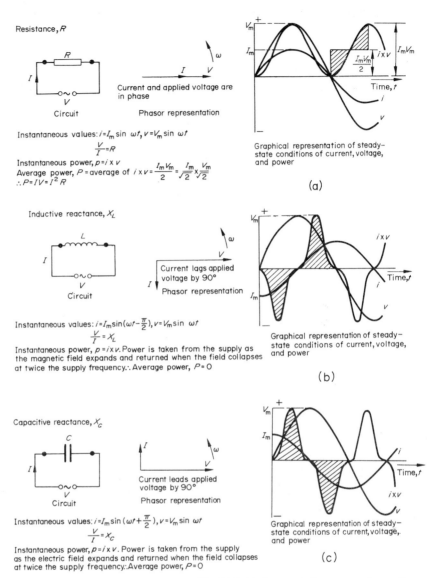

Resistance, R

R

Circuit

Current and applied voltage are in phase

Phasor representation

Instantaneous values: $i = I_m \sin \omega t$, $v = V_m \sin \omega t$

$$\frac{V}{I} = R$$

Instantaneous power, $p = i \times v$

Average power, $P = $ average of $i \times v = \dfrac{I_m V_m}{2} = \dfrac{I_m}{\sqrt{2}} \times \dfrac{V_m}{\sqrt{2}}$

$\therefore P = IV = I^2 R$

Graphical representation of steady-state conditions of current, voltage, and power

(a)

Inductive reactance, X_L

L

Circuit

Current lags applied voltage by 90°

Phasor representation

Instantaneous values: $i = I_m \sin(\omega t - \frac{\pi}{2})$, $v = V_m \sin \omega t$

$$\frac{V}{I} = X_L$$

Instantaneous power, $p = i \times v$. Power is taken from the supply as the magnetic field expands and returned when the field collapses at twice the supply frequency. $\therefore$ Average power, $P = 0$

Graphical representation of steady-state conditions of current, voltage, and power

(b)

Capacitive reactance, X_C

C

Circuit

Current leads applied voltage by 90°

Phasor representation

Instantaneous values: $i = I_m \sin(\omega t + \frac{\pi}{2})$, $v = V_m \sin \omega t$

$$\frac{V}{I} = X_C$$

Instantaneous power, $p = i \times v$. Power is taken from the supply as the electric field expands and returned when the field collapses at twice the supply frequency. Average power, $P = 0$

Graphical representation of steady-state conditions of current, voltage, and power

(c)

Fig. 12.5. Resistance, inductance, and capacitance

(d) If the frequency in part (b) is trebled what will be the effect on the voltage across the inductance in (c) if the current is to be maintained at the same value?

$$V = 3 \times 1\cdot005 \text{ V} = 3\cdot015 \text{ V}$$

(e) Calculate the capacitive reactance at 40 Hz in a circuit having a capacitance of 80 μF:

$$X_C = \frac{1}{2\pi f C} = \frac{1}{2\pi \times 40 \times 80 \times 10^{-6}}\ \Omega = \frac{10^6}{2\pi \times 40 \times 80}\ \Omega = 49\cdot73\ \Omega$$

137

(f) Calculate the p.d. across the capacitance in (e), when the circuit current is 1·4 A:

$$V = I \times X_C = 1·4 \times 49·73 \text{ V} = \underline{69·62 \text{ V}}$$

(g) If the frequency in part (e) is trebled what will be the effect on the voltage across the capacitance in (f)?

$$V = \frac{69·62}{3} \text{ V} = \underline{23·21 \text{ V}}$$

(h) Calculate the total opposition to current flow in a circuit in which an applied voltage of 110 V causes a current of 11 A to be set up:

$$Z = \frac{V}{I} = \frac{110}{11} \text{ } \Omega = \underline{10 \text{ } \Omega}$$

(i) What is the resistance of a circuit which takes 3 kW at a current of 5 A?

$$P = I^2 R$$
$$3000 = 5^2 \times R$$
$$R = \frac{3000}{25} \text{ } \Omega = \underline{120 \text{ } \Omega}$$

12.3 Series a.c. circuits

In a series circuit the current is used as the reference phasor since it is common to all parts of the circuit.

Resistance and inductance in series (Fig. 12.6)

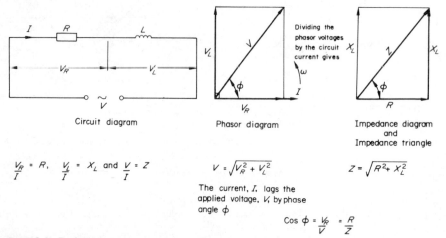

Circuit diagram   Phasor diagram   Impedance diagram and Impedance triangle

$\frac{V_R}{I} = R$, $\frac{V_L}{I} = X_L$ and $\frac{V}{I} = Z$ 　　$V = \sqrt{V_R^2 + V_L^2}$ 　　$Z = \sqrt{R^2 + X_L^2}$

The current, I, lags the applied voltage, V, by phase angle ϕ

$\text{Cos } \phi = \frac{V_R}{V} = \frac{R}{Z}$

Fig. 12.6. Resistance and inductance in series

Example 12.3. For the circuit shown in Fig. 12.6:

(a) Calculate the applied voltage, V, when V_R = 40 V and V_L = 50 V:

$$V = \sqrt{40^2 + 50^2} \text{ V} = \sqrt{1600 + 2500} \text{ V} = \sqrt{4100} \text{ V} = \underline{64·03 \text{ V}}$$

(b) Determine by means of a scaled phasor diagram the impedance, Z, when $R = 8\ \Omega$ and $X_L = 12\ \Omega$, Fig. 12.7(a).

(c) Calculate the phase angle, ϕ, of the circuit from (b):

$$\cos\phi = \frac{R}{Z} = \frac{8}{14\cdot4} = 0\cdot556: \phi = 56°\ 15'\text{ lagging}$$

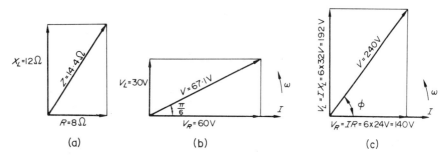

Fig. 12.7. Solution to examples 12.3(b) and (e), and 12.7

(d) Calculate the inductive reactance, X_L, when $V = 240$ V, $I = 12$ A, and $R = 10\ \Omega$:

$$Z = \frac{V}{I} = \frac{240}{12}\ \Omega = 20\ \Omega$$

$$Z = \sqrt{R^2 + X_L^2}$$

$$20 = \sqrt{10^2 + X_L^2}$$

$$20^2 = 10^2 + X_L^2$$

$$X_L = \sqrt{20^2 - 10^2}\ \Omega = \sqrt{400 - 100}\ \Omega = \sqrt{300}\ \Omega = 17\cdot32\ \Omega$$

(e) If the circuit has a phase angle of $\pi/6$ and the p.d. across the resistance, $V_R = 60$ V, draw a phasor diagram to determine the supply voltage, V, and the voltage across the inductance, V_L, Fig. 12.7(b).

(f) Calculate the power taken by the circuit when $I = 40$ A, $V = 410$ V, and $\phi = \pi/3$:

$$P = VI\cos\phi = 410 \times 40 \times \cos\pi/3\ \text{W} = 16400\cos 60°\ \text{W} = 16\ 400 \times 0\cdot5\ \text{W} = 8\cdot2\ \text{kW}$$

Example 12.4. Calculate the inductive reactance and circuit current when an inductance of $0\cdot12$ H is connected across a 200-V, 50-Hz sinusoidal supply:

$X_L =$ inductive reactance, $L = 0\cdot12$ H, $f = 50$ Hz

$$X_L = 2\pi fL$$
$$= 2\pi \times 50 \times 0\cdot12\ \Omega = 314 \times 0\cdot12\ \Omega$$
$$= 37\cdot7\ \Omega$$

139

I = circuit current, $V = 200$ V

$$X_L = \frac{V}{I}$$

$$I = \frac{V}{X_L}$$

$$= \frac{200}{37 \cdot 7} \text{ A} = \underline{5 \cdot 31 \text{ A}}$$

Example 12.5. An inductance of 0·2 H is connected across a 415-V sinusoidal supply. At what frequency will a current of 4 A flow in the circuit?

X_L = inductive reactance, $V = 415$ V, $I = 4$ A

$$X_L = \frac{V}{I}$$

$$= \frac{415}{4} \ \Omega = 103 \cdot 75 \ \Omega$$

f = frequency, $L = 0 \cdot 2$ H

$$X_L = 2\pi f L$$

$$f = \frac{X_L}{2\pi L}$$

$$= \frac{103 \cdot 75}{2\pi \times 0 \cdot 2} \text{ Hz}$$

$$= \underline{82 \cdot 5 \text{ Hz}}$$

Example 12.6. A sinusoidal current having a maximum value of 12 A flows in a circuit of resistance 10 Ω. Determine the p.d. across the resistor and the power dissipated. Write equations for the instantaneous circuit current and the p.d. across the resistor at a frequency of 50 Hz.

V = p.d. across the resistor, $I = 12 \times 0 \cdot 7071$ A $= 8 \cdot 49$ A, $R = 10 \ \Omega$

$$V = IR$$

$$= 8 \cdot 49 \times 10 \text{ V} = \underline{84 \cdot 9 \text{ V}}$$

P = power dissipated

$$P = I^2 R$$

$$= 72 \times 10 \text{ W} = \underline{720 \text{ W}}$$

$$\omega = 2\pi f = 2\pi \times 50 = 314, \ I_m = 12 \text{ A}, \ V_m = \frac{84 \cdot 9}{0 \cdot 7071} \text{ V} = 120 \text{ V}$$

$$i = I_m \sin \omega t = \underline{12 \sin 314 \ t}, \ v = V_m \sin \omega t = \underline{120 \sin 314 \ t}$$

Example 12.7. An air-cored coil takes a current of 10 A when connected across a 240-V d.c. supply and 6 A when connected across a 240-V sinusoidal supply at 50 Hz. Determine the resistance, impedance, and inductance of the coil. Sketch the circuit phasor diagram (Fig. 12.7(c)).

240 V d.c.: $R = $ coil resistance, $I = 10$ A

$$R = \frac{V}{I}$$

$$= \frac{240}{10} \; \Omega = 24 \; \Omega$$

240 V a.c.: $Z = $ coil impedance, $I = 6$ A

$$Z = \frac{V}{I}$$

$$= \frac{240}{6} \; \Omega = 40 \; \Omega$$

$L = $ coil inductance, $f = 50$ Hz

$$Z = (R^2 + X_L^2)^{1/2}$$

$$X_L = (Z^2 - R^2)^{1/2}$$

$$= (40^2 - 24^2)^{1/2} \; \Omega = (1024)^{1/2} \; \Omega = 32 \; \Omega$$

$$X_L = 2\pi f L$$

$$L = \frac{X_L}{2\pi f}$$

$$= \frac{32}{2\pi \times 50} \; H = 0 \cdot 102 \; H$$

Example 12.8. A heater, which may be regarded as purely resistive, dissipates 1·05 kW and takes a sinusoidal current of 8 A when operating at its rated values. Determine the inductance of a non-resistive choke which, when connected in series with the heater, across a 240-V, 50-Hz supply, will produce the correct working conditions.

L = inductance of choke, $P = 1 \cdot 05$ kW, $I = 8$ A, $V = 240$ V, $f = 50$ Hz

$$P = I^2 R$$

$$R = \frac{P}{I^2}$$

$$= \frac{1 \cdot 05 \times 10^3}{8^2} \, \Omega = 16 \cdot 4 \, \Omega$$

$$Z = \frac{V}{I}$$

$$= \frac{240}{8} \, \Omega = 30 \, \Omega$$

$$Z = (R^2 + X_L{}^2)^{1/2}$$

$$X_L = (Z^2 - R^2)^{1/2}$$

$$= (30^2 - 16 \cdot 4^2)^{1/2} \, \Omega = (631)^{1/2} \, \Omega = 25 \cdot 12 \, \Omega$$

$$X_L = 2\pi f L$$

$$L = \frac{X_L}{2\pi f}$$

$$= \frac{25 \cdot 12}{2\pi \times 50} \, \text{H} = \underline{79 \cdot 8 \text{ mH}}$$

Resistance and capacitance in series (Fig. 12.8).

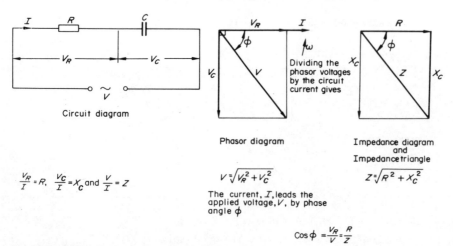

Circuit diagram

$\frac{V_R}{I} = R$, $\frac{V_C}{I} = X_C$ and $\frac{V}{I} = Z$

Phasor diagram

$V = \sqrt{V_R{}^2 + V_C{}^2}$

The current, I, leads the applied voltage, V, by phase angle ϕ

Dividing the phasor voltages by the circuit current gives

Impedance diagram and Impedance triangle

$Z = \sqrt{R^2 + X_C{}^2}$

$\cos \phi = \frac{V_R}{V} = \frac{R}{Z}$

Fig. 12.8. Resistance and capacitance in series

142

Example 12.9. For the circuit shown in Fig. 12.8:

(a) Draw to scale the phasor diagram when $I = 4$ A, $R = 2\ \Omega$, and $X_C = 3\ \Omega$:

$$V_R = IR = 4 \times 2\text{ V} = 8\text{ V},\ V_C = IX_C = 4 \times 3\text{ V} = 12\text{ V; (Fig. 12. 9(a))}$$

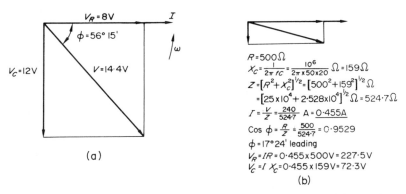

(a)

$R = 500\,\Omega$

$X_C = \dfrac{1}{2\pi fC} = \dfrac{10^6}{2\pi \times 50 \times 20}\,\Omega = 159\,\Omega$

$Z = [R^2 + X_C^2]^{1/2} = [500^2 + 159^2]^{1/2}\,\Omega$

$\quad = [25 \times 10^4 + 2\cdot528 \times 10^4]^{1/2}\,\Omega = 524\cdot7\,\Omega$

$I = \dfrac{V}{Z} = \dfrac{240}{524\cdot7}$ A $= \underline{0\cdot455\text{A}}$

$\text{Cos}\ \phi = \dfrac{R}{Z} = \dfrac{500}{524\cdot7} = 0\cdot9529$

$\phi = 17°24'$ leading

$V_R = IR = 0\cdot455 \times 500\text{V} = 227\cdot5\text{V}$

$V_C = I\,X_C = 0\cdot455 \times 159\text{V} = 72\cdot3\text{V}$

(b)

Fig. 12.9. Solutions to examples 12.9(a), and 12.11

(b) Use the phasor diagram from (a) to determine the applied voltage, V, and the circuit phase angle, ϕ:

$$V = 14.4\text{ V} \qquad\qquad \phi = 56°\ 15'$$

(c) Calculate the impedance, Z, of the circuit when $R = 20\ \Omega$ and $C = 40\ \mu\text{F}$ at a frequency of 60 Hz:

$$X_C = \frac{1}{2\pi fC} = \frac{1}{2\pi \times 60 \times 40 \times 10^{-6}}\ \Omega = \frac{10^6}{2\pi \times 60 \times 40}\ \Omega = 66\cdot31\ \Omega$$

$$Z = (R^2 + X_C^2)^{1/2} = (20^2 + 66\cdot31^2)^{1/2}\Omega = (400 + 4397)^{1/2}\ \Omega = (4797)^{1/2}\ \Omega = \underline{69\cdot26\ \Omega}$$

(d) Calculate the circuit current for the component values in (c) when a voltage of 100 V is applied to the circuit at 60 Hz:

$$I = \frac{V}{Z} = \frac{100}{69\cdot26}\text{ A} = \underline{1\cdot444\text{ A}}$$

(e) What is the power taken by the circuit in (d)?

$$P = I^2\,R = 1\cdot444^2 \times 20\text{ W} = \underline{41\cdot7\text{ W}}$$

(f) Write expressions for the instantaneous value of current and applied voltage in (d):

$$I_m = I \times \sqrt{2} = 1\cdot444 \times 1\cdot414\text{ A} = 2\cdot042\text{ A},\ \cos\phi = \frac{R}{Z} = \frac{20}{69\cdot26} = 0\cdot289,\ \therefore\phi = 1\cdot278\text{ rad}$$

$$V_m = V \times \sqrt{2} = 100 \times 1\cdot414\text{ V} = 141\cdot4\text{ V}$$

$$i = I_m \sin \omega t = 2\cdot042 \sin 2\pi \times 60t = \underline{2\cdot042 \sin 377t}$$

$$v = V_m \sin (\omega t - \phi) = \underline{141\cdot4 \sin (377t - 1\cdot278)}$$

Example 12.10. Determine the capacitance of a capacitor required to limit the current to 5 A, when it is connected across a 200-V, 400-Hz sinusoidal supply:

C = capacitance, $I = 5$ A, $V = 200$ V, $f = 400$ Hz

$$X_C = \frac{V}{I}$$

$$\frac{1}{2\pi f C} = \frac{V}{I}$$

$$C = \frac{I}{2\pi f V}$$

$$= \frac{5}{2\pi \times 400 \times 200} \text{ F} = \underline{9{\cdot}95 \ \mu\text{F}}$$

Example 12.11. A resistance of 500 Ω and a 20-pF capacitor are connected in series across a 240-V, 200-Hz supply. Determine the circuit current and its phase angle, and draw a phasor diagram. (Fig. 12.9(b)).

Example 12.12. A resistor of 0·05 MΩ and a 0·2-μF capacitor are connected in series across a sinusoidal 415-V, 50-Hz supply. Calculate the circuit current and the voltages across the resistor and the capacitor:

I = circuit current, V_R = voltage across resistor, V_C = voltage across capacitor,

$R = 0{\cdot}05$ M$\Omega = 0{\cdot}05 \times 10^6$ Ω, $C = 0{\cdot}2$ μF $= 0{\cdot}2 \times 10^{-6}$ F

$$X_C = \frac{1}{2\pi f C}$$

$$= \frac{1}{2\pi \times 50 \times 0{\cdot}2 \times 10^{-6}} \ \Omega = 15900 \ \Omega$$

$$Z = (R^2 + X_C^2)^{1/2}$$

$$= [(5 \times 10^4)^2 + (1{\cdot}59 \times 10^4)^2]^{1/2} \ \Omega$$

$$= 10^4 (25 + 2{\cdot}528)^{1/2} \ \Omega = 5{\cdot}247 \times 10^4 \ \Omega$$

$$I = \frac{V}{Z}$$

$$= \frac{415}{5{\cdot}247 \times 10^4} \text{ A} = \underline{7{\cdot}92 \text{ mA}}$$

$$V_R = IR$$

$$= 7{\cdot}92 \times 10^{-3} \times 0{\cdot}05 \times 10^6 \text{ V} = \underline{396 \text{ V}}$$

$$V_C = IX_C$$

$$= 7{\cdot}92 \times 10^{-3} \times 15900 \text{ V} = \underline{126 \text{ V}}$$

Resistance, inductance, and capacitance in series. Circuits comprising R, L, and C in series can be treated as either R-L or R-C circuits by reducing to an effective reactance $(X_L - X_C)$ and an effective reactance voltage $(V_L - V_C)$. A negative value simply indicating that the effective reactance is capacitive (Fig. 12.10).

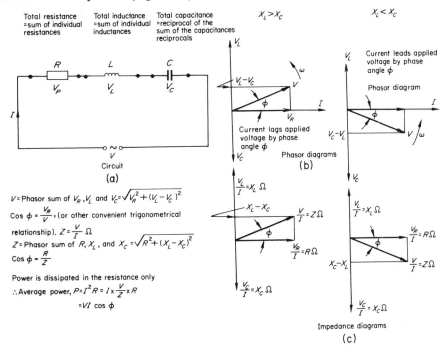

Fig. 12.10. R.L.C. series circuit

Example 12.13. For the circuit shown in Fig. 12.10:

(a) Calculate the circuit current, I, when $V = 240$ V, and $Z = 120 \, \Omega$:

$$I = \frac{V}{Z} = \frac{240}{120} \text{ A} = \underline{2 \text{ A}}$$

(b) Calculate the power taken, P, and phase angle, ϕ, for the circuit values in (a), when $R = 60 \, \Omega$:

$$P = I^2 \, R = 2^2 \times 60 \text{ W} = \underline{240 \text{ W}}$$

$$\cos \phi = \frac{R}{Z} = \frac{60}{120} = 0 \cdot 5 : \phi = \underline{60°}$$

(c) Calculate the effective reactance and state its nature when $L = 0 \cdot 2$ H and $C = 20 \, \mu F$ at a frequency of 60 Hz:

$$X_L = 2\pi f L = 2\pi \times 60 \times 0 \cdot 2 \, \Omega = 75 \cdot 41 \, \Omega$$

$$X_C = \frac{1}{2\pi f C} = \frac{1}{2\pi \times 60 \times 20 \times 10^{-6}} \, \Omega = \frac{10^6}{2\pi \times 60 \times 20} \, \Omega = 132 \cdot 6 \, \Omega$$

effective reactance $= (X_L - X_C) = (75 \cdot 41 - 132 \cdot 6) \, \Omega = \underline{57 \cdot 19 \, \Omega}$ capacitive.

(d) Calculate V_R, V_L, and V_C for the component values in (c) when $R = 100\ \Omega$, $I = 50$ mA, and the frequency remains at 60 Hz:

$$V_R = IR = 50 \times 10^{-3} \times 100\ \text{V} = \underline{5\ \text{V}}$$

$$V_L = IX_L = 50 \times 10^{-3} \times 75{\cdot}41\ \text{V} = \underline{3{\cdot}77\ \text{V}}$$

$$V_C = IX_C = 50 \times 10^{-3} \times 132{\cdot}6\ \text{V} = \underline{6{\cdot}63\ \text{V}}$$

(e) Draw to scale the phasor diagram for the values in (d) and indicate the value of the effective reactive voltage, supply voltage and phase angle. (Fig. 12.11(a)).

(f) What would be the effect on the values of R, X_L, and X_C in (b) if the frequency is doubled?

R, no change; X_L, doubled; X_C, halved

(g) If the effective reactance is capacitive, would the circuit current increase or decrease if the frequency is halved?

The current would decrease, since the opposition to current would increase due to the increase in effective reactance.

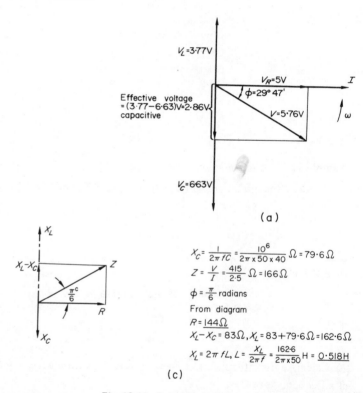

$$X_C = \frac{1}{2\pi fC} = \frac{10^6}{2\pi \times 50 \times 40}\ \Omega = 79{\cdot}6\ \Omega$$

$$Z = \frac{V}{I} = \frac{415}{2{\cdot}5}\ \Omega = 166\ \Omega$$

$$\phi = \frac{\pi}{6}\ \text{radians}$$

From diagram

$R = \underline{144\ \Omega}$

$X_L - X_C = 83\ \Omega,\ X_L = 83 + 79{\cdot}6\ \Omega = 162{\cdot}6\ \Omega$

$$X_L = 2\pi fL,\ L = \frac{X_L}{2\pi f} = \frac{162{\cdot}6}{2\pi \times 50}\ \text{H} = \underline{0{\cdot}518\text{H}}$$

(c)

Fig. 12.11. Solutions to examples 12.13(e), and 12.14

Example 12.14. An air-cored coil is connected in series with a 40-μF capacitor. The circuit takes a current of 2·5 A at a phase angle of $\pi/6$ when connected across a 415-V,

50-Hz sinusoidal supply. Determine by means of an impedance diagram, drawn to scale, the resistance and inductance of the coil (Fig. 12.11(c)).

Example 12.15. A series circuit consists of a resistance of 10 Ω, inductance 0·15 H, and a capacitance of 200 μF. The power consumed by the circuit is 2 kW when connected across a 50-Hz sinusoidal supply. Determine:

(a) the circuit current,
(b) the phase angle,
(c) the supply voltage,
(d) the circuit impedance.

I = circuit current, $R = 10\ \Omega$, $P = 2000$ W, $f = 50$ Hz, $L = 0\cdot15$ H, $C = 200\ \mu$F

(a)
$$P = I^2 R$$

$$I^2 = \frac{P}{R} = \frac{2000}{10} = 200$$

$$\underline{I = 14\cdot14\ \text{A}}$$

(b)
$$X_L = 2\pi f L$$

$$= 2\pi \times 50 \times 0\cdot15 = 47\cdot1\ \Omega$$

$$X_C = \frac{1}{2\pi f C}$$

$$= \frac{10^6}{2\pi \times 50 \times 200}\ \Omega = 15\cdot9\ \Omega$$

$$\tan\phi = \frac{X}{R} = \frac{47\cdot1 - 15\cdot9}{10} = 3\cdot12$$

$$\underline{\phi = 72° \ 14'}\ \text{lagging since}\ X_L > X_C$$

(c)
$$P = VI\cos\phi$$

$$2000 = V \times 14\cdot14 \times \cos 72° \ 14'$$

$$2000 = V \times 14\cdot14 \times 0\cdot3051$$

$$V = \frac{2000}{14\cdot14 \times 0\cdot3051} \quad \underline{V = 463\cdot6\text{V}}$$

(d)
$$Z = \frac{V}{I} = \frac{463\cdot6}{14\cdot14}\ \Omega$$

$$\underline{= 32\cdot79\ \Omega}$$

12.4 Series resonance

An *R-L-C* series circuit is said to be in a resonant condition when the supply voltage and current are in phase, Fig. 12.12. It can be seen from Fig. 12.13 that this will occur when $X_L = X_C$, hence $V_L = V_C$. Also, that the effective reactance $X_L - X_C$ will be zero, therefore $Z = R$ and $V = V_R$.

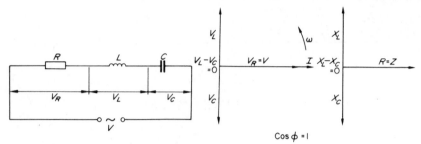

Fig. 12.12. Series resonance

A resonant condition can be produced by

(a) varying L ⎫
(b) varying C ⎬ until $X_L = X_C$
(c) varying f ⎭

Note: Varying L may also vary R due to the change in the number of turns on the coil.

Graphs of R, X_L, X_C, Z, and I against f are shown in Fig. 12.13.

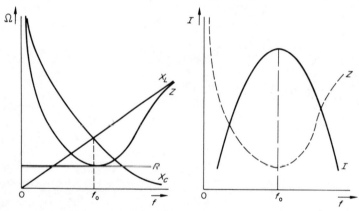

Fig. 12.13. Graphs of R, X_L, X_C, Z, and I against f

The resonant frequency, f_0, occurs when the current and power taken are a maximum, and can be calculated from

$$f_0 = \frac{1}{2\pi} \sqrt{\frac{1}{LC}}$$

Further effects of series resonance are that the circuit impedance is a minimum and that very high voltages can occur across the circuit reactances, even though the supply voltage may be relatively low.

Example 12.16. For an R-L-C series circuit:

(a) Which of the following quantites should be increased and which decreased to produce resonance if V_L is greater than V_C?

(i) frequency
(ii) inductance
(iii) capacitance
(iv) capacitive reactance.

Solutions:

(i) frequency, decreased
(ii) inductance, decreased
(iii) capacitance, decreased
(iv) capacitive reactance, increased.

(b) Calculate the value of the resonant frequency, f_0, for a circuit in which L = 80 mH and C = 3·125 μF:

$$f_0 = \frac{1}{2\pi}\sqrt{\frac{1}{LC}} = \frac{1}{2\pi}\sqrt{\frac{1}{80 \times 10^{-3} \times 3 \cdot 125 \times 10^{-6}}}\ \text{Hz} = \frac{1}{2\pi}\sqrt{\frac{10^9}{250}}\ \text{Hz}$$

$$= \frac{10^4}{10 \times \pi}\ \text{Hz} = \underline{318 \cdot 3\ \text{Hz}}$$

(c) When R = 20 Ω and the applied voltage is 100 V, what will be the value of the resonant current?

$$I = \frac{V}{Z}\text{, at resonance } Z = R\text{, therefore, } I = \frac{V}{R} = \frac{100}{20}\ \text{A} = \underline{5\ \text{A}}$$

(d) If X_L = 20 Ω and X_C = 30 Ω, what should be the proportional change in (i) L (ii) C, to produce resonance?
At resonance $X_L = X_C$:

$\qquad X_L$ must increase in the ratio $\frac{3}{2}$, hence L must increase $\frac{3}{2}$ times
$\qquad X_C$ must decrease in the ratio $\frac{2}{3}$, hence C must increase $\frac{3}{2}$ times

(e) What will be the effect on the resonant frequency value, f_0, if both L and C are increased?
f_0 would decrease, since $f \propto 1/LC$ which is unlikely to be fractional.

12.5 Parallel a.c. circuits

These consist of a number of series circuits called branches, each of which is connected across the same supply.
$\qquad$ Only two branch circuits consisting of:

(a) a coil having resistance and inductance,
(b) a capacitor,
will be considered.

The phasor diagram (Fig. 12.14) is drawn using the voltage as a reference phasor since it is common to all branches.

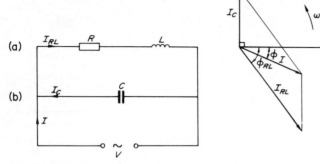

(a)

(b)

Fig. 12.14. Parallel a.c. circuits

I = phasor sum of I_C and I_{RL}

$$= \sqrt{(\text{sum of vertical components})^2 + (\text{sum of horizontal components})^2}$$

$$= \sqrt{(I_C - I_{RL} \sin \phi_{RL})^2 + (I_{RL} \cos \phi_{RL})^2}$$

(refer to section 2.7)

$$\cos \phi = \frac{I_{RL} \cos \phi_{RL}}{I}; \qquad Z = \frac{V}{I}$$

Power, P, $= VI \cos \phi$ or the sum of the power taken by each branch, in this case, $I_{RL}^2 R$.

Example 12.17. For the circuit shown in Fig. 12.14:

(a) Calculate I_{RL} and I_C, when a sinusoidal voltage of 200 V is applied at a frequency such that $Z_{RL} = 20\ \Omega$ and $X_C = 10\ \Omega$:

$$I_{RL} = \frac{V}{Z_{RL}} = \frac{200}{20}\ \text{A} = 10\ \text{A}; \qquad I_C = \frac{V}{X_C} = \frac{200}{10}\ \text{A} = 20\ \text{A}$$

(b) Determine the value of the coil-branch phase angle, ϕ_{RL}, when $R = 10\ \Omega$:

$$\cos \phi_{RL} = \frac{R}{Z_{RL}} = \frac{10}{20} = 0.5, \text{ therefore, } \phi_{RL} = 60° \text{ lagging}$$

(c) Calculate the value of the supply current, I, for the values in (a) and (b):

$$I = \sqrt{(I_C - I_{RL} \sin \phi_{RL})^2 + (I_{RL} \cos \phi_{RL})^2} = \sqrt{(20 - 10 \sin 60°)^2 + (10 \cos 60°)^2}\ \text{A}$$

$$= \sqrt{(20 - 10 \times 0.866)^2 + (10 \times 0.5)^2}\ \text{A} = \sqrt{11.34^2 + 5^2}\ \text{A} = \sqrt{128.6 + 25}\ \text{A}$$

$$= \sqrt{153.6}\ \text{A} = 12.39\ \text{A}$$

(d) Determine the power, P, taken for the values in (a), (b), and (c):

$$P = I_{RL}^2 R = 10^2 \times 10 = 1000 \text{ W} = \underline{1 \text{ kW}}$$

or

$$P = VI\cos\phi = 200 \times 12\cdot39 \times \frac{5}{12\cdot39} \text{ kW} = \underline{1 \text{ kW}}$$

(e) What would be the initial effect on the supply current, I, if the capacitance is increased, when the circuit phase angle is lagging?

I, would decrease since I_C would increase, therefore $(I_C - I_{RL} \sin\phi)$ would decrease.

(f) When $I = 12$ A, $\phi = 30°$ and $I_C = 6$ A, determine by means of a scaled vector diagram the value of the coil-current, I_{RL}. (Fig. 12.15(a)).

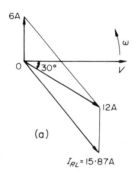

(a)

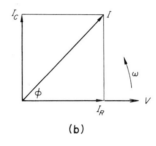

(b)

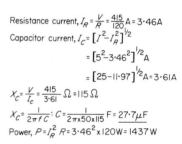

Resistance current, $I_R = \frac{V}{R} = \frac{415}{120} \text{A} = 3\cdot46\text{A}$

Capacitor current, $I_C = [I^2 - I_R^2]^{1/2}$

$= [5^2 - 3\cdot46^2]^{1/2}\text{A}$

$= [25 - 11\cdot97]^{1/2}\text{A} = 3\cdot61\text{A}$

$X_C = \frac{V}{I_C} = \frac{415}{3\cdot61}\Omega = 115\Omega$

$X_C = \frac{1}{2\pi f C}: C = \frac{1}{2\pi \times 50 \times 115}\text{F} = 27\cdot7\mu\text{F}$

Power, $P = I_R^2 R = 3\cdot46^2 \times 120\text{W} = 1437\text{W}$

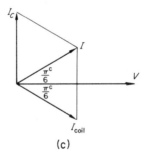

(c)

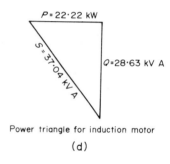

$P = 22\cdot22$ kW

$S = 37\cdot04$ kV A

$Q = 28\cdot63$ kV A

Power triangle for induction motor

(d)

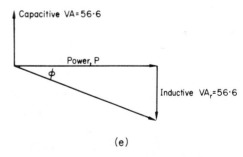

(e)

Fig. 12.15. Solutions to examples 12.17(f), 12.18, 12.19, 12.21, and 12.23

Example 12.18. A resistance of 120 Ω is shunted across a capacitor. The combination takes a current of 5 A when connected across a 415-V, 50-Hz sinusoidal supply. Determine the capacitance of the capacitor and the power taken. Sketch the phasor diagram for the circuit.(Fig. 12.15(b)).

Example 12.19. A coil of impedance 80 Ω and phase angle $\pi/6$ at a frequency of 50 Hz is shunted across a capacitor. Calculate the capacitance of the capacitor if the overall circuit phase angle is to be $\pi/6$ leading when the combination is connected across a 240-V, 50-Hz sinusoidal supply. Sketch the circuit phasor diagram in explanation (Fig. 12.15(c)).

Capacitor current, I_C = 2 x vertical component of coil current (refer to Fig. 12.15(c)).

$$= 2 \times \frac{V}{Z} \sin \phi_z$$

$$= 2 \times \frac{240}{80} \times \sin \frac{\pi}{6} = 2 \times 3 \times 0 \cdot 5 \text{ A} = 3 \text{ A}$$

$$X_C = \frac{V}{I_C}$$

$$= \frac{240}{3} \Omega = 80 \ \Omega$$

$$X_C = \frac{1}{2\pi f C}$$

$$C = \frac{1}{2\pi f X_C}$$

$$= \frac{1}{2\pi \times 50 \times 80} \text{ F} = \underline{39 \cdot 81 \ \mu\text{F}}$$

12.6 Effects of parallel phase resonance

For the circuit shown in Fig. 12.14 the supply current, I, will be in phase with the applied voltage, V, when the vertical component of, I_{RL} ($I_{RL} \sin \phi_{RL}$), equals I_C. The effects of this resonant condition are:

(a) The supply current, $I = I_{RL} \cos \phi_{RL}$ and is a minimum (Fig. 12.16).

(b) A large current could oscillate between the coil and capacitor, resulting in large branch currents compared with the supply current (Fig. 12.16).

(c) Slight changes from the resonant frequency could produce large changes in supply current (Fig. 12.16).

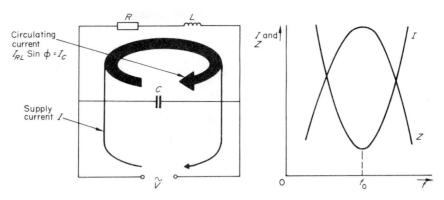

Fig. 12.16. Parallel phase resonance

Note: Both (b) and (c) depend on the relative values of R, L, C, and f.

Example 12.20. When the supply voltage, V, in the circuit shown in Fig. 12.16 is 200 V, and the coil impedance, $Z_{RL} = 40\ \Omega$, and resistance $R = 10\ \Omega$, calculate:

(a) the coil branch-current, I_{RL}:

$$I_{RL} = \frac{V}{Z_{RL}} = \frac{200}{40}\ \text{A} = \underline{5\ \text{A}}$$

(b) the coil branch phase angle ϕ_{RL}:

$$\cos\phi_{RL} = \frac{R}{Z} = \frac{10}{40} = 0{\cdot}25: \qquad \phi_{RL} = \underline{75°\ 31'\ \text{lagging}}$$

(c) the value of the capacitor current I_C if the circuit is in a resonant state:

$$I_C = I_{RL}\sin\phi = 5\sin 75°\ 31'\ \text{A} = 5 \times 0{\cdot}9682\ \text{A} = \underline{4{\cdot}84\ \text{A}}$$

(d) the value of the capacitance, C, at the resonant state, if the supply voltage was at a frequency of 100 Hz:

$$X_C = \frac{V}{I_C} = \frac{200}{4{\cdot}84}\ \Omega = 41{\cdot}32\ \Omega$$

$$C = \frac{1}{2\pi f X_C} = \frac{1}{2\pi \times 100 \times 41{\cdot}32}\ \text{F} = 0{\cdot}000\,038\,51\ \text{F} = \underline{38{\cdot}51\ \mu\text{F}}$$

12.7 Power, P, and power factor p.f.

In a.c. circuits power is a fluctuating quantity and is dissipated in the resistive parts only. The power at any instant, $p = i \times v$ or $i^2 R$. Figure 12.5 shows that the average power P in resistive circuits is given by $I^2 R$, but that in inductive or capacitive circuits power is taken from the supply as the magnetic or electric fields expand and is returned to the supply as the fields collapse, and the average power will be zero. Power factor is the factor by which the product of current and voltage is multiplied to give the power in watts.

$$\text{Volt amperes} \times \text{power factor} = \text{power in watts}$$

If the supply is sinusoidal then the power factor is $\cos\phi$:

$$\text{Power, } P = VI\cos\phi \text{ watts} = I^2R \text{ watts}$$

Active and reactive components. The component of current upon which the average power depends is the component in phase with the voltage and is called the active component of the current. The component of current at 90° to the voltage is called the reactive component, Fig. 12.17.

$$\text{Active component of current} = I\cos\phi$$
$$\text{Reactive component of current} = I\sin\phi$$

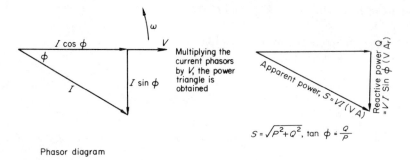

Multiplying the current phasors by V, the power triangle is obtained

$$S = \sqrt{P^2 + Q^2}, \quad \tan\phi = \frac{Q}{P}$$

Phasor diagram

Fig. 12.17. Active and reactive components

Example 12.21. A single-phase induction motor has an output of 20 kW and a p.f. of 0·6 when connected across a 240-V, 50-Hz sinusoidal supply. The efficiency of the motor at full load is 90%, calculate the active and reactive components of the motor current and sketch the power triangle of the motor (Fig. 12.15(d)):

$$\text{Active component of current} = \frac{P}{V} = \frac{22 \cdot 22 \times 10^3}{240} = 92 \cdot 58 \text{ A}$$

$$\text{kV A} = \frac{\text{kW}}{\cos\phi} = \frac{22 \cdot 22}{0 \cdot 6} = 37 \cdot 04$$

$$\text{kV Ar} = \text{kV A} \times \sin\phi = 37 \cdot 04 \times 0 \cdot 8 = 28 \cdot 63$$

$$\text{Reactive component of current} = \frac{\text{V Ar}}{\text{V}}$$

$$= \frac{28 \cdot 63 \times 10^3}{240} = 119 \cdot 27 \text{ A}$$

Power factor correction. Nearly all consumer loads are inductive-resistive and therefore have lagging power factors. Figure 12.18(a) shows that if a leading current device such as a capacitor is placed in parallel with, and as near to, the load as possible, the

154

overall power factor is improved, i.e., increased in value from say 0·8 to 0·9, and the supply current up to that point is reduced without affecting the load current. Consequently, generation and transmission losses are minimized and switchgear can either be smaller or more fully utilized.

Since generation and transmission losses are the responsibility of the supply authority and not directly that of the consumer, consumers are persuaded to improve their power factor toward unity by means of selective tariffs. Figure 12.18(b) and (c) shows that power factor improvement past 0·96 is not very economical since beyond this value the reduction in supply current is small compared with the capacitive kV Ar required to bring about the reduction. It can also be seen that over correction will increase the supply current again. However for the purpose of calculation simplification all correction problems in this book will be correction to unity power factor.

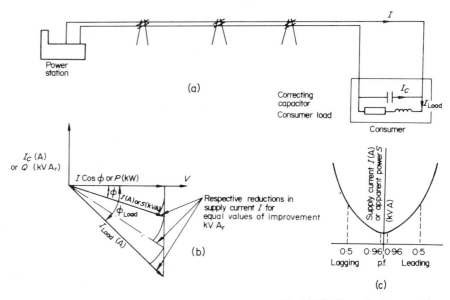

Fig. 12.18. Power factor correction

$$\text{Correcting kV Ar} = \text{Power taken by the load} \times \tan \phi_{\text{Load}}$$
$$\text{kV Ar} = P \times \tan \phi_{\text{Load}}$$

Example 12.22. A 500-kW factory load operates at a p.f. of 0·6 lagging from a 240-V, 50-Hz supply. Calculate:

(a) the reactive kV Ar of a capacitor, in parallel with the load, required to improve the p.f. to unity:

$$\cos \phi = 0·6, \quad \phi = 53° 8'$$

kV Ar of capacitor $= P \times \tan \phi = 500 \times 1·334 = 667$

(b) the capacitor current:

$$I_C = \frac{\text{kV Ar}}{V} = \frac{667 \times 100}{240} \text{ A} = \underline{278 \text{ A}}$$

(c) the capacitance of the capacitor:

$$X_C = \frac{V}{I_C} = \frac{240}{278}\,\Omega = 0{\cdot}863\,\Omega$$

$$C = \frac{1}{2\pi \times f \times X_C} = \frac{1}{2\pi \times 50 \times 0{\cdot}863}\,F = 0{\cdot}003\,69\,F = 3{\cdot}69\,mF$$

Example 12.23. A factory load on a 415-V, 50-Hz sinusoidal supply has an effective resistance of 1000 Ω and inductance 1·19 H. Determine the V A rating of a capacitor, in parallel with the load, which will improve the factory's power factor to unity. (Fig. 12.15(e)):

$$\text{Inductive reactance, } X_L = 2\pi f L$$

$$= 1{\cdot}19 \times 314\,\Omega = 374\,\Omega$$

$$\text{Impedance, } Z = (R^2 + X_L^2)^{1/2}$$

$$= (1000^2 + 374^2)^{1/2}\,\Omega$$

$$= (10^6 + 139\,900)^{1/2}\,\Omega = 1067{\cdot}7\,\Omega$$

$$I = \frac{V}{Z}$$

$$= \frac{415}{1067{\cdot}7}\,A = 0{\cdot}389\,A$$

To improve the p.f. to unity:

$$\text{Capacitor kV A} = \text{inductor kV Ar}$$

$$\text{Capacitor V A} = VI\sin\phi = 415 \times 0{\cdot}389 \times \frac{374}{1067{\cdot}7}$$

$$= 56{\cdot}6$$

Problems

1. A sinusoidal voltage has an equation $v = 80 \sin 314t$. Find for this supply:

(a) the maximum value, V_m
(b) the r.m.s. value, V
(c) the angular velocity of electrical generations, ω
(d) the frequency, f
(e) the periodic time, τ

2. Write an equation for a sinusoidal current of r.m.s. value 20 A at a frequency of 40 Hz. Draw a phasor for this current and sketch the waveform.

3. Sketch on the same axes the waveforms $v = 100 \sin(20\pi t + \pi/3)$ and $i = 10 \sin 20\pi t$ using the current as a reference phasor. Indicate on the waveforms, the maximum value, the periodic time and the phase.

4.   Calculate the values of the voltage and current in problem (3) when $t = 0.02$ s, and indicate these values on the waveforms.

5.   Explain, with reference to a sinusoidal current, the meaning of the terms:

(a) frequency
(b) periodic time
(c) amplitude.

Write down the mathematical expression representing a sinusoidal current having an r.m.s. value of 100 mA and a frequency of 1 kHz. The r.m.s. voltage across an inductor of negligible resistance is 10 V when this current flows in it. Deduce an expression for this voltage. Using the same axes, sketch these current and voltage waveforms showing clearly the phase relationship between them. Mark approximate scale values on the axes.

(C.G.L.I.)

6.   Explain the meaning of r.m.s., peak and average values, and frequency as applied to an alternating waveform. Show, by a neat diagram, the production of a sinusoidal waveform by a coil rotating in a uniform magnetic field. Draw a diagram of a single loop alternator showing two slip rings, the coil, the N−S poles and two brushes.

(U.E.I.)

7.   A sinusoidal voltage has an equation $v = 80 \sin 314t$. Determine:

(a) the r.m.s. value
(b) the average value over half a wave
(c) the periodic time.

8.   Draw phasors to represent the following currents:
$i_1 = 6 \sin \omega t$
$i_2 = 10 \sin (\omega t + \pi/4)$
$i_3 = 4 \sin (\omega t - \pi/3)$.
Determine the resultant current $i_1 + i_2 + i_3$ in the form $i = I_m \sin (\omega t + \phi)$.

9.   The p.d. applied to a circuit is $v = 120 \sin 628t$, the p.d. across one part of the circuit is $v_1 = 80 \sin (628t - \pi/4)$. Calculate:

(a) the p.d. across the rest of the circuit in the form $v_2 = V_m \sin (628t + \phi)$
(b) the frequency of the supply.

10.   A sinusoidal voltage of 100 V causes a current of 20 A to flow in a purely resistive circuit. Calculate the value of the resistance.

11.   Determine the voltage required to produce a current of 5 A in an inductance of 0.4 H at a frequency of 50 Hz.

12.   What would be the effect on the current in problem (11) if the supply frequency were halved and the voltage maintained at the same value?

13.   Calculate the capacitance of a capacitor, such that when a voltage of 12 V is applied at a frequency of 60 Hz, a current of 6 mA is established.

14.   Determine the frequency in problem (13) in order to double the current.

15.   Calculate the power taken by a circuit of resistance 10 Ω, when a current, $i = 40 \sin \omega t$, flows in the circuit.

16.   Determine by means of a phasor diagram drawn to scale, the voltage across the resistive part of an $R-L$ series circuit when, $V_L = 60$ V and supply voltage, $V = 80$ V.

157

17. Calculate the phase angle for the circuit in problem (16).

18. If a current of 5 A flows in the circuit in problem (16), calculate:
(a) the resistance
(b) the inductive reactance
(c) the impedance.
Sketch the impedance triangle.

19. Calculate the impedance, Z, of a series circuit having a resistance, $R = 3\ \Omega$ and inductive reactance, $X_L = 4\ \Omega$.

20. Calculate the impedance of an $R-L$ series circuit having a resistance, $R = 20\ \Omega$, when the power taken from a 100-V, 50-Hz supply is 2 kW.

21. Determine the inductive reactance and impedance of a coil having a resistance of 40 Ω and an inductance of 80 mH, when connected across:
(a) a d.c. supply
(b) an a.c. supply at frequencies of 50 Hz, 1000 Hz, and 1 MHz.

22. A coil of resistance 60 Ω and inductance 0·4 H is connected to a 240-V, 50-Hz sinusoidal supply. Determine the circuit current and phase angle. Sketch one cycle of the current and voltage waveforms and write the equations for instantaneous current and voltage.

23. A coil having a phase angle of $\pi/3$ dissipates 2 kW when connected to a 240-V, 50-Hz sinusoidal supply. Determine the resistance and inductance of the coil. Draw to scale the circuit phasor diagram.

24. Two coils connected in series have r.m.s. voltages of 60 V and 80 V across them but differing in phase by 40°. Determine the maximum value of the sinusoidal supply voltage.

25. Two coils A and B are connected in series across a 415-V, 50-Hz sinusoidal supply. Coil A has a p.f. of 0·6 and impedance 40 Ω, coil B has a p.f. of 0·8 and impedance 60 Ω. Determine:
(a) the circuit current
(b) the circuit power and p.f.
(c) the p.d. across each coil.
Sketch the circuit phasor diagram.

26. A coil takes a current of 4 A when connected to a 200-V d.c. supply and 2·5 A when connected to a 200-V, 50-Hz sinusoidal supply. Explain the reasons for the difference and calculate the power taken in each case. Determine also the inductance and impedance of the coil, and sketch the phasor diagram.

27. In an $R-C$ series circuit, $V_C = 5$ V, and supply voltage, $V = 13$ V. A current of 0·6 A flows in the circuit. Determine the values of resistance, R, capacitive reactance, X_C, and impedance, Z.

28. Use the values in problem (27) to construct a scaled phasor diagram. Determine from the diagram the circuit phase-angle.

29. A series circuit consists of a resistance, $R = 10\ \Omega$, and capacitive reactance, $X_C = 15\ \Omega$. A current of 5 A flows in the circuit. Determine the power taken and the voltages, V_R and V_C.

30.   In problem (29), what would be the effect on the power taken of:

(a) halving the resistance

(b) halving the capacitance, the circuit current being kept constant?

31.   Explain the meaning of phase angle in an a.c. circuit.

(a) Complete the following table:

Frequency (Hz)	Inductive reactance $X_L(\Omega)$	Capacitive reactance $X_C(\Omega)$
100	2	10
50		
200		
150		

(b) A circuit comprises a pure inductor in series with a pure capacitor across an a.c. supply. Draw one complete cycle of: the voltage across the capacitor, the voltage across the inductor, and the supply current. Show clearly the phase angle between each voltage and the current. Make the horizontal axis the time (or degrees) scale.

(c) Sketch the voltage and current waveforms for a loss-free capacitor connected to a sinusoidal a.c. supply and show graphically that the average power over one cycle is zero.

(U.E.I.)

32.   A series circuit consists of a 40-μF capacitor and a non-resistive inductor of 0·2 H. Calculate the impedance of the circuit at sinusoidal frequencies of 50 Hz and 400 Hz.

33.   A capacitor of 6 μF is in series with a 200-Ω resistor. Determine the maximum sinusoidal supply voltage at 50 Hz if the circuit current is to be limited to 0·5 A.

34.   What is the value of a resistor which when connected in series with a capacitor of 10 μF across a 240-V, 25-Hz sinusoidal supply will result in a circuit current of 0·2 A? Sketch the phasor diagram.

35.   The voltage across a reactance carrying an alternating current $i = 10 \sin 200\pi t$ is given by: $v = 20 \sin (200\pi t + \pi/2)$. State:

(a) the peak values of current and voltage

(b) the frequency

(c) the sign and magnitude of the phase angle of the voltage relative to the current.

Determine, from the given expressions, the magnitude of the reactance. Is it capacitive or inductive? Sketch the waveforms of the current and voltage on one pair of axes, showing the scale values.

(C.G.L.I.)

36.   Draw the waveforms of the currents $i_1 = 8 \sin (10\pi t + \pi/2)$ and $i_2 = 6 \sin (10\pi t - \pi/6)$. Plot the waveform of the resultant current, i, in each case, giving the principal values and stating the scales of the axes.

37.   Plot the waveform of the voltage $v - v_1$ over one cycle where $v = 200 \sin (60\pi t)$ and $v_1 = 100 \sin (120\pi t + \pi/4)$, giving the main values of voltage and time.

38.   An $R-L-C$ series circuit where, $R = 10 \ \Omega$, $L = 0·2$ H, and $C = 25 \ \mu$F, has a voltage, $V = 240$ V at 50 Hz connected across the circuit. Calculate:

(a) the values of inductive reactance, X_L, and capacitive reactance, X_C

(b) the impedance, Z

(c) the circuit current, I

(d) the voltages, V_R, V_L, and V_C

(e) the circuit phase angle, ϕ

(f) the power taken, P

(g) the energy, W, absorbed in 5 minutes.

Draw to scale:

(h) the current-voltage phasor diagram

(i) the impedance triangle.

39.   What would happen to the voltages, V_R, V_L, and V_C in problem (38) if the 240-V supply frequency is reduced?

40.   What precautions should be taken in a piece of switchgear having resistance, inductance, and capacitance in series if supplies at various frequencies are likely to be connected?

41.   A coil has a resistance of 20 Ω and an inductive reactance of 30 Ω, when connected across a 100-V, 50-Hz supply. Calculate:

(a) the value of the capacitance to be connected in series with the coil to produce a resonant condition

(b) the value of the resonant current.

42.   Sketch the curve of $X_C - X_L$ as the frequency of a supply connected across an $R-L-C$ series circuit is increased from zero to beyond the resonant value.

43.   Calculate the resonant frequency of a series circuit having an inductance of 0·4 H and a capacitance of 40 μF.

44.   Sketch typical phasor diagrams for a coil and capacitor in parallel:

(a) on a low-frequency supply

(b) on a high-frequency supply.

45.   A circuit consists of a coil, having a resistance, $R = 200$ Ω, and inductance, $L = 0·25$ H in parallel with a capacitance of 30 μF connected across a 240-V, 50-Hz supply. Calculate:

(a) the inductive reactance, X_L, of the coil

(b) the capacitive reactance, X_C

(c) the branch currents, I_{RL} and I_C

(d) determine by means of a scaled phasor diagram the supply current, I

(e) the power taken by the circuit.

46.   A parallel circuit has two branch currents $i_{RL} = 20 \sin (14\pi t - \pi/6)$ and $i_C = 15 \sin (14\pi t + \pi/2)$. Draw the waveform of the supply current over a complete cycle giving the periodic time and maximum, r.m.s. and mean values of the current.

47.   A 400-pF capacitor is connected in parallel with a coil across a 415-V, 10^4-Hz supply. The coil has an impedance of 5 Ω and phase angle of 60°. Determine the branch and supply currents, and the power taken.

48.   A circuit consisting of a coil in parallel with a capacitor is connected across 20-V, 400-Hz supply. The power consumed is 40 W and the circuit phase angle 50°. Determine the supply current and the coil resistance.

49.   Describe the effects of parallel phase resonance. What are the dangers which may result from varying the frequency of the supply across a circuit consisting of a coil in parallel with a capacitor?

50.   A series circuit takes a current of 5 A at a phase angle of 30°. Calculate the active and reactive components of the current.

51.   Define the term 'power factor'. Draw a circuit diagram showing how the volt-ampere and power input can be measured for a single-phase inductive load. In such a test the voltage was 240 V and the current was 22 A. The wattmeter in the circuit indicated a power input of 3·538 kW. Calculate:

(a) the volt-amperes

(b) the power factor

(c) sketch the phasor diagram showing current and voltage phasors. Indicate their sizes and write in the value of the phase angle between them.

If the load was an induction motor, calculate the power output assuming an efficiency of 90%.   (U.E.I.)

52.   A coil is energized by a source of a.c. voltage and the circuit incorporates an ammeter, voltmeter, and wattmeter. Draw the circuit diagram showing how the three instruments are connected in order to carry out a test on the coil. If the readings on the instruments are 1·5 A, 250 V, and 300 W respectively, calculate:

(a) the impedance of the coil

(b) the volt-amperes in the circuit, and

(c) the power factor of the coil.

Without making any calculations, state and explain what would have been the effect if the circuit had been connected across a d.c. supply in error.

53.   Find the active and reactive components of the current taken by a series circuit consisting of a coil of inductance 0·1 H and resistance 8 Ω and a capacitor of 120 μF, connected to a 240-V, 50-Hz sinusoidal supply. Draw, to scale, a phasor diagram showing the voltages across the coil and capacitor, the supply voltage and current, and the components of the current.   (U.L.C.I.)

54.   A single-phase induction motor develops 2 kW at an efficiency of 88% and p.f. of 0·6 when connected across a 240-V sinusoidal supply. Determine the active and reactive components of the motor current and construct the power triangle.

55.   (a) Explain the meaning of the term power factor.

(b) Two consumers operate at power factors of 0·6 and 0·8 respectively. The power taken by both loads is the same. Explain which will cost the most to supply and why?

56.   (a) What are the advantages to a consumer of improving the power factor of his load?

(b) Explain the means by which the supply authority can persuade a consumer to improve the power factor of his load.

57.   (a) Why is it uneconomical to improve the power factor of a load to unity?

(b) What are the advantages to the authority of consumers operating at high power factors?

(c) Explain, using diagrams, why the supply authority does not fit power factor correcting capacitors at the generating end of the transmission lines.

58.   A customer has a maximum demand of 600 kW and an annual consumption of 800 MW h at an average power factor of 0·6. The supply authority offer a choice of two tariffs:

(a) £4 per kV A of maximum demand, plus 0·75p per unit

(b) a flat rate of 1·3p per unit.

Which should he choose? Explain, giving values, why the choice was made.

59. A single-phase induction motor operating from a 240-V, 50-Hz supply, has a full load output of 20 kW at a p.f. of 0·6, and is 85% efficient. Determine the kV Ar rating of a capacitor required to improve the overall power factor to unity.

60. (a) Explain, with the aid of a phasor diagram, the meaning of power factor in an alternating current circuit. Why is a low power factor undesirable?

(b) A single-phase factory load of 400 kW operates at a power factor of 0·8. The supply is 240-V, alternating current. Calculate the decrease in supply current if the power factor is changed to unity with the same kW loading.

61. During an experiment a 100-W fluorescent tube had its capacitor removed. The tube was then paralleled with a variable capacitor bank and connected across a 110-V, 50-Hz supply. Determine the capacitance needed to improve the uncorrected p.f. of 0·6 to unity. Neglect choke losses.

Note: All problems assume sinusoidal waveforms.

Answers

1. (a) 80 V   (b) 56·57 V   (c) 314 rad/s   (d) 50 Hz   (e) 0·02 s
2. 28·29 sin 251·4 t
3. $V_m = 100$ V; $I_m = 10$ A; 0·1 s; $\pi/3$ lagging
4. 71·85 V; 9·616 A
5. $i = 0·1414$ sin $6284t$; $v = 14·14$ sin $(6284t + \pi/2)$
7. 56·57 V; 50·96 V; 0·02 s
8. $i = 15·5$ sin $(\omega t + 0·244)$
9. $v_2 = 85$ sin $(628t + 0·7296)$, 100 Hz
10. 5 Ω 11. 628·5 V
12. Current would be doubled.   13. 1·33 μF   14. 120 Hz
15. 8 kW   16. 52·9 V
17. 48° 36' lagging   18. (a) 10·58 Ω (b) 12 Ω (c) 16 Ω
19. 5 Ω 20. 10 Ω
21. (a) 0·40 Ω (b) 25·14 Ω, 47·23 Ω; 502·8 Ω, 503·6 Ω; 502 400 Ω, $\approx$ 502 800 Ω
22. 1·725 A; 64° 28' lagging; $i = 2·44$ sin $314t$; $v = 339$ sin $(314t + 1·125)$
23. 7·2 Ω; 39·4 mH   24. 186 V
25. 4·19 A; 1268 W; 0·7275 lagging; 167·6 V; 251·4 V
26. 800 W; 312·5 W; 0·198 H; 80 Ω
27. R 20 Ω; $X_C = 8·33$ Ω; $Z = 21·67$ Ω
28. $\phi = 57° 25'$ leading   29. 250 W; $V_R = 50$ V; $V_C = 75$ V
30. (a) the power is halved   (b) no change
31. at 50 Hz : $X_L = 1$ Ω; $X_C = 20$ Ω
     at 200 Hz : $X_L = 4$ Ω; $X_C = 5$ Ω
     at 150 Hz : $X_L = 3$ Ω; $X_C = 6·67$ Ω
32. 16·84 Ω; 492·9 Ω 33. 283·3 V
34. 1017 Ω 35. 10 A, 20 V, 100 Hz, the current
                                                          lags the voltage by 90°, 2 Ω
                                                          inductive
38. (a) $X_L = 62·4$ Ω; $X_C = 127·1$ Ω (b) $Z = 65·03$ Ω (c) $I = 3·69$ A
     (d) $V_R = 36·9$ V; $V_L = 231·87$ V; $V_C = 469$ V   (e) 81° 20' leading
     (f) 136·16 W   (g) 40·84 kJ
39. All voltages decrease
40. Insulation should be able to withstand the voltages at the resonant condition.
41. (a) 106·1 μF   (b) 5 A   43. 39·78 Hz
45. (a) 78·55 Ω (b) 106·1 Ω (c) $I_{RL} = 1·117$ A, $I_C = 2·26$ A   (d) $I = 1·118$ A
     (e) 249·5 W
46. $I_m = 18·03$ A; $I = 12·75$ A; $I_{av} = 11·48$ A. Periodic time = 0·143 s
47. $I_{coil} = 83$ A; $I_C = 95·86$ A; $I = 47·92$ A; $P = 17·22$ kW

48. $I = 2 \cdot 38$ A; $R = 7 \cdot 06 \, \Omega$
49. The supply ammeter may be recording a small current, but large currents may be circulating between components.
50. Active components of current = $4 \cdot 33$ A; reactive component = $2 \cdot 5$ A
51. 5280 V A; $0 \cdot 67$ lagging; $3 \cdot 178$ kW
52. $166 \cdot 7 \, \Omega$; 375 V A; $0 \cdot 8$ lagging; power and current values would increase
53. $21 \cdot 82$ A; $13 \cdot 38$ A   54. $7 \cdot 06$ A; $9 \cdot 44$ A
58. The customer should choose the two part tariff, saving £400 p.a.
59. $31 \cdot 39$ kV Ar   60.   (b) $416 \cdot 7$ A
61. $220 \cdot 5 \, \mu$F

Laboratory work

1. To show the difference between a.c. and d.c. supplies applied to:

(a) resistance and inductance. Connect:

(a) 110-V d.c.

(b) 110-V, 50-Hz a.c.

supply to a circuit comprising a resistor of approximately 40 Ω and having negligible inductance in series with a 0·15-H inductor of negligible resistance and having provision for the insertion of an iron core.

Record, in both cases, the supply current and p.d. across the two components. Repeat with an iron core inserted in the inductor.

List the quantities which increase and those which decrease when the a.c. supply is connected.

Comment on results, suggesting reasons for any change in values.

Investigate the relationship between the supply voltage and the voltage drops across the components.

(b) capacitance. Using a signal generator and secondary cells connect

(a) 6 V d.c.

(b) 6 V a.c. at 50 Hz, across a 20 μF capacitor.

Record the circuit current in each case and explain the reasons for any difference.

2. Inductive reactance.
Connect a 0·2-H air-cored inductance of negligible resistance via a multi-range ammeter to a variable frequency source, such as a signal generator. Keeping the voltage constant at about 5 V, vary the frequency from 50 Hz to 300 Hz.

Record the current taken by the coil on the ammeter at 25-Hz intervals.

Calculate the inductive reactance from V/I and the reciprocal of the frequency at each interval.

Tabulate the results and plot graphs of I v. f, I v. $1/f$, X_L v. f.

Do the shapes of the graphs confirm the formulae relating these quantities? List the formulae and the proportionalities confirmed by the graphs.

3. Capacitive reactance.
Repeat experiment (2) using a 20-μF capacitor in place of the inductive coil.

Calculate the capacitive reactance.

Tabulate the results and plot graphs of I v. f, X_C v. f, X_C v. $1/f$.

163

4. Series resonance.

(a) Connect a coil of approximately 40-Ω resistance and 0·15-H inductance in series with an 8-μF capacitor to a signal generator, as shown in the circuit diagram, Fig. 12.19(a). Keep the supply voltage constant at about 4 V and determine the resonant frequency by adjusting the frequency control for maximum current.

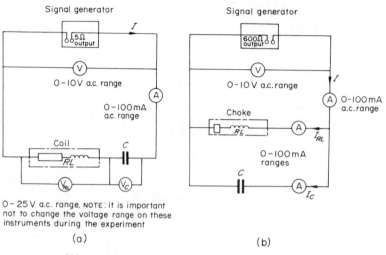

0 – 25 V a.c. range. NOTE: it is important not to change the voltage range on these instruments during the experiment

(a)　　　　　　　　　　(b)

All instruments are multi-range and the values given are nominal values

Fig. 12.19. Circuit diagrams for laboratory experiments 4 and 5

Take four sets of readings at intervals of 10 Hz then three at 20 Hz, either side of the resonant condition.

Record values of circuit current, I, capacitor voltage, V_C, and coil voltage, V_{RL}. Calculate values of circuit impedance, Z, from V/I.

Tabulate the values and plot graphs of, I, V_C, and V_{RL}, against a base of frequency, also I and Z against frequency.

Indicate the resonant frequency f_0 on the graphs. Compare the graphs of I and Z. Why are the voltages V_C and V_{RL} not quite equal when the current is a maximum?

(b) Connect, in series, a 100-Ω resistor of negligible inductance, a 0·4 inductance of negligible resistance, and a 15-μF-35-μF variable capacitor bank, having 1 μF switching increments, across a fixed 110-V, 50-Hz a.c. supply.

Record the values of the circuit current, I, and the p.d. across the resistance, inductance, and capacitor bank for capacitance values from 15 μF to 35 μF in 1-μF stages.

Tabulate the values and plot graphs of I, V_R, and V_C against a capacitance base.

Indicate the resonant condition. Compare the graphs and the power taken at resonance from VI and I^2R.

5. Parallel resonance.

Connect a 0·3-H choke in parallel with a 6-μF capacitor to a variable frequency supply, as shown in the circuit diagram, Fig. 12.19(b). Keep the supply voltage constant at 4 V, and vary the frequency from as low a value as possible to 200 Hz, in 10-Hz stages.

Record values of supply current, I, and branch currents I_{choke} and I_C.

Tabulate the recorded values and the circuit impedance, Z, calculated from V/I.

Plot graphs of I, I_{choke}, I_C, and Z, against a frequency base. Indicate the approximate resonant current. Compare the graphs.

Why is this type of circuit called a rejector circuit?

6. Power factor correction. Connect a load consisting of an 80-W fluorescent tube, which has had its capacitor removed, in parallel with a $\frac{1}{2}$ μF-15 μF variable capacitor bank, having $\frac{1}{2}$-μF switching stages, across a 240-V, 50-Hz, a.c. supply, as shown in the circuit diagram, Fig. 12.20.

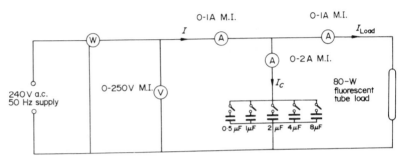

Fig. 12.20. Circuit diagram for laboratory experiment 6

After the instruments have reached steady readings increase the capacitance from 0–15 μF, in steps of 0·5-μF.

Record the instrument readings at each step and tabulate the values together with values of power factor, p.f., capacitor reactive voltamperes, V Ar, and supply voltamperes V A, calculated from P/VI, VI_C, and VI. Plot graphs of p.f., I, I_{load}, and I_C against capacitance, also capacitor V Ar and supply V A against p.f.

Draw vector diagrams for:

(a) lagging p.f.

(b) unity p.f.

(c) leading p.f., from sets of experimental results.

Why is it not economical to improve the p.f. beyond about 0·96?

What are the effects of over correction?

Comment on the transmission losses at unity power factor.

Note: Some of the experiments can be done on a theoretical basis in associated studies.

13. Cathode ray oscilloscope

13.1 The cathode ray tube (C.R.T.)

The cathode ray tube is the main component of the cathode ray oscilloscope (C.R.O.), which is used to display waveforms of alternating currents and voltages or shapes representing electrical quantities. It consists of a glass tube from which the air has been evacuated and into which components are fitted to provide the following requirements:

(A) a supply of electrons

(B) a control of the quantity of electrons emitted

(C) a means of accelerating the electrons toward the far end of the tube

(D) a means of focusing the stream of accelerated electrons into a converging beam

(E) a means of deflecting the beam in both the vertical and horizontal directions

(F) a display screen

(G) a return path for the electrons.

Letters A, B, C, etc., refer to Fig. 13.1 which shows a basic tube layout with relative potentials applied to the components.

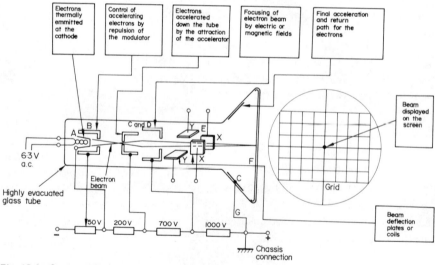

Fig. 13.1. Construction and operation of C.R.O.

Students should not be confused by the many and varied representations of the C.R.T., or the variation in potential differences applied to components, since these result from specific design features for special applications and not fundamental principles.

(A) The supply of electrons is obtained by indirectly heating an oxide-coated nickel cathode by means of a heating element connected to a low voltage a.c. supply.

(B) Control of the quantity of electrons emitted is provided by surrounding the cathode with a cylindrical metal tube closed at one end except for a small central hole. This is called a modulator and is at a variable negative potential with respect to the cathode. The negatively-charged electrons therefore tend to be repelled by the modulator as they are attracted down the tube by the accelerator. The potential difference between the modulator and cathode controls the quantity of electrons which are allowed to pass down the tube and hence determines the brightness of the screen trace.

(C) Acceleration of the electrons is necessary in order to give them sufficient kinetic energy so that when they strike the screen the energy transferred will be sufficient to produce a glow on the screen. The acceleration is caused by the attracting force of the accelerators C which are at a relatively high positive potential with respect to the cathode.

(D) Focusing. The electric field between the cathode, modulator, and first accelerator causes the beam to cross over just before the first accelerator. The diverging beam is then focused into a spot on the screen by the action of either an electrostatic field between C and D or by the magnetic field of a focusing coil wound round the outside of the tube, Fig. 13.2(a) and (b).

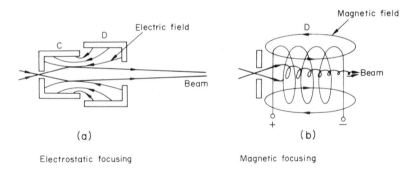

(a)

Electrostatic focusing

(b)

Magnetic focusing

Fig. 13.2. Focusing of electron beam

(E) Beam deflection. The vertical and horizontal deflection of the beam from the central axis of the tube is produced by the action of either an electric field, or magnetic field, set up by the voltages applied to the X and Y plates or coils as shown in Fig. 13.3(a) and (b). The symbols X and Y are used since the components to which they apply produce beam deflections in the same directions as the x and y axes of a graph.

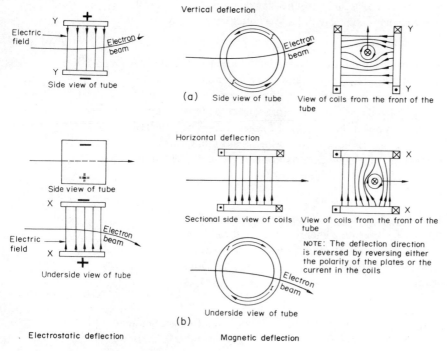

Fig. 13.3. Deflection of electron beam

(F) Display screen. The end of the tube is coated on the inside with a metallic salt or similar material to form a screen. When the electron beam strikes the screen electrons are displaced and emit light which appears as a fluorescent glow on the screen. The colour and the time for which the glow stays after the electron beam has moved depends on the material used for the coating.

(G) A return path for spent or displaced electrons is provided through the oscilloscope chassis via the second accelerator as shown, or by a conducting coating on the inside of the tube extending to a second accelerator positioned after the focusing cylinder.

13.2 Display of electrical waveforms

In order to display an electrical quantity on the oscilloscope screen, a voltage, proportional to the quantity to be represented, must be connected across the Y plates (or coils), one of which is connected via internal amplification circuitry to the chassis. When a d.c. voltage is applied the spot on the screen will move up or down depending on the polarity of the other plate, when an a.c. voltage is applied the spot moves up and down and a vertical line is displayed. A voltage is now connected to the X plates. With a d.c. voltage applied to the Y plates, the X plates' voltage is applied so that the beam swings from left to right, then cuts off and repeats. For an a.c. voltage applied to the Y plates, a synchronized voltage is connected across the X plates which starts at a maximum negative, increasing through zero to a maximum positive, which swings the beam from left to right during one waveform of the voltage being represented. The resultant display now has a vertical displacement proportional to the magnitude of the quantity being measured and a horizontal displacement proportional to time. Figure 13.4 shows the connections necessary to display an a.c. waveform.

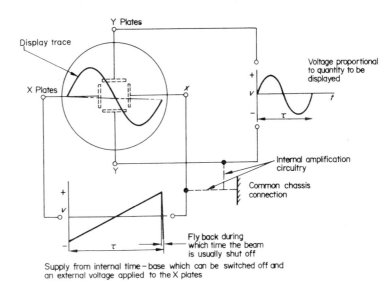

Fig. 13.4. Display of electrical waveforms

13.3 Measurement of voltage and time

Oscilloscopes normally have a grid of 10 mm x 10 mm squares in front of the screen. The oscilloscope is so designed that the voltage applied to the Y plates can be multiplied up or down. A switch on the oscilloscope enables the value in volts that each vertical 10 mm is to represent to be selected. The X plate is synchronized to the period of the Y plate waveform, the width of the waveform being equal to the periodic time. A switch enables various times of sweep, ranging from about 1 ps to 1 s, thus enabling the width of the waveform to be increased, or reduced, to display more than one cycle of the waveform.

The value of the voltage v at any time t from the origin can be determined from the oscilloscope. The voltage is determined by multiplying the number of grid squares between the x axis and the waveform by the number of volts per 10 mm, and the time by multiplying the number of grid squares between the origin and t by the number of seconds per 10 mm.

Problems

1. Make a sketch showing an arrangement of the grid, first accelerator, and focusing component of an oscilloscope. Indicate on the diagram the relative potentials applied to each component.

2. Describe the function of the oscilloscope modulator.

3.   With the oscilloscope switches set so that each vertical grid square represents 50 V and the horizontal sweep time covering 8 squares is 0·001 s, sketch on a grid the following waveforms:

(a) an a.c. voltage of r.m.s. value 80 V at a frequency of 50 Hz;

(b) a d.c. current of 2 A flowing through a resistor of 40 Ω, across which the Y plates are connected;

(c) an a.c. voltage represented by 120 sin 618t;

(d) an a.c. current of r.m.s. value 4 A flowing in a resistance of 20 Ω across which the Y plates are connected.

4. Sketch the circuit and Y plate connections of a C.R.O. in order to display an a.c. current waveform on the screen.

5.   Sketch the X and Y deflecting plates of a C.R.O., with a common chassis connection.

With the time-base out of circuit draw the waveform that will be displayed on the screen when the following supplies of equal magnitude are connected:

	X *plates*	Y *plates*	
(a)	–	V volts a.c.	
(b)	V volts a.c.	V volts a.c.	supplies in phase
(c)	V volts a.c.	V volts a.c.	supplies 90° out of phase

6.   Sketch the X and Y deflecting plates as in problem 5, and indicate the supplies required to produce the waveforms shown in Fig. 13.5(a).

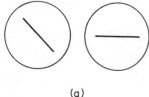

(a)   (b)

Fig. 13.5. Diagram for problems 6 and 9

7.   Describe the functions of the accelerators and the focusing elements of a C.R.O.

8.   What would be the choice of switch settings in order to best display two cycles of an a.c. voltage of maximum value 20 V at 1 kHz on a grid 6 vertical squares by 8 horizontal squares. Sketch the resulting waveform.

9.   A double-beam oscilloscope (Fig. 13.5(b)) is to be used to display the current and voltage waveforms of a coil connected to an a.c. supply.

(a) Draw a circuit diagram for the coil and any additional component required in order to measure the current on Y_1 and the voltage across the coil on Y_2.

(b) If Y_1 has a sensitivity of 10 mV/mm, Y_2 a sensitivity of 400 mV/mm and the screen traces of current and voltage have amplitudes of 20 mm and 35 mm respectively, sketch the waveforms on an 80 mm x 60 mm grid with the current lagging the voltage by 30°.

(c) Calculate the maximum values of current and voltage and indicate them on the waveforms.

Answers
6.   X and Y plates, supplies of equal magnitude, 180° out of phase
8.   Y sensitivity 10 V/10 mm: X sweep 0·001 s

Laboratory work

1. **Calibration of scales.** Connect an a.c. voltage of known r.m.s. value and frequency, between the Y terminal and the common terminal of the oscilloscope.

Calculate the maximum value of the supply and the periodic time. Adjust the oscilloscope to display the best stable trace of the waveform.

Use the calculated values to determine the sensitivity of the X and Y scales for this particular setting.

Adjust the a.c. input to about half the initial value. Use the oscilloscope to write the equation of the new waveform.

2. **Measurement of an a.c. current.** Connect a resistor of known value in series with an ammeter across an a.c. supply.

Take connections from across the resistor to between the Y and common terminals on the oscilloscope.

Adjust the switch settings on the scope to display the best stable waveform, using the switch sensitivities of the X and Y scales in s/mm and V/mm respectively.

Calculate:

(a) the maximum and r.m.s. values of the current using

$$I = \frac{V}{R}$$

(b) the frequency of the supply.

Write an equation for the instantaneous current.

3. **Rectification and smoothing** (refer to section 14.1). Using a circuit similar to that shown in Fig. 13.6 carry out the following tests:

(a) With change over switch E switched to the transformer output, switch on the supply by closing switch A.

Adjust the oscilloscope sensitivities to obtain the best stable trace of the unrectified transformer output. Make a sketch approximately to scale of the voltage waveform.

(b) To view the half-wave rectified load supply waveform connect the change over switch to the load.

With switches B, C, and D open and the inductor shorted out repeat the procedure carried out in (a).

(c) Switch in the reservoir capacitor by closing switch C and repeat the procedure carried out in (a).

(d) Connect the filter circuit by removing the inductor short-circuiting link and closing switch D. Repeat the procedure carried out in (a).

(e) To view the full-wave load supply waveform close switch B and repeat tests (c) and (d).

Compare the resultant waveforms and estimate the value of the a.c. ripple in each case.

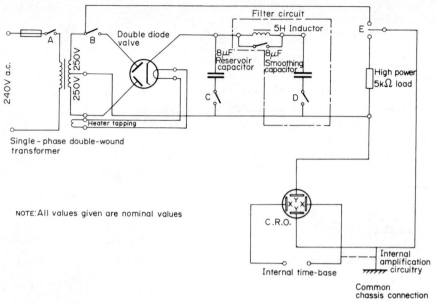

Fig. 13.6. Circuit for laboratory experiment 3

4. **Oscilloscope test traces.** With the internal time-base switched off, connect the following supplies as indicated and record the oscilloscope traces:

Oscilloscope terminals

Y –*common*	X – *common*		
—	V volts a.c.		
V volts a.c.	—		
V volts a.c.	V volts a.c.	supplies in phase	all supplies having equal magnitude
V volts a.c.	V volts a.c.	90° out of phase	
V volts a.c.	V volts a.c.	180° out of phase	

14. Rectifiers

There are many appliances that require operating from a direct current supply, some common examples being certain variable-speed machine drives, electric traction motors, electroplating, and many electronic circuits. Since the majority of supply systems are alternating current it is necessary to be able to change or rectify the alternating current into direct current.

14.1 Rectification

A rectifier is a device which offers a very low resistance to the passage of an electric current through it in one direction, known as the forward direction, and a very high resistance to the passage of current in the opposite direction, known as the reverse direction. These devices enable alternating current to be changed into direct current, the process being known as rectification.

Half-wave
The simplest type of rectifier circuit. It allows only each alternate half-wave of the alternating current to pass, Fig. 14.1(a).

Full-wave
By using either two or four rectifier units, full-wave rectification can be obtained. If only two rectifier units are used the supply is taken from a centre-tapped transformer where the e.m.f. output of each half-winding is equal to the e.m.f. required across the load. Each of the two circuits supplies the current in turn during alternate half-cycles, Fig. 14.1(b). An alternative method of full-wave rectification is to use a bridge circuit. This requires four rectifier units but does not require a centre-tapped transformer (Fig. 14.1(c)).

Output voltage
The forward voltage and the current flowing in a rectifier element consists of a series of pulses, the waveform of the forward pulses being similar to the input waveform over one half-cycle. For a sinusoidal input, the output voltage and current waveforms will therefore be a series of sinusoidal half-waves in the same direction, Fig. 14.1(d) and (e). The average value of the output voltage for a full-wave rectifier, operating from a sinusoidal input, is calculated from:
Average value of output voltage = maximum value of output voltage x 0·637 (refer to section 12.1).

For half-wave rectification, since every alternate pulse is missing, the average output voltage is calculated from:

$$\text{average value of output voltage} = \frac{\text{maximum value of output voltage} \times 0.637}{2}$$

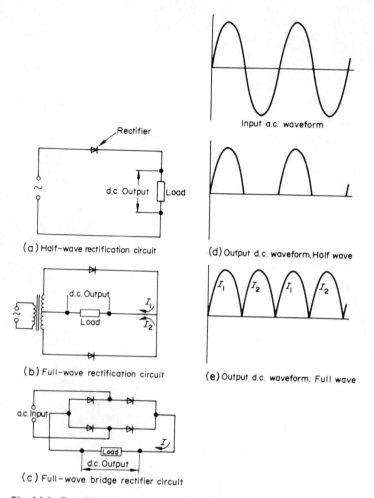

Input a.c. waveform

(a) Half-wave rectification circuit

(d) Output d.c. waveform. Half wave

(b) Full-wave rectification circuit

(e) Output d.c. waveform. Full wave

(c) Full-wave bridge rectifier circuit

Fig. 14.1. Rectification

Smoothing

The pulsating waveform obtained directly from a rectifier is unsuitable for many applications and requires smoothing. The smoothing circuit is composed of a capacitor, Fig. 14.2(a), or a combination of capacitors and inductors, Fig. 14.2(b). If smoothing of the output is required full-wave rectification should be used.

Ripple

As stated previously rectifiers have a very low forward resistance and a high reverse resistance. Since the reverse resistance of most rectifiers is not infinite, a small reverse current will normally flow, so that the rectifier will be passing a small amount of alternating current. The alternating voltage that is passed by a rectifier will also affect the output waveform. The variation in output voltage is termed the a.c. ripple. Characteristics showing typical values of reverse current for various types of rectifiers are given in section 14.2

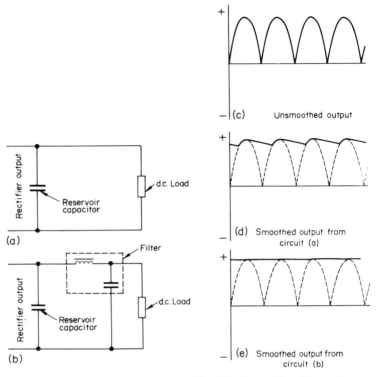

Fig. 14.2. Smoothing of d.c. pulsations

14.2 Types of rectifiers

Semiconductor diodes, metal rectifiers, vacuum and gas-filled diodes, are all used as rectifiers. Each of these devices can be connected to provide half- or full-wave rectification, and the output from each device can be smoothed by the methods described in section 14.1.

Semiconductor diodes. These can be used for most rectification purposes and have replaced thermionic diodes, metal rectifiers and mercury arc rectifiers in many applications. They have the advantage over all other rectifying devices of very small size. Two types of semiconductor devices are in common use:

(a) silicon,

(b) germanium.

The forward and reverse characteristics of typical diodes are compared in Fig. 14.3. The majority of semiconductor rectifiers are made from silicon. Silicon diodes are manufactured which are capable of withstanding peak reverse voltages up to 3000 volts and carry currents of over 500 amperes. A typical diode operating at these voltage and current values would be less than three inches in diameter and under three inches high. The forward peak voltage drop of a silicon diode is normally between 1·1 and 1·6 volts.

Germanium diodes have the advantage of a smaller forward voltage drop but will not withstand high reverse voltages. They are therefore mainly used where very large currents at low voltages are required, such as in plating processes, to give a higher operating efficiency.

Semiconductor diodes are not capable of withstanding surge currents and in applications where surges are likely to occur they must be protected by surge-limiting devices.

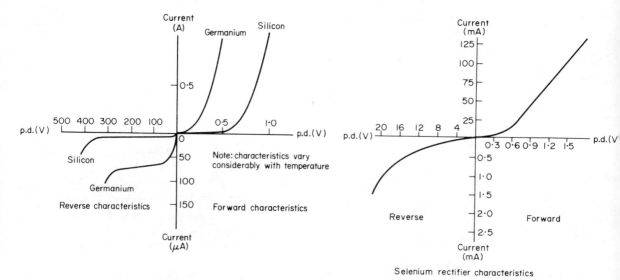

Fig. 14.3. Rectifier characteristics

NOTE change of scales for forward and reverse characteristics

Metal rectifiers. Modern metal rectifiers are of the selenium type, the copper oxide rectifier being virtually obsolete. A single selenium rectifier element is not capable of operating at voltages above 20 V r.m.s. and maximum current ratings are in the region of 10 A. They can however be connected in series-parallel combinations to operate at higher voltages and currents.

Selenium rectifiers have the advantage over semiconductor diodes in that they are capable of withstanding voltage and current surges without the addition of surge protection equipment. Typical characteristics for a selenium rectifier are given in Fig. 14.3.

Heat sinks. When metal rectifiers or semiconductor diodes are operating, heat is produced which will cause a temperature rise of the component. To prevent an excessive temperature rise the components are usually fastened to a metal plate, called a heat sink, which will conduct the heat away from the rectifier. The units must be mounted so that air can circulate over the plate and so remove the heat by convection.

Vacuum diodes. A thermionic valve containing one anode and one cathode is termed a diode valve. Current will only flow one way across the valve. If a diode valve is connected as shown in Fig. 14.4(a) then current will only flow during the half-cycles when the anode is positive and the cathode negative, thus giving half-wave rectification.

Full-wave rectification can be obtained by the use of two diodes connected as shown in Fig. 14.1(b), but it is usual to use a double diode—two anodes in one envelope—as shown in Fig. 14.4(b). Note that the transformer also has a separate winding to supply the low voltage required by the cathode heater.

Waveform outputs are as shown in Fig. 14.1(c) and (d) and the static characteristics are shown in Fig. 14.4(c).

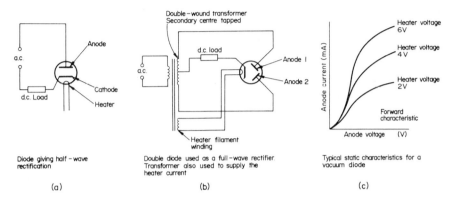

(a)

Diode giving half – wave rectification

(b)

Double diode used as a full-wave rectifier. Transformer also used to supply the heater current

(c)

Typical static characteristics for a vacuum diode

Fig. 14.4. Thermionic vacuum diode rectifier

Gas-filled diodes. The gas-filled diode contains a heated cathode and an anode, usually carbon, the envelope being filled with mercury vapour. As with the vacuum diode, current will only pass in one direction, but far larger currents can be handled than is possible with vacuum diodes. The circuit for half-wave rectification is shown in Fig. 14.5(a) and a typical characteristic in Fig. 14.5(b). Two gas-filled diodes can be arranged as shown in Fig. 14.1(b) to give full-wave rectification.

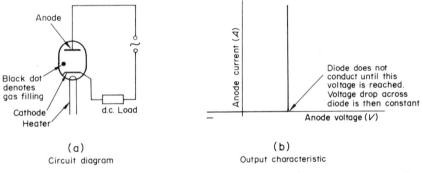

(a)
Circuit diagram

(b)
Output characteristic

Fig. 14.5. Gas-filled diode rectifier

Problems

1. Sketch typical characteristic curves for:
(a) a silicon diode
(b) a germanium diode.

2. Explain the advantages of full-wave rectification over half-wave rectification.

3. Sketch a circuit diagram for full-wave rectification using silicon diodes.

4.   What is meant by the ripple voltage of a rectifier?

5.   A rectifier is to be installed to supply an electroplating plant requiring a current of 2000 A. What type of rectifier would you choose? Give reasons for your choice.

6.   A mercury arc rectifier has been used for many years to supply power to a number of large variable-speed motors. The rectifier is now obsolete and is to be replaced. What type of rectifier would you choose and what protective equipment would you install?

7.   What advantages and disadvantages have selenium rectifiers over silicon diodes?

8.   What is a heat sink, and what purpose does it serve when fitted to a rectifier?

9.   A d.c. supply is required for a small electronic process controller which requires a supply of 0·2 A at 100 V. It is decided to use a vacuum diode as the rectifier. Draw the complete circuit diagram with the necessary smoothing components connected in the circuit.

15. Transformers

A transformer is an alternating current, electro-magnetic device, which takes in energy on one side, called the primary, and delivers it at another called the secondary, usually at a different voltage.

15.1 Construction

Single-phase double-wound transformers. These consist of two electrically separate coils of insulated conducting wire, the primary and the secondary. The coils are assembled on a common magnetic circuit called the core.

There are two main types of assembly, the core type and the shell type, Fig. 15.1.

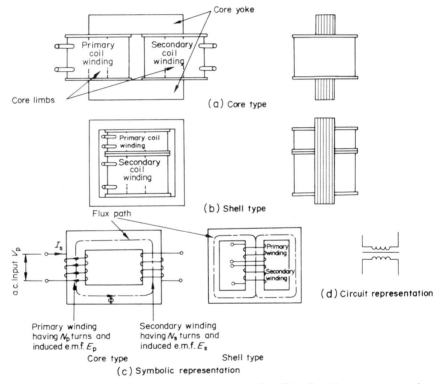

Fig. 15.1. Transformer representation

Three-phase double-wound transformers. These are mainly used in power transmission and are nearly always core type. They consist basically of three pairs of single-phase windings mounted on one core, thus giving a considerable saving in the amount of iron used, Fig. 15.2(a).

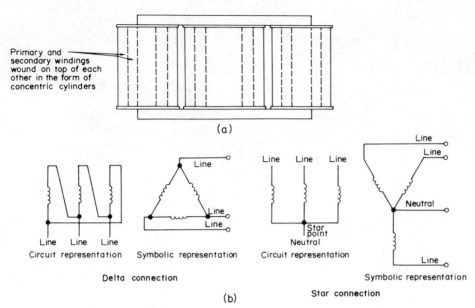

Primary and secondary windings wound on top of each other in the form of concentric cylinders

(a)

Line

Circuit representation   Symbolic representation   Circuit representation   Symbolic representation

Line   Line   Line   Line   Line   Line   Line   Line
                                        Line   Star   Neutral
                                                                                point
                                                                                Neutral   Line

Delta connection   Star connection

(b)

Fig. 15.2. Three-phase transformers

The most common method of connecting the three coils of the primary or secondary windings are star and delta as shown in Fig. 15.2(b). The usual sequence is delta-star or delta-delta although other combinations can be used.

Auto-transformers. These consist of a single core-mounted winding, the primary and secondary connections being tapped off this winding, Fig. 15.3.

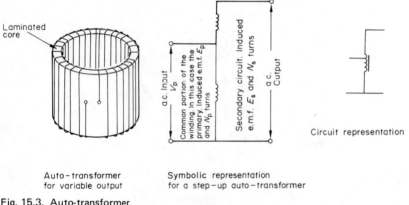

Laminated core

a.c. Input V_p

Common portion of the winding. In this case the primary. Induced e.m.f. E_p and N_p turns

Secondary circuit. Induced e.m.f. E_s and N_s turns

a.c. Output

Circuit representation

Auto-transformer for variable output

Symbolic representation for a step-up auto-transformer

Fig. 15.3. Auto-transformer

Auto-transformers use less material, are smaller and have lower losses and smaller percentage voltage regulation (refer to section 15.3) than equivalent double-wound transformers. Their disadvantage being direct connection between primary and secondary circuits which could result in large voltages on the secondary side of step-down transformers should the common winding become open circuited. In some circumstances I.E.E. Regulations prohibit their use for this reason.

Transformer cores. These can be solid in the case of small experimental transformers being made of a low reluctance steel. Practical transformers however have laminated cores (refer to section 15.4), made from grain oriented or low loss silicon steels. The laminations are usually built up in two parts which are interleaved together after the windings have been fitted. Certain small high-frequency transformers may have air or dust cores.

Transformer windings. In small transformers these are usually made of round-section copper wire, but in larger transformers the conductors are often multi-stranded and rectangular-sectioned.

Insulation:

(a) Core laminations are insulated on one side by either surface oxidization, spraying with an insulating substance, or by natural surface insulation due to the method of manufacture.

(b) Windings are insulated between turns, layers, and between coils. The materials used vary considerably, some of the more usual being enamel, oil impregnated cellulose paper, cloth, plastic, and pressboard.

Cooling. The cooling requirements of a transformer depends partially on design but mainly on size. Small transformers are cooled by natural conduction of heat to the surface where it is dissipated by convection. Progressively larger transformers use air ducts or oil with natural or forced circulation through radiating tubes, in hot countries the oil itself may be water-tube cooled. The oil also acts as an insulator and serves to absorb some of the transformer iron noise, that in large transformers would otherwise be prohibitive.

15.2 Transformer operation

No-load operation. An a.c. supply of V_p volts connected to the primary causes a small no-load current I_0 to flow in the primary winding. This current has two components, the magnetizing component I_m which lags V_p by $90°$ (refer to section 12.7) and is in phase with the magnetic flux which it sets up, and the loss component I_l in phase with V_p which occurs due to the iron losses (refer to section 15.4) and small copper losses. The alternating flux induces an equal e.m.f. in each turn of both windings. The total windings e.m.f.s E_p and E_s act so as to oppose their cause (refer to Lenz's law) and are therefore $180°$ out of phase with V_p, also if flux leakage and the resistive voltage drop in the primary are neglected the magnitude of E_p is the same as that of V_p.

Using the flux as a reference, since it is common to both windings, the resultant phasor diagram is shown in Fig. 15.4(a), the no-load p.f. being low since I_m is large compared with I_l.

On-load operation. When a load is connected across the secondary winding a current I_s flows in the secondary winding, the direction of which is due to the secondary e.m.f. The resultant secondary m.m.f. therefore acts so as to tend to reduce the core

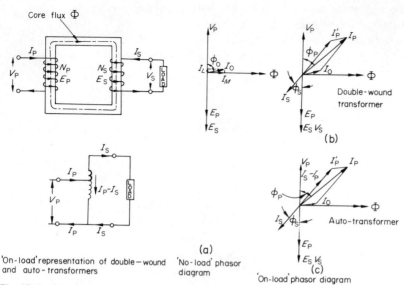

Core flux Φ

I_P N_P N_S I_S
V_P E_P E_S V_S LOAD

(b) Double-wound transformer

Auto-transformer

(a)

'On-load' representation of double-wound and auto-transformers

'No-load' phasor diagram

(c)

'On-load' phasor diagram

Fig. 15.4. Transformer 'no-load' and 'on-load' phasor diagrams

flux, this however does not happen since reduction of the core flux reduces E_p, hence a reflected increase in primary current I_p' occurs which provides a restoring m.m.f. therefore at all loads primary and secondary m.m.f.s are equal but in opposition and the core flux remains constant.

$$I_p' \times N_p = I_s \times N_s$$

Also, since the e.m.f. induced per turn is equal:

$$\frac{E_p}{N_p} = \frac{E_s}{N_s}$$

$$\frac{N_p}{N_s} = \frac{E_p}{E_s} = \frac{I_s}{I_p'} \quad \text{and} \quad \simeq \frac{V_p}{V_s} \text{ and } \frac{I_s}{I_p}$$

The resulting phasor diagram is shown in Fig. 15.4(b), the secondary p.f. being dependent on the type and size of load.

The auto-transformer consists of a single core-mounted winding. The primary voltage is applied across the whole or part of this winding, depending on whether a step-down or step-up transformer is required. The secondary circuit is also tapped off this winding as shown in Fig. 15.3 and Fig. 15.4. This is usually a close voltage-ratio transformer and since the common portion of the winding carries the **difference** between I_p and I_s the conductor section of the common portion can be considerably reduced and hence there is a saving in cost and size. The e.m.f. per turn in all parts of the winding is the same, therefore, neglecting losses,

$$V_p I_p = V_s I_s \quad \text{and} \quad \frac{V_p}{N_p} = \frac{V_s}{N_s}$$

hence

$$\frac{N_p}{N_s} = \frac{V_p}{V_s} = \frac{I_s}{I_p}$$

182

Example 15.1. A double-wound single-phase transformer has a primary to secondary turns ratio of 1:8. Determine the primary voltage necessary to supply a load at 160 V. If the load current is 5 A what will be the primary current? Neglect the no-load current and internal volt drops.

V_p = primary voltage, I_p = primary current, $\dfrac{N_p}{N_s} = \dfrac{1}{8}$, V_s = 160 V, I_s = 5 A

For the assumptions made, $\quad \dfrac{N_p}{N_s} = \dfrac{V_p}{V_s} = \dfrac{I_s}{I_p}$

$$\frac{1}{8} = \frac{V_p}{160} = \frac{5}{I_p}$$

therefore, $\qquad\qquad V_p = \dfrac{160}{8} \text{ V} = \underline{20 \text{ V}}$ and $I_p = 8 \times 5 \text{ A} = \underline{40 \text{ A}}$

Example 15.2. Draw to scale:

(a) the no-load phasor diagram for a single-phase double-wound 2:1 step-up transformer, that takes a no-load current of 2 A at a power factor of 0·27 at a supply voltage of 200 V. From the diagram determine the magnetizing and loss components of the no-load current. Fig. 15.5(a).

(b) the on-load phasor diagram, when a load connected across the secondary takes a current of 6 A at a p.f. of 0·8 lagging. Use the diagram to find the primary current and phase angle. Neglect internal volt drops. Fig. 15.5(b).

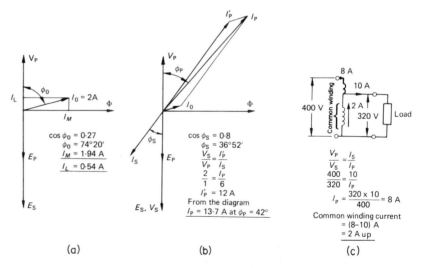

cos ϕ_0 = 0·27
ϕ_0 = 74°20'
I_M = 1·94 A
I_L = 0·54 A

cos ϕ_S = 0·8
ϕ_S = 36°52'
$\dfrac{V_S}{V_P} = \dfrac{I'_P}{I_S}$
$\dfrac{2}{1} = \dfrac{I_P}{6}$
I'_P = 12 A
From the diagram
I_P = 13·7 A at ϕ_P = 42°

$\dfrac{V_P}{V_S} = \dfrac{I_S}{I_P}$
$\dfrac{400}{320} = \dfrac{10}{I_P}$
$I_P = \dfrac{320 \times 10}{400} = 8 \text{ A}$
Common winding current
= (8–10) A
= 2 A up

(a)   (b)   (c)

Fig. 15.5. Solutions to examples 15.2 and 15.3

Example 15.3. Make a representative sketch of an auto-transformer on load, having a step-down voltage ratio of 400/320. What will be the current in the common section of the winding when the load current is 10 A. Fig. 15.5(c).

15.3 Regulation

The output of a transformer is not constant but depends on the size and type of load. Voltage regulation is the ratio of the difference between the voltage on no-load and the voltage on-load, to the no-load voltage, and is usually expressed as a percentage:

$$\text{Regulation} = \frac{E_s - V_s}{E_s} \times 100\%$$

Example 15.4. A tap changing mechanism (refer to section 15.5) is set to operate when the percentage regulation of a power transformer drops below 2%. The open-circuit voltage of the transformer is 415 V. Determine the load voltage at which the mechanism operates:

V_s = operating load voltage, E_s = 415 V, regulation = 2%

$$\text{Regulation} = \frac{E_s - V_s}{E_s} \times 100\%$$

$$2 = \frac{415 - V_s}{415} \times 100$$

$$\frac{2}{100} \times 415 = 415 - V_s$$

$$8 \cdot 3 = 415 - V_s$$

$$V_s = (415 - 8 \cdot 3)\text{ V} = \underline{406 \cdot 7\text{ V}}$$

15.4 Losses and efficiency

Transformer losses can be divided into two groups:

1. Constant losses
These are losses which are independent of the transformer load. They are called iron losses since they are due to:

(a) Hysteresis loss, which is the heating of the core as a result of the internal molecular structure reversals that take place as the magnetic flux alternates, Fig. 15.6. The loss is proportional to the frequency and a power of the flux density. Hysteresis loss is minimized by using steel having a low reluctance.

(b) Eddy current loss, is the heating of the core due to electromagnetic induced e.m.f.s in the core which set up circulating currents in the core, perpendicular to the direction of the flux, Fig. 15.6. This is proportional to the square of the maximum flux density, the frequency and the thickness of laminations. Eddy current loss is minimized by using thin laminations of high resistance steel, usually about 0·35 mm thick plus 0·025 mm of insulation. In both cases the losses are constant because the core flux is constant.

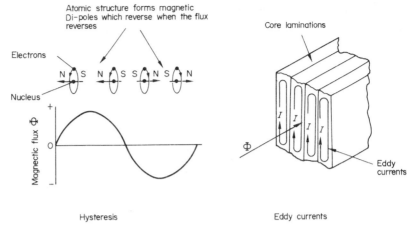

Fig. 15.6. Hysteresis and eddy currents

2. Variable losses

These are losses which vary with the load. They are called copper losses since they are due to the heating of the windings by the flow of the primary and secondary currents. Copper losses = $I_p{}^2 R_p + I_s{}^2 R_s$, the total variable losses are therefore proportional to the square of the kV A output.

Transformer efficiency (η). The efficiency of a transformer is given by:

$$\eta = \frac{\text{output}}{\text{input}} \times 100\% = \frac{V_s \times I_s \times \text{p.f.}}{V_s \times I_s \times \text{p.f.} + \text{iron losses} + \text{copper losses}} \times 100\%$$

The efficiency is usually based on the values of the losses. The iron losses are determined from a wattmeter connected in the primary circuit at normal voltage and frequency when the secondary is on open circuit. The copper losses are determined from the wattmeter in the primary winding with normal current but very low voltage, this is obtained by short-circuiting the secondary winding.

Example 15.5. The hysteresis loss in a transformer is 200 W at 50 Hz. Calculate the loss at the same flux density and at a frequency of 20 Hz.
Hysteresis loss is proportional to frequency:

$$\text{Hysteresis loss at } 20 \text{ Hz} = 200 \times \frac{20}{50} \text{ W} = \underline{80 \text{ W}}$$

Example 15.6. A transformer has an eddy-current loss of 600 W. Calculate the loss in a similar transformer due to:

(a) halving the lamination thickness

(b) doubling the frequency.

Eddy current loss is proportional to the square of both the lamination thickness and the frequency:

(a) Eddy current loss = $600 \times \left(\frac{1}{2}\right)^2$ W = $\underline{150 \text{ W}}$.

(b) Eddy current loss = $600 \times (2)^2$ W = $\underline{2.4 \text{ kW}}$.

185

Example 15.7. The wattmeter in the primary of a 120 kV A transformer on a short-circuit test read 800 W. What will be its copper loss at outputs of 60 kV A and 30 kV A?

Copper loss is proportional to $(kV A)^2$:

at 60 kV A output $\qquad$ Copper loss $= 400 \times \left(\dfrac{60}{120}\right)^2$ W $= \underline{100\ W}$

at 30 kV A output $\qquad$ Copper loss $= 400 \times \left(\dfrac{30}{120}\right)^2$ W $= \underline{25\ W}$

Example 15.8. A 200-kV A transformer has full-load iron and copper losses of 1·2 kW and 2 kW respectively. Calculate its efficiency at full- and half-load and unity power factor.

$$\text{Full-load efficiency, } \eta, = \frac{\text{output}}{\text{output} + \text{iron loss} + \text{copper loss}} \times 100\%$$

$$= \frac{200}{200 + 1\cdot2 + 2} \times 100\% = \frac{200}{203\cdot2} \times 100\% = \underline{98\cdot4\%}$$

$$\text{Half-load efficiency, } \eta, = \frac{100}{100 + 1\cdot2 + 2 \times (\tfrac{1}{2})^2} \times 100\%$$

$$= \frac{100}{100 + 1\cdot2 + 0\cdot5} \times 100\%$$

$$= \frac{100}{101\cdot7} \times 100\% = \underline{98\cdot3\%}$$

Note: The efficiency of all large transformers must be very high since only a small percentage drop in efficiency results in considerable extra running costs.

15.5 Transformer tappings

Due to variation in supply voltages, voltage drops due to cables and type of load, and the need to provide a variable supply it is often desirable to be able to alter the transformer ratio. This is done by making a connection called a tapping at some point on the windings other than the ends.

Tappings can be made on either the primary or the secondary windings and can be carried out by:

(a) A connection panel just blow the oil level to which external connections are usually permanently made. This method is used for definite supply changes where specific change in operating voltage is required.

(b) Fairly close tapping points are brought out through a link system to an external off-load tapping switch, this method is used when fairly regular minor adjustment of input or output voltage is required.

(c) An on-load tapping switch arranged by the connection of a reactance between the new tapping point and the supply during the switching period. This method of tapping is the one usually used in the voltage variation of distribution power transformers and is often automatic in operation.

15.6 Instrument transformers (refer also to section 16.9)

The high voltages and currents of many a.c. power supplies usually make it unrealistic to operate the voltage and current coils of switchgear, instruments, and relays directly. To reduce the supply values and also isolate the instrument panels from the power bus-bars, voltage and current transformers are used.

Voltage transformers, these transformers are similar to power transformers, except that the secondary voltage is standard at 110 V (115 V in America) and a great deal more attention is given to insulation, since breakdown could result in voltages such as 132 kV being connected to the switchgear framework. The internal voltage drops, losses, and winding ratio errors must also be minimized to give very accurate voltage ratios and reduce phase displacement errors.

Current transformers. As with the voltage transformer the operation is similar to that of a power transformer. In the case of the current transformer however the secondary current is standardized at 5 A and mechanical strength is an important factor due to mechanical forces between turns on the primary winding under overload conditions. To reduce stresses and to ease construction and mounting problems the bus-bar itself is often used as the primary. The same accuracy factors apply but are more difficult to maintain due to variation in the load.

15.7 Mass and cost calculations

Estimates of the overall mass and cost of transformers is usually based on previous designs. However for the main individual components, calculations can be made using the following formulae:

Mass = volume x the mass per unit volume in kg/m^3 (refer to section 2.9)
Weight = mass (in kilogrammes) x 10 N
Cost = (volume x material cost per unit volume) + production costs

Example 15.9. A transformer winding 120 mm high and 80 mm diameter has a square core-hole 25 mm x 25 mm along its length. Determine for the winding:

(a) its volume
(b) its mass, if the average density is 4 g/cm^3
(c) its weight
(d) the cost if the average material cost is 120p/kg and production costs are $\frac{4}{5}$ of the material costs.

Calculate also the number of square metres of timber required for a reasonable crate in which to transport 40 coils in two layers of 5 x 4:

(a) Volume = $(\pi \times 40^2 \times 120 - 25 \times 25 \times 120)$ mm$^3 \simeq$ 528·3 cm^3
(b) Mass = 528·3 x 4 g = 2·11 kg
(c) Weight = 2·11 x 10 N = 21·1 N
(d) Cost = 2·11 (120 + $\frac{4}{5}$ x 120) = £4·56

Packing-crate timber, allowing 10 mm space all round for packing and 10 mm for overlap:

$$= \{2[(5 \times 80) + 40] \, [(4 \times 80) + 40] + 2 \, [120 + 120 + 20] \, [(5 \times 80) + 40]$$

$$+ \, 2[120 + 120 + 20] \, [(4 \times 80) + 20]\} \, \text{mm}^2$$

$$= 0.3168 \, \text{m}^2 + 0.2288 \, \text{m}^2 + 0.1768 \, \text{m}^2 = \underline{0.7224 \, \text{m}^2}$$

Problems

1. The power taken by a 400/200-V single-phase double-wound transformer on no-load is 100 W at a p.f. of 0·2. Draw the no-load phasor diagram and calculate the magnetizing component of the current.

2. A 240/12-V double-wound single-phase transformer takes a load current of 20 A at a p.f. of 0·6 lagging. Neglecting internal volt-drops calculate:

(a) the transformer turns ratio

(b) the reflected primary current.

The components of the no-load current are $I_L = 0.1$ A and $I_M = 0.4$ A. Draw to scale the on-load phasor diagram and hence determine the primary current.

3. A 210-kV A auto-transformer is used to step up a distribution voltage from 10·5 kV to 11 kV. Determine the current in the common portion of the winding.

4. Sketch the no-load phasor diagram for a single-phase double-wound transformer. What factors determine the no-load current?

5. Draw a symbolic diagram of a single-phase double-wound transformer on-load. Mark on the diagram the primary and secondary currents and voltages. Explain the on-load operation of the transformer.

6. Explain the advantages and disadvantages of an auto-transformer over a double-wound transformer.

7. The open-circuit secondary voltage of a transformer is 240 V; the voltages on-load due to three different types of load are 234 V, 236 V, and 244 V respectively. Determine in each case the transformer regulation.

8. Sketch the circuit representation for star and delta connections of a three-phase transformer.

9. A transformer has a hysteresis loss of 400 W at 60 Hz. Complete the following table:

Hysteresis loss, W	Frequency, Hz
150 W	
	30
	90

10. The eddy-current loss in a transformer is 200 W at 100 Hz. Determine the loss at a frequency of 50 Hz.

What would be the loss at 100 Hz of a similar transformer having laminations $1\frac{1}{2}$ times as thick?

11. The efficiency of a 20-kV A transformer is 94%. Calculate the iron loss and copper loss if the variable losses equal the constant losses at this efficiency and unity p.f.

12. A 50-kV A transformer has an iron loss of 800 W and copper loss of 600 W at half-load. Calculate the full-load efficiency. Assume unity p.f. in each case.

13. Calculate the mass and cost of a single-phase double-wound core-type transformer core having a constant cross-section of $0 \cdot 12$ m x $0 \cdot 12$ m and inside window dimensions of $0 \cdot 18$ m x $0 \cdot 48$ m. The mass per unit volume for the core material is 8 g/cm^3, and the cost including production 40p/kg.

Answers

1. $I_M = 1 \cdot 225$ A
2. (a) 20/1   (b) $I_p' = 1$ A; $I_p = 1 \cdot 39$ A
3. $I_{common} = 0 \cdot 9$ A
7. $2 \cdot 5\%$; $1 \cdot 67\%$; $1 \cdot 67\%$ up
9. Frequency at a hysteresis loss of 150 W = $22 \cdot 5$ Hz
    Hysteresis loss at a frequency of 30 Hz = 200 W
    Hysteresis loss at a frequency of 90 Hz = 600 W
10. 50 W; 450 W
11. Iron loss and copper loss = $0 \cdot 64$ kW
12. 94%
13. $207 \cdot 36$ kg; £82·94

Laboratory work

1. Transformer ratios. Using four transformer-core assemblies having different known primary and secondary turn ratios:

(a) Connect the voltmeters across the primary and secondary winding terminals. Switch on the supply and record V_p and V_s.

Tabulate the turns ratio $\dfrac{N_p}{N_s}$ and the corresponding voltage ratio $\dfrac{V_p}{V_s}$

Compare the relationships $\dfrac{N_p}{N_s}$ and $\dfrac{V_p}{V_s}$

(b) Connect a suitable resistive load across the secondary winding. Connect ammeters in the primary and secondary circuits. Switch on the supply and record I_p and I_s.

Tabulate the turns ratio $\dfrac{N_p}{N_s}$ and the corresponding current ratio $\dfrac{I_s}{I_p}$

Compare the relationships $\dfrac{N_p}{N_s}$ and $\dfrac{I_s}{I_p}$

2. Transformer losses and efficiency. Using a small 240/110-V single-phase power transformer of about 1 kV A rating and a variable voltage supply:

(a) With the secondary on open-circuit connect a voltmeter, ammeter, and wattmeter in the primary circuit. Increase the supply to normal voltage and record the primary voltage, primary current, and input power. The power taken is approximately the iron loss since the no-load primary current is small and consequently the copper loss is negligible.

(b) With the supply switched off, short-circuit the secondary winding. Increase the supply voltage until the ammeter indicates the current at which it is required to calculate the efficiency. Record the primary voltage, primary current, and power input, and calculate the the secondary load current from the transformer ratio.

The wattmeter now indicates the copper loss since the supply voltage required to cause normal currents on short-circuit is relatively small and consequently the iron loss is negligible.

Assuming a unity power factor load, the efficiency at the particular load current of the short-circuit test can be calculated from:

$$\text{efficiency} = \frac{V_s I_s}{V_s I_s + \text{iron loss} + \text{copper loss}} \times 100\%$$

3. Transformer regulation. Using a 220/110-V single-phase power transformer at normal supply voltage:

(a) Measure the no-load secondary voltage V_{NL}.

(b) Measure the secondary load voltage, V_L, across:

(i) a resistive load

(ii) a capacitive load

(iii) an inductive load at the same load current.

Calculate the percentage regulation for each type of load from:

$$\frac{V_{NL} - V_L}{V_{NL}} \times 100\%$$

Comment on the relative values.

16. Measurements and instruments

Indicating instruments

Electrical instruments such as voltmeters, ammeters, wattmeters, ohmmeters, etc., are called indicating instruments since they indicate the conditions existing in the circuit at any particular instant. These instruments have three essential features:

(a) a means of deflecting the pointer over the scale,

(b) a means of controlling the movement of the pointer

(c) a means of damping the movement of the pointer.

16.1 Instrument control

The controlling device ensures that the amount of deflexion depends on the magnitude of the quantity being measured, and also ensures that the pointer returns to zero when the deflecting force is removed. Modern instruments use spring control, as shown in Fig. 16.4.

16.2 Instrument damping

An instrument movement is damped to ensure that the pointer comes to rest quickly at the correct reading without excessive oscillation.

Air damping is obtained by attaching to the spindle a thin metal vane which moves within a closed box. As the pointer moves, the vane compresses the air in the box thus slowing down the pointer movement, Fig. 16.1(a).

Eddy current damping is obtained by attaching either an aluminium disc (Fig. 16.1(b)) or an aluminium frame (Fig. 16.1(c)), to the spindle and arranging that the disc or frame moves in a magnetic field. When the disc or frame rotates an e.m.f. will be induced which will cause eddy currents to flow. In accordance with Lenz's law these eddy currents will cause a force to be exerted opposing the movement of the disc or frame.

Oil damping has been recently introduced by one manufacturer where damping is obtained by means of a thin film of oil between the spindle and a specially designed fixed collar, Fig. 16.1(d).

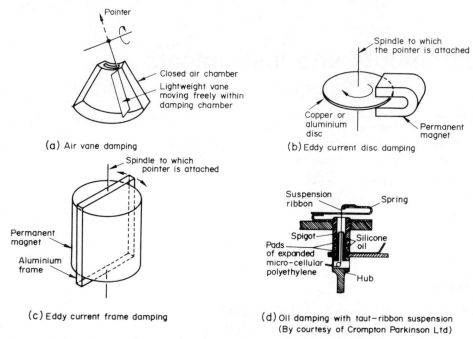

(a) Air vane damping

(b) Eddy current disc damping

(c) Eddy current frame damping

(d) Oil damping with taut–ribbon suspension
(By courtesy of Crompton Parkinson Ltd)

Fig. 16.1. Instrument damping arrangements

16.3 Moving coil instruments

These consist of a lightweight coil, wound on an aluminium frame, which is free to rotate through approximately $120°$ around the poles of a permanent magnet. If current flows in the coil a force will be exerted on the coil sides which will cause the coil to be deflected (refer to section 9.5). The deflexion is proportional to the current flowing in the coil. Control is by two springs which also act as current connexions to the coil. Damping is by the eddy current frame method since the frame is also required as a supporting former for the coil. The scale is linear and the instrument can be calibrated to read various electrical quantities and values depending on the method of circuit connection (refer to section 16.8). It is not suitable for use on alternating current circuits since the direction of deflexion depends on the direction of current in the coil (refer to section 16.4).

16.4 Rectifier instrument

To enable a moving coil instrument to work on alternating current a rectifier can be inserted in the coil circuit. Since the current flowing through the coil of a moving coil instrument is only a few milliamperes for full-scale deflexion (refer to section 16.8) the rectifier is only a very small unit. This is the method adopted in multi-range moving coil instruments which operate on either a.c. or d.c. supplies.

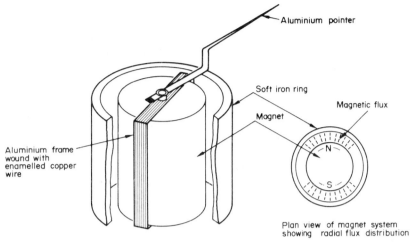

Aluminium pointer

Soft iron ring

Magnetic flux

Magnet

Aluminium frame
wound with
enamelled copper
wire

Plan view of magnet system
showing radial flux distribution

Fig. 16.2. Moving coil instrument

16.5 Thermocouple instrument

If two conductors of different metals are formed into a closed loop, and a difference
in temperature maintained between the two junctions, then an e.m.f. will be produced. This e.m.f. will cause a current to flow round the circuit, the magnitude of
the current increasing with an increase in temperature differential between the
junctions. This type of circuit is called a thermocouple.

If a resistor is connected so that the current to be measured flows through it, and
one of the junctions of the thermocouple is fastened to the resistor, then the heat
produced in the resistor will cause a current to flow in the thermocouple circuit. This
current can be used to operate a microammeter. The instrument can be calibrated
using direct current, and can then be used to measure the r.m.s. value of alternating
current over a wide range of frequencies without recalibration being necessary, Fig. 16.3.

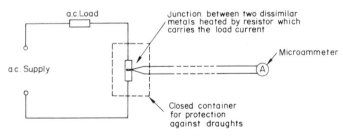

a.c.Load

Junction between two dissimilar
metals heated by resistor which
carries the load current

Microammeter

a.c. Supply

Closed container
for protection
against draughts

Fig. 16.3. Thermocouple instrument

16.6 Electrodynamic instruments.

In electrodynamic or dynamometer instruments the deflecting torque is produced
by two current carrying coils, one fixed, and the other, to which the pointer is
attached, free to move, Fig. 16.4(a). When current flows in both coils magnetic

fields are created round both coils and the interaction of these two magnetic fields causes a force to be exerted between the coils resulting in the deflexion of the moveable coil. The deflecting torque is dependent on the strengths of the two magnetic fields. Since the field strengths are proportional to the currents flowing in the two coils:

deflecting torque $\propto$ current in fixed coil x current in moving coil

This type of instrument is mainly used as a wattmeter, the fixed coil carrying the circuit current and the moving coil being connected across the supply through a non-inductive resistor, Fig. 16.4(b). The instrument can be used on either a.c. or d.c. supplies. When used on a.c. supplies:

deflecting torque $\propto$ instantaneous value of current through load x instantaneous p.d.
across the load

Since the instrument cannot follow the change in instantaneous power over one cycle the pointer will take up a position which indicates average power, the scale being calibrated accordingly.

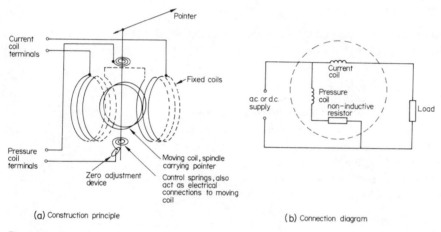

(a) Construction principle

(b) Connection diagram

Fig. 16.4. Electrodynamic instrument

16.7 Moving iron instruments

The majority of modern moving iron instruments are of the repulsion type, in which two pieces of nickel-iron alloy are placed side by side inside a stationary coil. One piece of iron is fixed and the other is free to move with the pointer. When current flows in the coil both pieces of iron are magnetized in the same direction and therefore repel each other, causing the pointer to deflect. In which ever direction the current flows in the coil the pointer will always be deflected in one direction, and the instrument can therefore be used on alternating or direct current circuits. The amount of deflexion depends on the square of the current flowing in the coil, and by suitable design of the shape of the fixed and moving elements, the scale can be made almost linear except for the lower end which is normally compressed, Fig. 16.5.

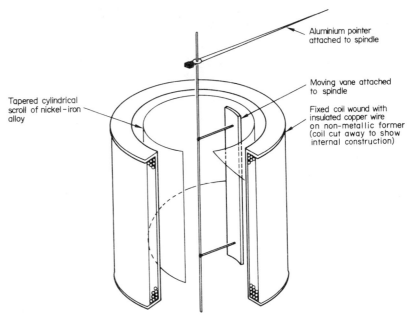

Aluminium pointer
attached to spindle

Moving vane attached
to spindle

Fixed coil wound with
insulated copper wire
on non-metallic former
(coil cut away to show
internal construction)

Tapered cylindrical
scroll of nickel–iron
alloy

Fig. 16.5. Moving iron instrument

16.8 Extension of instrument ranges

The ranges of instruments can be extended by using shunts or series resistors.

Ammeters. To enable the instrument to read higher values of current a low value resistor—called a shunt—is connected in parallel with the instrument coil, Fig. 16.6. Shunts are normally not fitted to moving iron instruments since the fixed coil can be wound with large gauge wire to carry the full circuit current.

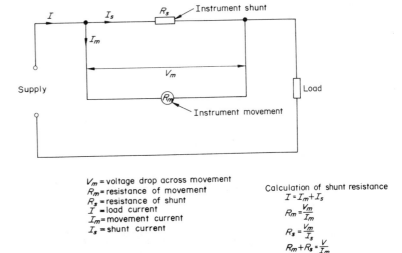

V_m = voltage drop across movement
R_m = resistance of movement
R_s = resistance of shunt
I = load current
I_m = movement current
I_s = shunt current

Calculation of shunt resistance
$$I = I_m + I_s$$
$$R_m = \frac{V_m}{I_m}$$
$$R_s = \frac{V_m}{I_s}$$
$$R_m + R_s = \frac{V}{I_m}$$

Fig. 16.6. Instrument shunt

Voltmeters. To enable the instrument to read higher voltages a high value resistor—called a multiplier—is connected in series with the instrument coil, Fig. 16.7

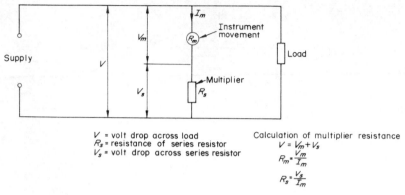

V = volt drop across load
R_s = resistance of series resistor
V_s = volt drop across series resistor

Calculation of multiplier resistance
$$V = V_m + V_s$$
$$R_m = \frac{V_m}{I_m}$$
$$R_s = \frac{V_s}{I_m}$$

Fig. 16.7. Instrument multiplier (part 1 and part 2)

Example 16.1. A moving coil galvanometer has a coil of resistance 5 Ω and gives full-scale deflexion with a current of 15 mA in the coil. How can it be made to read 2 A full-scale deflexion? Referring to Fig. 16.6:

$$I = 2 \text{ A}, I_{\mathrm{m}} = 15 \text{ mA} = 0 \cdot 015 \text{ A}, R_{\mathrm{m}} = 5 \text{ } \Omega$$

$$I = I_{\mathrm{m}} + I_{\mathrm{s}}$$

$$2 = 0 \cdot 015 + I_{\mathrm{s}}$$

$$I_{\mathrm{s}} = 1 \cdot 985 \text{ A}$$

$$R_{\mathrm{m}} = \frac{V_{\mathrm{m}}}{I_{\mathrm{m}}}$$

$$5 = \frac{V_{\mathrm{m}}}{0 \cdot 015}$$

$$V_{\mathrm{m}} = 5 \times 0 \cdot 015 \text{ V} = 0 \cdot 075 \text{ V}$$

$$R_{\mathrm{s}} = \frac{V_{\mathrm{m}}}{I_{\mathrm{s}}}$$

$$R_{\mathrm{s}} = \frac{0 \cdot 075}{1 \cdot 985} \text{ } \Omega$$

$$= 0 \cdot 0377 \text{ } \Omega$$

To convert to a 2-A instrument connect a 38 mΩ resistor in parallel.

Example 16.2. A moving coil instrument has a resistance of 4 Ω and gives full-scale deflexion when a potential difference of 50 mV is applied. How can it be made to read up to 100 V?
Referring to Fig. 16.7:

$V = 100$ V, $V_m = 50$ mV $= 0.05$ V, $R_m = 4\ \Omega$

$$V = V_m + V_s$$
$$100 = 0.05 + V_s$$
$$V_s = 99.95 \text{ V}$$

$$R_m = \frac{V_m}{I_m}$$

$$4 = \frac{0.05}{I_m}$$

$$I_m = \frac{0.05}{4} \text{ A}$$
$$= 0.0125 \text{ A}$$

$$R_s = \frac{V_s}{I_m}$$

$$R_s = \frac{99.95}{0.0125} \ \Omega$$
$$= 7996 \ \Omega$$

To convert to a 100-V instrument connect a 7·996-kΩ resistor in series with the instrument coil.

16.9 Instrument transformers

When measuring high values of alternating current and voltage, instrument transformers are often used.

Current transformers. For currents in excess of about 100 A a current transformer is normally used. In a double-wound transformer the primary and secondary currents are inversely proportional to the primary and secondary turns. Since the primary and secondary currents will always be in the same ratio it is possible to measure the secondary current and then calculate the primary current. In current transformers the primary usually consists of one or two turns whilst the secondary consists of several hundred turns. If, for example, a current transformer is constructed as shown in Fig. 16.8(a) with 2 turns on the primary and 200 turns on the secondary, then for a current of 500 A in the primary the secondary current will be:

$$\frac{500 \times 2}{200} \text{ A} = 5 \text{ A}$$

Thus the value of the primary current can be obtained from

$$\text{Primary current} = \text{secondary current} \times \frac{\text{secondary turns}}{\text{primary turns}}$$

For very large currents the transformer core can be mounted round the conductor or bus-bar which then acts as a one-turn primary, Fig. 16.8(b); (refer also to section 15.6).

Current transformers must never be operated with the secondary winding open-circuited since this would give rise to excessive values of flux in the core, with consequent overheating and possibly dangerously high voltages induced in the secondary. If it is necessary to remove the instrument from a current transformer the secondary terminals must first be short-circuited.

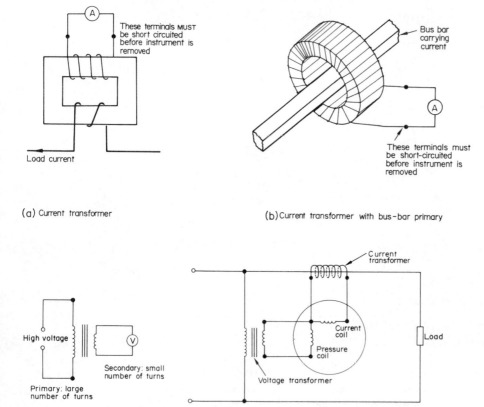

(a) Current transformer

(b) Current transformer with bus-bar primary

(c) Voltage transformer

(d) Wattmeter connections for large currents at high voltages

Fig. 16.8. Measurement of large voltages and currents

Voltage transformers. When the voltage of an a.c. system exceeds 500 V it is often safer to use a voltage transformer to measure the voltage. Voltage transformers are normal double-wound transformers with a large number of turns on the primary, which is connected to the high voltage supply, and a small number of turns on the secondary (refer also to section 15.6). If, for example, a voltage transformer is constructed as shown in Fig. 16.8(c) with 5000 turns on the primary and 25 turns on the secondary then for a voltage of 10 000 V on the primary the instrument would only have

$$\frac{10000 \times 25}{5000} \, V = 50 \, V$$

across its terminals. Since the ratio of the primary to secondary voltages will always be the same, the primary voltage can be obtained from:

$$\text{Primary voltage} = \text{secondary voltage} \times \frac{\text{primary turns}}{\text{secondary turns}}$$

16.10 Instrument errors

When instruments are used to measure quantities in electrical circuits it is essential that the current taken by the instruments does not affect unduly the existing circuit conditions.

Ammeters should have a very low resistance.

Voltmeters should have a very high resistance.

The actual values required will depend on the circuit being tested, as shown in the following example.

Example 16.3. Calculate the change in current taken from the battery in Fig. 16.9 when a voltmeter having a resistance of

(a) 200 Ω

(b) 20 kΩ

is connected across the 200-Ω resistor.

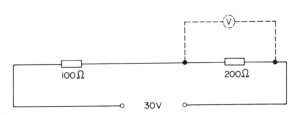

Fig. 16.9. Circuit for example 16.3

R_a = resistance of 200-Ω resistor and 200-Ω voltmeter in parallel

$$\frac{1}{R_a} = \frac{1}{R_1} + \frac{1}{R_2}$$

$$= \frac{1}{200} + \frac{1}{200}$$

$$= \frac{2}{200}$$

$$R_a = \frac{200}{2} \, \Omega = 100 \, \Omega$$

199

R_b = resistance of 200-Ω resistor and 20000-Ω resistor in parallel

$$\frac{1}{R_b} = \frac{1}{R_1} + \frac{1}{R_2}$$

$$= \frac{1}{200} + \frac{1}{20000}$$

$$= \frac{100 + 1}{20000}$$

$$R_b = \frac{20000}{101}\ \Omega = 198\ \Omega$$

Current taken from battery with no voltmeter connected:

$$I = \frac{V}{R} = \frac{30}{(100 + 200)} = \frac{30}{300}\ \text{A} = 0 \cdot 1\ \text{A}$$

Current taken from battery with 200-Ω voltmeter connected:

$$I = \frac{V}{R} = \frac{30}{(100 + 100)} = \frac{30}{200}\ \text{A} = 0 \cdot 15\ \text{A}$$

This is a 50% change in current so that this voltmeter would be completely unsuitable for checking the p.d. in this circuit.

Current taken from the battery with 20 kΩ voltmeter connected:

$$I = \frac{V}{R} = \frac{30}{(100 + 198)} = \frac{30}{298}\ \text{A} = 0 \cdot 1007\ \text{A}$$

This is only a 0·7% change in current which can therefore be neglected since it is not possible to read instruments to within this degree of accuracy.

16.11 Instrument sensitivity

An instrument with high sensitivity will cause very little change in the circuit current when it is connected to the circuit. It is particularly important that instruments used on circuits carrying only very small values of current should have a high sensitivity. Typical values of sensitivity for instruments such as portable multi-range instruments are 20000 ohms per volt on d.c. and 1000 ohms per volt on a.c. circuits.

16.12 Valve voltmeters

When normal moving coil instruments are used on electronic circuits the power required to operate the instrument may be more than the circuit can produce, and even though a reading is indicated on the instrument it may be nowhere near the actual voltage present under normal working conditions.

Under these conditions the valve voltmeter is useful since the power taken from the circuit being tested is negligible and the input impedance is several megohms.

These instruments can be used for measuring d.c. voltages of several thousand volts and a.c. voltages with frequencies as high as 800 MHz. When this instrument is used to measure a.c. voltages, the input must be rectified. The rectifier may be housed in the instrument or in the end of the test probe.

16.13 Resistance measurement by the Wheatstone bridge

The resistance of a resistor can be accurately measured by means of a Wheatstone bridge circuit as shown in Fig. 16.10. P and Q are known resistances or ratio arms,

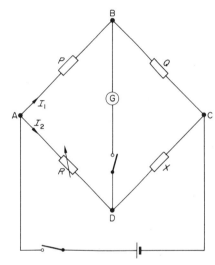

Fig. 16.10. Wheatstone bridge circuit

R is a decade resistor, and X is the unknown resistance. R is adjusted until the galvanometer gives zero deflexion. The bridge is then said to be balanced. Points B and D are now at the same potential, so that the

$$\text{p.d. across AB} = \text{p.d. across AD and}$$

$$\text{p.d. across BC} = \text{p.d. across DC}$$

therefore, $\qquad PI_1 = RI_2$ $\qquad\qquad$ (16.1)

and $\qquad QI_1 = XI_2$ $\qquad\qquad$ (16.2)

Dividing (16.1) by (16.2) $\qquad \dfrac{P}{Q} = \dfrac{R}{X}$

therefore, $\qquad X = R \times \dfrac{Q}{P}$

The ratio arms P and Q normally consist of resistors of either 10 Ω, 100 Ω, or 1000 Ω resistance and by varying the ratios of $P{:}Q$ the values indicated on the decade resistor at balance can be divided or multiplied by 10 or 100.

Example 16.4. A Wheatstone bridge circuit is connected as shown in Fig. 16.10 with $P = 10 \ \Omega$ and $Q = 1000 \ \Omega$. Balance is obtained when the decade resistor reads 1492 Ω. What is the value of X?

X = unknown resistance, $P = 10 \ \Omega$, $Q = 1000 \ \Omega$, $R = 1492 \ \Omega$

$$X = R \times \frac{Q}{P}$$

$$= 1492 \times \frac{1000}{10} \ \Omega = 149\,200 \ \Omega$$

$$= \underline{149 \cdot 2 \ \text{k} \ \Omega}$$

Example 16.5. A Wheatstone bridge circuit is connected as shown in Fig. 16.10. Balance is obtained when the decade resistor is adjusted to read 2846 Ω. If the resistance of P is 1000 Ω and the resistance of Q is 100 Ω, calculate the value of the unknown resistor:

X = unknown resistance, $P = 1000 \ \Omega$, $Q = 100 \ \Omega$, $R = 2846 \ \Omega$

$$X = R \times \frac{Q}{P}$$

$$= \frac{2846 \times 100}{1000} \ \Omega = \underline{284 \cdot 6 \ \Omega}$$

16.14 Cable fault location

It is often necessary to be able to accurately locate the position of a fault on a buried cable. For an earth fault on one core when a sound core is also available a Murray loop test can be used to locate the fault position. The cable ends are connected as shown in Fig. 16.11. The variable resistors P and Q are adjusted until there is no deflexion on the galvanometer. When balance is obtained

$$\frac{P}{Q} = \frac{2L - X}{X}$$

$$XP = 2\,LQ - QX$$

$$XP + QX = 2LQ$$

$$X(P + Q) = 2LQ$$

$$X = \frac{2\,LQ}{P + Q}$$

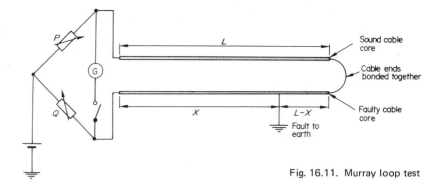

Fig. 16.11. Murray loop test

Note: Since accurate location of the fault requires accurate resistance measurement it is essential that the fault between the cable core and earth must have negligible resistance. It may therefore be necessary to 'burn out' the fault by passing a large current across the fault to weld the core to the earthed sheath.

Problems

1. Draw a circuit diagram to show how a voltmeter, ammeter, and wattmeter should be connected to measure the voltage, current, and power taken by a d.c. motor.

2. On what type of circuit would the following instruments be used: moving iron voltmeter, moving coil voltmeter, valve voltmeter?

3. On what types of circuit would the following instruments be used: moving coil ammeter, rectifier ammeter, thermocouple ammeter?

4. Explain how the deflecting torque is obtained in a moving iron instrument, and show how this torque varies with current. Sketch and explain the type of scale expected for this instrument. What is the main use of the moving iron instrument?

5. With the aid of a diagram, describe an ammeter that can be used to measure current on either direct or alternating current circuits. Why is damping of the movement necessary and how is it achieved? What limits the use of this instrument on alternating current?

6. Sketch the construction of a moving coil indicating instrument. Explain how the deflecting and control torques are produced. Why is damping necessary, and how is it achieved? What are the main advantages and disadvantages of this instrument compared with a moving iron instrument?

7. A moving coil instrument gives a full-scale deflexion when a current of 15 mA passes through it. If the instrument coil has a resistance of 5 Ω, calculate the value of series resistor to enable it to read up to 240 V. What type of materials are used to manufacture these resistors? Give the reasons for their use.

8. A moving coil movement has a resistance of 50 Ω and full-scale deflexion of 15 mA. Calculate the value of resistor that would convert the movement into:

(a) an ammeter with maximum indication of 30 A

(b) a voltmeter to read up to 250 V.

Make a diagram of connexions for both (a) and (b).

(C.G.L.I.)

9.　A moving coil voltmeter has a resistance of 100 Ω. The scale is divided into 150 equal divisions. When a potential difference of 1 V is applied to the terminals of the voltmeter, a deflexion of 100 divisions is obtained. Explain how the instrument could be used for measuring up to 300 V. Give a diagram of connexions. Determine the value of the component used.

(C.G.L.I.)

10.　(a) Draw a labelled diagram to show the construction of a moving coil instrument.

(b) A moving coil instrument has a resistance of 75 Ω and gives a full-scale deflexion of 100-scale divisions for a current of 1 mA. The instrument is connected in parallel with a shunt of resistance 25 Ω and the combination is then connected in series with a load and a supply. What is the current in the load when the instrument gives an indication of 80 scale divisions?

(C.G.L.I.)

11.　A type of voltmeter in common use has a sensitivity of 500 Ω/V and full-scale deflexion of 100 V. What will be the current taken for full-scale deflexion and the resistance of the meter? A resistance of 50 kΩ is connected in series with a resistance of 25 kΩ across a 90-V supply, and the above voltmeter is used to measure the voltage across the 50-kΩ resistor. What will be the reading on the voltmeter? What is the voltage across the 50-kΩ resistor before the voltmeter is connected? Why does this differ from the voltmeter reading?

(C.G.L.I.)

12.　A moving coil meter gives full-scale deflexion with a current of 15 mA. The resistance of the coil is 5 Ω. The instrument is connected in series with a 495-Ω resistor and gives a deflexion of half full-scale. Calculate:

(a) the supply voltage

(b) the deflexion for a supply voltage of 5 V

(c) the power taken by the instrument for full-scale deflexion.

13.　A current transformer has a turns ratio of 800:1. What current will flow in an ammeter connected to the secondary side of the transformer when the load current is 2000 A?

14.　A voltage transformer has a turns ratio of 500:1. What will be the supply voltage when the voltage across a voltmeter connected to the secondary side is 70 V?

15.　Explain the precautions to be taken, with reasons, when the ammeter is removed from the secondary winding of a current transformer.

16.　Two resistors of 200 Ω and 400 Ω are connected in series across a 48-V d.c. supply. A voltmeter having a resistance of 400 Ω is connected across the 400-Ω resistor. What reading will be indicated on the voltmeter?

17.　Explain, with the aid of circuit diagrams, how to extend the ranges of the following instruments:

(a) A 0 - 1 A d.c. ammeter to read: (i) 10 A　(ii) 1000 A

(b) A 0 - 1 A a.c. ammeter to read: (i) 10 A　(ii) 1000 A

(c) A 0 - 110 V a.c. voltmeter to read: (i) 500 V　(ii) 5 kV

18.　Explain, with a suitable diagram, how a Wheatstone bridge can be used to measure the value of an unknown resistor. If a variable resistor of 0-10 kΩ in 1-Ω steps is available together with two 10-Ω, one 100-Ω, and one 1000-Ω resistor, tabulate the ranges of resistance that can be measured. In each range state the accuracy that can be obtained.

19. Draw a circuit diagram for a Wheatstone bridge circuit for measurement of resistance. If the ratio arms can be set at 10 Ω, 100 Ω, or 1000 Ω mark on the diagram suitable values of resistors for measuring 4·36 Ω. The variable resistor is 0-10 kΩ in 1-Ω steps.

20. Explain how a core to earth fault could be located on a twin underground cable.

Answers

7. 15·995 kΩ
8. (a) 0·025 Ω (b) 16·616 kΩ
9. 19·900 kΩ
10. 3·2 mA
11. 0·002 A; 50 kΩ; 45 V; 60 V
12. 3·75 V; $\frac{2}{3}$ full scale; 1·125 mW
13. 2·5 A
14. 35 kV
16. 24 V

Index

LABORATORY WORK

Printed by William Clowes & Sons, Limited, London, Colchester and Beccles